LOS ANGELES CITY HALL
AN AMERICAN ICON

LOS ANGELES CITY HALL
AN AMERICAN ICON

STEPHEN GEE

FOREWORD BY ERIC GARCETTI
MAYOR OF LOS ANGELES

CONTEMPORARY PHOTOGRAPHY BY SANDRA STOJANOVIĆ

ACP
ANGEL CITY PRESS

To Dorothy and Harry Gee

CONTENTS

CITY OF LOS ANGELES
FOUNDED 1781

FOREWORD

L**os Angeles City Hall** is not just an architectural gem—it's a place to reflect on our city's past and glimpse its future. So much history has been made beneath these muraled ceilings. So many people have walked these marble floors and transformed our city with their ideas, energy, and passion. And that work continues today, because this great, global city is in the midst of a decade of historic growth.

L.A. was experiencing a big growth spurt back when this building went up in the post-war boom of the 1920s. Its construction materials were distinctly Californian: concrete mixed with sand from every one of our state's fifty-eight counties and water from each of our twenty-one missions. But its architectural style is a true mix—with its classical elements, art deco glamour, and Spanish-style roofing.

It's been called "Modern American," but to me, it's pure Los Angeles. Our City of Angels is incredibly diverse and inclusive, and that's reflected in our City Hall. People have always understood the connection between this place and the people it was built for: A program for the opening celebration in 1928 described our new City Hall as "the spirit of Los Angeles—the spirit of a forward-looking people."

You can still feel that spirit in the Council Chambers where Angelenos are active partners in charting a course for our city. You can still see it when you go up to the tower for sweeping 360-degree views of our beautiful city. (City Hall hasn't been the tallest building in L.A. since 1966, but it has the advantage of *location*. And that tower? It's named after our greatest mayor, Tom Bradley.)

And you can find, on one side of the majestic rotunda, an Olympic torch. That's our legacy—it's our past and our future. The Games have brought the world here at pivotal moments in our city's growth and allowed us to share, and export, our extraordinary spirit.

We hosted the Games first in 1932 and then again in 1984—the year that torch was delivered to its permanent home near the Spring Street entrance. Now we're gearing up for the 2028 Olympic and Paralympic Games.

I can't wait for people from across the globe to see what Los Angeles is all about, and I know just the place for them to go.

—Eric Garcetti
Mayor of Los Angeles, 2018

INTRODUCTION

> ***It is our greatest hope that we can give the city of Los Angeles an efficient city hall that will stand for years as a monument to the citizens of this community.***
>
> —Mayor George E. Cryer, March 4, 1926[1]

Los Angeles City Hall is more than a building; it is a bold symbol of the forward-thinking ambition of America's most progressive city, while gracing California as one of its most enduring landmarks. It is a proud vision of progress imagined by long-ago civic leaders to usher in a new era of prosperity and provide powerful physical evidence that Los Angeles's remarkable transition from an outpost to the dominant metropolis on the West Coast was complete.

The towering, futuristic—and monumental—edifice, completed in 1928, could not have been further removed from the rambling, dusty adobe acquired to serve as Los Angeles's first city-owned municipal home just seventy-five years earlier. The population then was around two thousand residents; by the time the current City Hall opened, it exceeded 1.4 million.

The gleaming white structure was the tallest in the city, more than three times the 150-foot legal limit set by a 1911 charter amendment, and on a par with any other city hall in any leading city across America.

In the ninety years since it was put into service, the purpose, ambitions, and dreams of the city have evolved to become more open and inclusive, and decisions made within its storied walls now make an impact on a diverse population set to exceed four million. City Hall is no longer the tallest building in Los Angeles; the height limit was removed by voters in 1956, and it was later surpassed by the forty-two-story Union Bank Square. It is now dwarfed by numerous skyscrapers, yet it maintains its majesty, proving a survivor in a city that has abandoned too many landmarks in the name of progress.

The building has hosted world leaders; survived earthquakes; and witnessed riots, suicides, and more than its share of bitter arguments. Its grounds have been occupied; its leaders vilified in protest; and if its walls could talk, they would tell the story of a city coming of age and a people looking for opportunity in a place perpetually wrestling over issues of economics, politics, and justice affecting the everyday lives of its citizens.

Within its magnificent rotunda, titans of local government have laid in state, including Senator Frank Flint, a powerful voice in building the Los Angeles Aqueduct and bringing water from the Owens Valley to Los Angeles; Mayor George E. Cryer, who was instrumental in the effort to build City Hall; Mary Foy, the first woman to lead the Los Angeles Public Library; controversial Police Chief William H. Parker, notorious for clashes with minority groups; and Mayor Fletcher Bowron, who guided Los Angeles through World War II and led a crackdown on corruption.

Ironically, the creation of City Hall pitted two of its most important future tenants against each other in an unprecedented political showdown. The City Council and the Board of Public Works both believed it was their right to choose an architect to design the monumental structure. The responsibility ultimately would belong to a trio of the city's most celebrated and prolific architects. John C. Austin, Albert C. Martin, and John Parkinson were close friends with synergistic skills and a determination to do the best job possible for a city they loved.

Together, they created a remarkable structure that blended architectural styles and spoke to an altogether new vision of what Los Angeles architecture could be. It would be decorated by leading California artists who created numerous exceptional works intended to remind the building's inhabitants of the ideals borne of their responsibility in conceiving a new symbol for the city.

Over the years, many have attempted to describe the building's architecture; it has been called Romanesque, Greek, Greco-Roman, Modern, and art deco. However, like the city in which it was constructed, it is made up of an inspired blend of influences.

Today, Los Angeles City Hall is intertwined with the identity of the city. Since 1940, the building has been the central image on the official badge worn by the men and women of the Los Angeles Police Department. One of the world's most recognizable structures, its celebrity has been enhanced by a local film industry that regularly makes use of the building to identify a location as Los Angeles. It was immortalized as the offices of the *Daily Planet* in the *Adventures of Superman* TV show, played a starring role in *Dragnet,* and was destroyed by aliens in *War of the Worlds.* It regularly hosts more than fifty productions each year and more recently appeared in *Gangster Squad* and *Hail Caesar,* as well as playing cameo roles in the Amazon TV shows, *Bosch* and *Goliath.*

It is such an integral part of Los Angeles that it is hard to imagine the city without it. And yet, there were those in the 1980s and 1990s who questioned whether it had outlived its relevance as the city's municipal headquarters. Its subsequent renovation was a rebuttal to the notion that Los Angeles is a city that inevitably fails to recognize its own history.

The restoration, led by A.C. Martin & Associates, the firm created by one of the building's original architects, introduced a new kind of innovation to the structure, an impressive base isolation system to help protect the building from future earthquake damage.

The incredible effort it took to restore the building was a demonstration of the faith a new generation of Angelenos had in their City Hall, not only as a cherished architectural gem, but even more, as an important reminder of the aspirations of a unique city always ready to keep moving forward.

—Stephen Gee

TIN

CHAPTER 1

OUTPOST TO METROPOLIS

In the block bounded by Temple, Main, First, and Spring streets, the new City Hall is a conspicuous landmark, covering twenty acres of floor space at a cost of $9,000,000. During my childhood, on this same property, a little one-story, dingy adobe was large enough to house the business of the pueblo. So to me, the City Hall of today is symbolic of the growth of Los Angeles.

—BOYLE WORKMAN, Los Angeles City Council President[1]

El Pueblo de Nuestra Señora la Reina de los Ángeles was established as a Spanish pueblo by forty-four settlers in 1781; however, it wasn't until 1853 that City and County offices shared the same building and not until 1884, when the population had exceeded eleven thousand, that the first purpose-built city hall was constructed.

In the early years of Los Angeles, local affairs were organized by the Mission of San Gabriel. Its priests kept records of births, deaths, marriages, and taxes, and its churches provided venues to resolve disputes. Under subsequent Mexican rule, Los Angeles was administered by a mayor, four councilmen, and a treasurer.[2] When American forces arrived in 1846, they found residents governed from a rugged adobe on the northeast corner of what is now West Cesar Estrada Chavez Avenue and Spring Street.

Mayor Stephen C. Foster

Under military control, Los Angeles was organized jointly from U.S. Army headquarters at Aliso and Los Angeles streets and a flat-roofed structure further down Los Angeles Street.

It was in this humble headquarters, also housing shops and rooms for lodgers, that Stephen Clark Foster, a Yale graduate from Maine, led a population of fewer than 1,600 as the first American mayor of Los Angeles. Foster, who had traveled to California as an interpreter for the Mormon Battalion, was appointed to the position in 1847.

Massachusetts native Abel Stearns, commonly known as Don Abel Stearns, who had served as city assessor and tax collector, took over the role and basic quarters when he was elected mayor on May 17, 1849. He was followed by Alpheus P. Hodges, the first mayor to serve after California became a state and the pueblo became an incorporated city in 1850. A respected physician, Hodges was also the coroner.

The next mayor to govern while the unpretentious quarters were still in use was former council member Benjamin D. Wilson, who, during his term in office from 1851 to 1852, organized the first volunteer police force. Los Angeles would not have a paid police department until 1877.[3] While in power, Wilson witnessed the creation of the first local newspaper, *La Estrella—The Star*, printed in both Spanish and English.

Wilson was succeeded by John G. Nichols, who had the distinction of living in the first brick house

in Los Angeles and fathering the first American child (a son) in the city. He would serve as mayor until 1853, the same year the city's municipal headquarters moved into an adobe structure on New High Street (later Spring Street).

When it was purchased for three thousand dollars, the Antonio J. Rocha adobe became the first City-owned city hall used jointly by the City and the County of Los Angeles. Built in 1828, the single-story structure had a large yard that housed a small building used as a jail, behind which the local gallows were located.

"I was a little lad when Father first took me to a council session in the old one-story adobe that stood at Spring and Jail (Franklin) streets," Councilmember Boyle Workman, the son of Mayor William H. Workman, wrote in his 1936 memoir. "The council room was dingy and dark, and made darker by the porch across the front. However, it was considered quite elegant because it had a floor, even though that floor was of rough planks which were not nailed any too closely together. There were no chairs. The only provision for citizens who had business to present to that august body was a splintery old bench that stood against the adobe wall."[4]

With limited space to discuss civic matters, it was common for community leaders to conduct City of Los Angeles business at the Bella Union Hotel, the city's first boarding house, which opened on Main and Temple in 1849, or elsewhere in private residences.

In 1867, county and district courts moved into the upper floor of the Temple Market Building, located on a small block then bounded by Spring, Main, Court, and Market streets, now the location of the current Los Angeles City Hall. Soon afterward, the City, which had used up all the space in its nearby adobe, rented additional space on the lower floor, thus occupying offices in two locations.

The building, constructed for investor John Temple in 1859, became commonly known as the Clock-tower Courthouse, thanks to the four-sided cupola displaying a clock's face on each side, added shortly after the building opened. Locals came to rely on the tower to tell time.[5]

John Temple, or Don Juan Temple as he was known to early American settlers, had arrived in California in 1827 from Honolulu. Born in Reading, Massachusetts, in 1798, he became a naturalized citizen of Mexico in 1830. Those who knew him described him as "a very shrewd businessman, not easily flattered or deceived, although he was of a genial, affable disposition and easily accessible."[6]

Temple paid $35,000 to erect the structure in the center of town. "The architect's name was Deering, who was a very thorough and competent man," local historian H.D. Barrows wrote in 1894.[7] Deering would also design the southwestern portion of the neighboring Temple Block.

Before the City moved in, the lower floor had served as a market and the upper level, a theater, which opened in November 1860 with a performance by the Great Star Company of Stark and Ryer. It was promoted as "the first advent of a theatrical company here."[8] When President Lincoln was assassinated in 1865, it was in this space that the community came together to mourn the nation's loss.

Following Temple's death in 1866, the property was sold to a syndicate led by John S. Griffen for $14,000. The County purchased it in 1869 for $20,000.[9] In 1890, real estate investor John A. Bullard bought the property for $100,500, then knocked it down, building the Bullard Block in its place. Likewise, the Bullard Block would eventually be demolished to make way for the new city hall.

Between 1860 and 1870, the population of Los Angeles grew by just over one thousand residents, as the Civil War kept young men occupied. In 1874, the first horse car arrived in the city, and the following year, Mayor Prudent Beaudry moved the municipal offices into a privately owned brick structure nearby at 136 North Spring St., believing it to be a more dignified location. The

During military control, army headquarters were located at the southeast corner of Los Angeles and Aliso streets (the two-story structure at center of image).
Pages 12–13: The first city hall under American rule located on Los Angeles Street.

Los Angeles City Hall 1853–1884

following year, he changed his mind and returned the City's headquarters to the adobe on Spring and Franklin streets.[10]

In 1878, the first telephone poles appeared in Los Angeles. By the early 1880s, larger buildings of brick or masonry, designed by trained architects, were being built. The city now had a number of small hotels, the three-story Pico House being the most significant. As the city grew, more buildings were being built, including the Phillips Block and the Nadeau Hotel.

In 1884, architect Robert B. Young was commissioned to design Los Angeles's first purpose-built city hall on the northeast corner of Second and Spring streets on a lot that once had been home to the first public school, built in 1855.

Young, who was born in Huntingdon County, Quebec, on April 1, 1855, was one of the pioneer architects of Los Angeles. He developed his knowledge of architecture and construction in Denver, Colorado, before moving to San Francisco in 1881.

He came to Los Angeles in 1883, the same year the Southern Pacific Railroad completed its second transcontinental line (via Yuma). Two years later, the Santa Fe Railroad arrived, and Young took full advantage of the boom that followed. Among the structures in Los Angeles that carried his architectural imprimatur were the Hollenbeck Hotel, the Braum Building (which was on South Broadway and once the tallest building in Los Angeles), and the Lankershim Block.[11]

According to the *Los Angeles Herald,* the brick city hall Young designed with a stone foundation was expected to cost $65,000. It would be three stories high with a tower and a weather vane on top. "There will be two halls for public speaking; one on Spring Street and one on Second Street, supported on iron pillars, with beams, and concrete-and-tile floor," the newspaper reported. "The building will have a heavy galvanized iron cornish [*sic*], painted and sanded like sandstone. The whole of the building throughout will be fire-proof, with all the latest improvements."[12]

The structure would include space for Confidence Fire Company No. 2, the police headquarters, and

Temple Market Building in 1867. Located in the space where the tower of City Hall now stands.

the jailer's office. When completed, the *Herald* predicted it would "compare favorably with any on the coast, and fill a long-felt want in Los Angeles, besides being an ornament to Second and Spring streets."[13]

In 1885, the City moved in, but barely a year had passed before its leaders began to lobby for an even larger facility. As Boyle Workman described, the structure was "a decided improvement on the old adobe but far from elegant." His father, William H. Workman, served as mayor from 1886 to 1888 while the building operated as the City Hall. "There was no room for the mayor's office, so Father had to rent quarters on First Street," he remembered.[14]

In 1887, the first paved streets could be found in Los Angeles. As the city grew, local government officials became scattered as City-owned office space was exhausted. "It makes the transaction of business very inconvenient, both for the public and the officers themselves, but until a new city hall can be erected, nothing better can be done," the *Los Angeles Times* opined.[15]

A number of different locations were considered for a new city hall, including lots on Spring and Sixth streets, Second and Hill streets; Fort Street (Broadway) and First Street; two lots on the west side of Fort Street, opposite the county jail; and a lot offered by William H. Workman on Boyle and Park avenues.[16]

Ultimately, a City-owned site on the southwest corner of Fort Street, between Second and Third streets, was selected. The property, according to the records of the Title Guarantee and Trust Company, was first owned by Francisco Figueroa, who paid $382 to the Treasury of the Ayuntamiento of the Pueblo of Los Angeles in 1849 for a lot that extended from Calle Fortin (Fort Street) to Calle Primavera (Spring Street).[17]

In 1886, the City acquired the site, then occupied by cottages, from investors L.H. Titus, M.L. Wicks, and Howard M. Mills. The $54,000 purchase was made possible through the financial support of local residents. As real estate investor J.A. Graves revealed, he and Wicks both made "liberal" contributions to a city hall purchase fund before "strenuous canvassing" among their friends made up the "difference between the price asked for the property and that which the Council was willing to pay."[18]

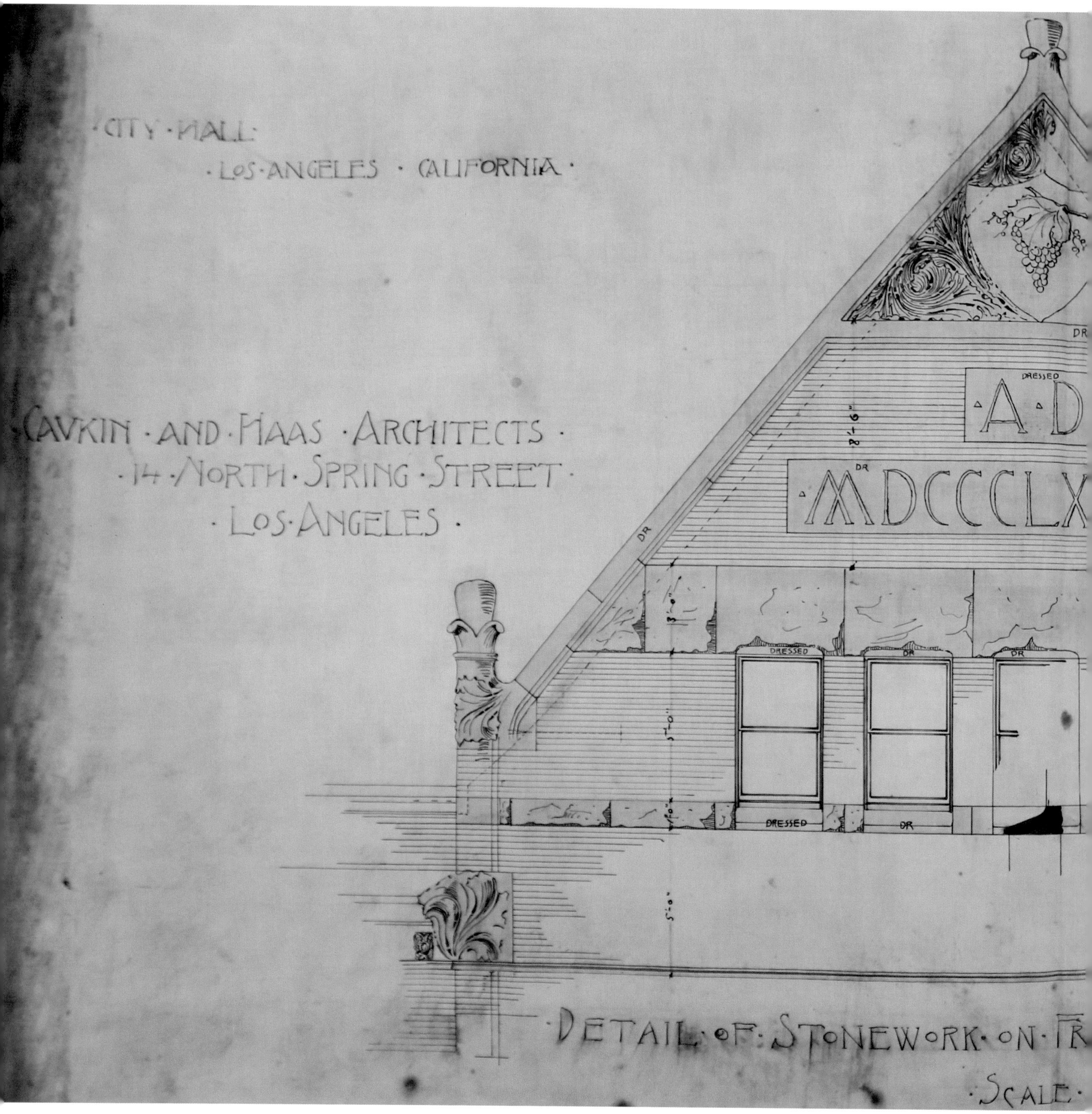
·CITY·HALL·
·LOS·ANGELES · CALIFORNIA·
·CAUKIN ·AND·HAAS ·ARCHITECTS ·
·14·NORTH·SPRING·STREET·
·LOS·ANGELES ·
DRESSED
A·D
MDCCCLX
DR
DRESSED
·DETAIL·OF·STONEWORK·ON·FR
·SCALE·

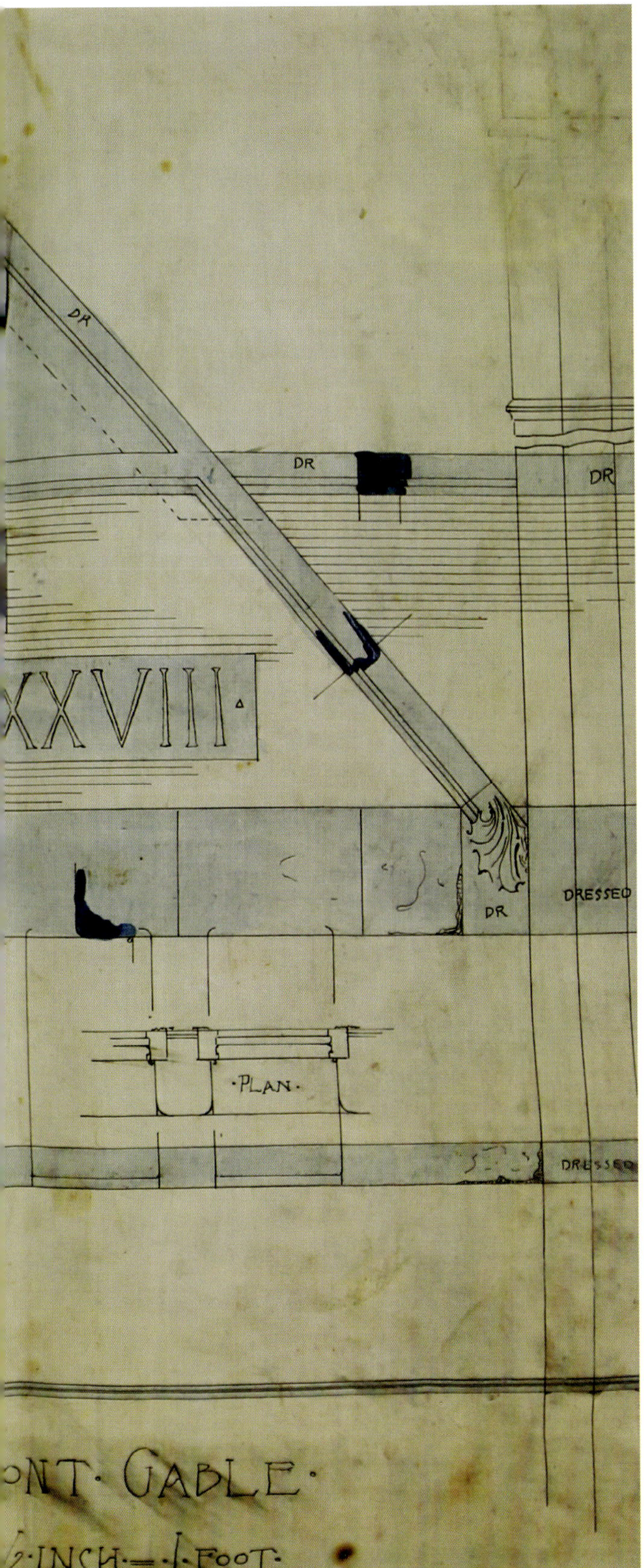

Early maps recorded Fort Street as Calle Fortin, named after the U.S. military base, Fort Moore, situated at its north end. When Americans began calling it Fort Street, the name stuck. It was renamed Broadway in 1889, thanks in large part to George D. Rowan, who owned considerable property on the thoroughfare and believed it to be a more fitting moniker.[19]

The location of the new city hall had once been described as the "choicest residence neighborhood" in the city.[20] To make room for the structure, Broadway was widened, leading to protests from local residents concerned their flower gardens and "stately" pepper trees would be destroyed. And in fact, the new building would signal the end of the street's time as a residential neighborhood.

The effort to design the structure began in May 1887 when the building committee of the City Council issued a circular to architects, advising them of the need for a building not to exceed $150,000.

"The lot is situated on the east side of Fort Street, having a frontage of said street of 180 feet by a depth of 165 feet, the building to occupy that portion of the lot as noted on plan below, and set flush with the property line of the street and south side of lot, and shall not exceed 130 feet frontage or 140 depth of lot," the notice read. "Principal entrance to be in center of street frontage. The street frontage and return on the east back to same return to be of face brick or cut stone, either sandstone, or limestone, or terra cotta. The entire structure, including the roof, to be made as safe against fire as possible."[21]

The firm of Caukin and Haas was selected in July 1887 among several local architects who put up bids for the work. According to the *Los Angeles Times,* the architects, who operated from offices at 14 North Spring St. in the heart of downtown, had done "a large amount of the finest work" performed in the city in the previous year. "Their masterpieces are to be found in many localities," the newspaper reported, referring to their work on the soon-to-be-completed Times Building, the Garvanza Park Hotel, the Grand View Hotel in Monrovia, and the Hotel Arcadia in Santa Monica.[22]

John Galen Howard, who was employed by the architects as their head designer during this period, later described Eugene L. Caukin, a Michigan native, as a "very pleasant, slight, pallid man, gentlemanly—maybe forty or fifty."[23]

Solomon Irmscher Haas, born in Galena, Illinois, had arrived in Los Angeles in 1880 soon after completing college. He stayed in the city until 1893, when he left to manage the California State Exhibit at the Chicago World's Fair before continuing his career as an architect in Pittsburgh. When he returned to Los Angeles in 1926 at the age of seventy, he observed, "The

Los Angeles City Hall, Broadway Plan

changes that amazed Rip Van Winkle are nothing compared with the changes I see here."[24]

Caukin and Haas's design for the new city hall was heavily influenced by architect Henry Hobson Richardson, whose unique interpretation of Romanesque design was widely recycled across the nation for grand municipal buildings, churches, and libraries throughout the 1870s and 1880s.

In Los Angeles, Caukin and Haas followed Richardson's emphasis on thick masonry walls, rounded arches over windows, and vast entryways to design a three-story structure of Arizona red sandstone, brick, and terra cotta, with a red-and-brown Spanish tile roof the *Los Angeles Times* predicted would be "a monument to the taste and liberality of the city"[25] and "one of the finest buildings in Southern California."[26]

The building's design was considered so elaborate, Mayor Workman and the City Council were forced to defend themselves against criticism they were funding a structure that was "much too big" for the City's needs and a "waste of public funds."[27]

Reached by a flight of granite steps, the building was entered through a triple-arched porch. Inside, visitors were greeted by a twenty-foot-square vestibule that offered a glimpse of the grand staircase hall, the connection to various offices and meeting rooms.

On the first floor, space was allocated for the office of the clerk of the council; a vault for storage of

Los Angeles City Hall, 213 W. 2nd Street. Built 1884. • *Inset:* Robert B. Young, Architect

Los Angeles City Hall, Broadway between 2nd and 3rd streets, built 1888, served until 1928.

records; and the offices of the tax collector, treasurer, *zanjero* (in charge of water distribution), fire chief, board of public works, and building inspector.

The second floor housed the Council Chamber (which extended to the third floor), the office of the mayor and his secretary, two committee rooms, a coat room, and the offices of the board of education, city surveyor, city attorney, and superintendent of streets.

In 1889, the Los Angeles Public Library moved in with its six thousand volumes, occupying the majority of space on the third floor. The library was connected to the city librarian, whose office, along with the library's reference room, was located in the tower that also housed a ladies' reading room, space for the historical society, and a courtroom.

The floors were all connected by a passenger elevator. The attic also offered room for storage and a meeting space. The Grand Hall and vestibule had marble tile floors with a six-foot-high wainscot of colored Georgia marble.

The Council Chamber, Grand Hall, and vestibule all boasted elaborate columns and pilasters of red oak. Red oak was also used for the Council Chamber ceiling and the room's ten-foot-high wainscoting. The space was illuminated by ornate stained-glass windows in the south gable opposite a public gallery. Attention was drawn to a grand twenty-five-foot-high and ten-foot-wide buff terra cotta mantel with a hood.

The architects paid particular attention to fireproofing the building. The supporting walls were brick, and "all the partitions of hollow fire-clay tile and all the floor and ceiling joists are covered with the same kind of tile."[28] The architects anticipated future additions eventually would be built, including an engine house.[29]

The contractor for the project was John Hanlon; Willard and Wadsworth, the mason for the cut stone; H. Clement and Company provided the terra cotta and ornamental brick; Los Angeles Terra Cotta and Pressed Brick Company, the interior fireproofing; and the roof tiles were supplied by the San Francisco firm Gladding, McBean.[30]

The final cost of the structure was $230,000. It was decided funds for construction would be raised through the sale of bonds. However, the uptake was slow, and the City was short of money, resulting in the building being only partially complete when employees moved in. The upper floors were not finished until 1893.[31]

Still, the building represented a significant step forward for the city and provided a dignified venue to welcome investors and visiting dignitaries to Los Angeles. Within its walls, leaders promoted the ambitions of the region to three successive U.S. presidents—William McKinley, Theodore Roosevelt, and William Taft.

While the initial design was praised, it soon became apparent there were problems with the finished structure. In 1898, after large cracks began to appear in partition walls, concerns grew that the building was settling. "A distinct vibration not unlike that of a slight earthquake is frequently felt in the offices on the north side of the building and while it is not supposed that the structure is at all unsafe, it is the intention of the Council to put it in perfect repair, provided the cost is not too great," the *Los Angeles Times* reported.[32]

The following year, the building committee recommended the height of the tower be reduced by twenty feet, although no action was taken.[33] In 1903, architects John Parkinson and John C. Austin were appointed to a special commission to examine the structure. They concluded three rooms in the library were overloaded and recommended additional columns for support that would extend from the basement to the ceiling of the rooms used by the library.

Although Parkinson calculated that a floor in one of the rooms was fifty percent overloaded, he concluded the structure was "nevertheless safe." He explained, "At least there is a factor of safety that enters into the computation. But the floors are not rigid."[34] Adding to the stress on the tower was the weight of an "immense" bell that sounded every time the fire department was called into action. In 1917, after damage caused by various earthquakes loosened the bricks in the tower, the decision was made to reduce its height by seventy-six feet to a height of 107 feet, and the work was completed in September 1918.[35]

In 1900, the beginning of a new millennium, more than 100,000 citizens called Los Angeles home. As the population multiplied, politicians began to examine ways to reorganize how the city was governed. Rapid population and industrial growth had led to fears that without proper planning, many American cities would become crowded and chaotic.

The City Beautiful Movement, a reform philosophy advocating grand city planning with parks, boulevards, and inspirational architecture, had developed in major East Coast cities in the 1890s and early 1900s. Its followers believed a more beautiful city would lead to a more motivated, harmonious society. The philosophy made its way to Los Angeles, and an art committee was established in 1903 to promote interest in the civic development of the city; by 1905, it was formally recognized as the city's Municipal Art Commission. In 1907, celebrated urban theorist Charles Mulford Robinson was commissioned to create plans to beautify the city, including establishing an administrative center that would group together public buildings such as the city hall, courthouse, county jail, and federal building, all to be connected by small parks.[36]

Robinson, who held the first professorship of civic design in the country at the University of Illinois, gained recognition for conceptualizing city plans for Denver, Omaha, and Honolulu and was the organizer of the National Alliance of Civic Organizations. In Los Angeles, he recommended locating the city hall on the site of a row of buildings, including the Bullard Block on North Spring Street. The proposed civic center would be located north of First Street and south of the Plaza and between Broadway and Main Street, where the county jail, courthouse, and federal building were already located.[37]

Robinson's plan had a significant influence on city leaders who, in 1909, took the first step toward building a civic center and a new city hall by beginning the process of acquiring the Temple Block at the intersection of Spring and Main streets from investors Robert A. Rowan and Cal Hunter, who owned the property. The $500,000 purchase, to be paid in installments over seven years, was aided by $125,000 in contributions from nearby business owners.[38,39]

News of the acquisition triggered a frenzy of activity among local architects, eager to jockey for the chance to design a new municipal home for the city. In order to gain public approval, voters would twice be asked to give their permission to sell the existing building in favor of the new site on the Temple Block.

On June 30, 1910, Los Angeles voters overwhelmingly responded "yes." The *Los Angeles Times* reported the 4,714 majority who voted in favor was "so palpable in its result that the council will at once consider undertaking a sale."[40]

Despite enthusiastic support, legal and political obstacles soon emerged, delaying the project. The city charter would have to be amended to allow the current building to be sold, and the newly elected City Council members were more critical of the idea compared to their predecessors; they also voiced concern over the way funds would be raised to acquire a new location.

The debate over whether to build a new city hall led to what the *Times* described as "verbal fireworks" in the Council Chamber that "at times threatened a general oratorical conflagration." The council argued over how to pay for a new structure and whether to also acquire the nearby Bullard Block to allow for a larger building.

In February 1914, City Attorney Stephens gave his opinion the City could move ahead with a proposal to acquire the Bullard Block from Dr. John Anson Bullard, though he made clear the title to the property could be acquired only once the fee was paid in full. No construction should begin, Stephens maintained, until the title was secured.[41] It was hoped the sale of the city hall structure could raise as much as $600,000.

Former Chief of Police Charles E. Sebastian attempted to reinvigorate the effort to build a new city hall shortly after he was elected the city's thirtieth mayor in 1915. However, as World War I took hold in Europe, the project was met with declining interest. "While many contend this is not an opportune time to start work on a new city hall, there are equally strong arguments in favor of doing this work right now when the activity is needed most," he argued.[42] When the United States entered the conflict in 1917, many costly construction projects in the city were placed on hold indefinitely.

TO THE VOTER

Do you want to see Los Angeles have a new City Hall like this or some other beautiful design, one which Los Angeles may be justly proud of?

Do you want to save the city from paying out $42,955.80 yearly for rent for offices for various departments of the city now located outside of our inadequate old City Building?

Do you want to continue to pay out $42,955.80 in rent annually when this sum will pay the interest at 4½ per cent annually on a sum sufficient to build a new City Hall?

Do you know that money realized from the sale of the old City Hall site will be almost sufficient to build a new City Hall which contains ten times as much space for offices?

Do you want to have a City Hall big and commodious enough to accommodate all of the departments of the city in one building; where you can transact all your city business by paying one car fare?

If you do—VOTE YES to authorize the sale of the old City Hall property. on Thursday, Junc 30th, 1910.

A SUGGESTED PLAN FOR THE NEW CITY HALL

Voter Instruction Card, 1910

CHAPTER 2

MAYOR GEORGE E. CRYER

For the last two years I have been urging upon the people the necessity of providing a new adequate City Hall. I hope that they will seize this opportunity to supply a long-felt want. The present building is shabby, antiquated, and poorly adapted to the business of a metropolitan city.

—Mayor George E. Cryer, May 30, 1923[1]

Los Angeles city leaders understood that to keep pace with a relentless population boom, they needed a new city hall worthy of a burgeoning metropolis. George E. Cryer was elected mayor in 1921 with a mandate to clean up city politics, but he knew that to be considered a successful leader, he would have to reinvent and reorganize the way Los Angeles did business—beginning with the construction of a new municipal home.

Cryer's incumbency would coincide with the greatest growth and development in Los Angeles history. By 1920, the population was approaching 600,000, and in the coming decade, it would more than double. Immediately after taking office, Cryer began pushing for a new city charter and an executive budget. His administration laid the groundwork for an ambitious series of bond issues to significantly expand the Los Angeles Harbor and to acquire the site for, and pay for the construction of, a new city hall.

George E. Cryer

During Cryer's time in office, Los Angeles would construct the Los Angeles Memorial Coliseum, Olympic Auditorium, and the new Central Library, and dedicate the Mulholland Highway. Considerable new investments were made to manage traffic, water, and power, and to construct a series of branch city halls, public libraries, and police and fire stations.

In 1928, Cryer gained national attention as Los Angeles assumed prompt culpability for the St. Francis Dam disaster that claimed more than four hundred lives. With his guidance, the City settled the many claims for damages without legal dispute. It was also during his administration that Los Angeles secured the 1932 Summer Olympic Games.

Born on May 13, 1875, on a farm in Waterloo, Nebraska, George Edward Cryer had a childhood dream to someday work with horses.[2] He moved to California in 1885 with his parents, John and Elizabeth (Grange) Cryer, who had both grown up in Yorkshire, England. His father had been a merchant during the frontier days in Sioux City, Iowa, and according to family legend, helped provide supplies for Lieutenant Colonel George Armstrong Custer's notorious Black Hills Expedition.[3]

Cryer studied at public schools in Redlands and Pasadena before graduating from Los Angeles High School. In 1898, he was an early volunteer, serving in California's Seventh Los Angeles Regiment in the Spanish-American War. By the end of the conflict, he was a respected sergeant, determined to pursue his passion for the law.

After his discharge, he enrolled in the University of Michigan at Ann Arbor, where he served as assistant editor of the *Michigan Law Review*. He was known as "Judge" to fellow students because of his judicial temperament.[4] After graduation in 1903, he returned to Los Angeles and began practicing law.[5] He met his future wife, Grace Gay of Franklin, Pennsylvania, at a Michigan alumni event in California, despite the fact they had graduated the same year.[6] They married on September 5, 1906,[7] and they later had two children, Edward Gay and Catherine Christine.

Cryer's slim build, gray eyes, and brown hair often led to comparisons to Woodrow Wilson. The *Los Angeles Examiner* noted he had a "frank engaging disposition," although he was, the newspaper reported, "not at all a pretty man, his face just escaping being rugged, a visage in which kindliness perhaps exceeds strength, but with a chin sufficiently prognathous to show that he has a will that will find a way."[8]

A Republican, Presbyterian, Mason, Elk, and Knight of Pythias,[9] Cryer quickly established himself in the legal field, and by 1911, he was a federal district attorney under A.I. McCormick. The following year, Judge John W. Shenk appointed him chief assistant city attorney. From 1915 to 1919, Cryer served as chief district attorney.

His transition from the legal world to politics was heavily backed by *Los Angeles Times* newspaper publisher Harry Chandler, who supported Cryer's opposition to municipally owned power utilities and saw the forty-six-year-old as the ideal candidate to take on incumbent Meredith Pinxton Snyder. "I had no idea of becoming a candidate until a few days before the primaries, when I entered the race at the earnest solicitation of a number of friends," Cryer later reflected.[10]

Snyder, a Democrat born in Winston-Salem, North Carolina, had the support of Chandler's arch rival, magnate William Randolph Hearst, publisher of the *Los Angeles Examiner* and *Herald*. He also had a formidable resume, having served as the city's police commissioner from 1891 to 1894 and later on the city council. He had also served as mayor from 1896 to 1898, and again from 1900 to 1904. Following the death of his son, Ross, from injuries sustained at the Battle of Chateâu Thierry during World War I,[11] he returned to politics and was re-elected in 1919 with the support of organized labor and the two local Hearst newspapers, the *Los Angeles Herald* and the *Examiner*.

Meredith Pinxton Snyder

After beginning his latest term, Snyder identified a new city hall as a top priority. "The one or two public buildings constructed a score of years ago, supposedly for half a century, are ridiculously inadequate and new sites and buildings are imperative," he declared in his annual mayor's message on July 7, 1919. "We are without an adequate city hall, a public service building, a police administration building, and a jail, a library building, an auditorium, so much needed for conventions and large gatherings, an art gallery and museum, and other public structures."[12]

Despite his appeals, Snyder struggled to deliver new infrastructure, yet he remained a formidable incumbent. To energize his own campaign, Cryer recruited former University of California football star Kent Kane Parrot, known for his "imposing physique and personal magnetism."[13] A native of Kennebunkport, Maine, Parrot came to Los Angeles in 1907 to attend law school and was admitted to the California bar in 1909. He would trade a promising legal career to pursue his political ambitions with the encouragement of his mentor, USC law professor and Superior Court Judge Gavin Craig.

Even before Cryer was elected, critics noted how much control Parrot exercised over his boss. When Cryer, at the urging of Parrot, withdrew from a series of written debates in the *Los Angeles Record* and instead allowed his campaign manager to take on the mayor directly, Snyder asked Cryer, "Who is Kent Parrot? Is he your mouthpiece? If so, are the promises he is reported to have made to Spring Street gamblers also uttered with your knowledge and consent?"[14]

Later described as a "sinister"[15] political "wire-puller" and the man "who brought machine politics to Los Angeles,"[16] Parrot lobbied to secure the support of the Central Labor Council, the Better America Foundation and the Anti-Saloon League, as well as influential church leaders who became convinced that gambling and vice had prospered during Snyder's administration. He frequently accused Snyder of failing to enforce the city's "most important laws" and playing "favorites."[17]

When the polls opened on a typically warm, sunny, Southern California day on June 7, 1921, a record number of voters were expected to head to the polls. Although Snyder had narrowly defeated Cryer in the May primary, both candidates were confident of success. However, fifteen minutes after the polls closed, Cryer's camp was claiming victory.[18]

Los Angeles City Hall, Broadway

Shortly before midnight, a hundred-strong parade of Cryer-for-Mayor-decorated vehicles led by a triumphant band began a procession through downtown. Their candidate ultimately won by more than seven thousand votes (Cryer 55,422, Snyder 48,274).[19] Snyder waited until morning to concede the election. "I have no ill feeling in this matter," he said. "I am today forwarding to Mr. Cryer my felicitations, wishing for him a successful administration."[20] And with that, Snyder vowed never again to run for political office.

Cryer was sworn in on July 4, 1921, at a ceremony in the mayor's office. In his first post-election interview, he told the *Los Angeles Examiner*, "I feel the city has outgrown the limitations of the present charter."[21] A new charter would give him more authority to influence civic affairs and more control over the effort to build a new city hall.

Almost immediately, the new mayor began to agitate for a bond issue to pay for a new municipal building. It was estimated that more than eighty percent of the office space occupied by City employees was outside of the current city hall.[22] The new structure, he insisted, should be "adequate for our present and future needs and which shall be in keeping with the wealth and dignity of one of America's largest and most rapidly growing cities."[23]

As a temporary solution, Cryer advocated demolishing the city hall on Broadway and in its place, erecting a modern twelve-story structure. "The need for additional offices all under one roof is imperative," he argued. "The City is paying thousands of dollars annually for scattered rented quarters for City departments. Why not build on the present city hall site a modern office building, not particularly designed for a city hall, but which will serve for the next few years?

"Such a building could be built for $1,000,000 and then, when the new city hall is ready, the office building can be sold for its full or even increased value, as it will be primarily an up-to-date Broadway office building."[24]

Cryer's suggestion for a temporary city hall failed to gain traction, but his efforts to raise funds for a permanent structure through a bond issue would prove more successful. On March 7, 1923, City Council President Ralph L. Criswell presented and obtained the adoption of a resolution, calling on voters to approve a $7.5 million bond issue to pay for a new city hall during the upcoming June 5 election; $5 million would be used to pay for the structure and the remainder to acquire the site.

The resolution also called for a "straw vote" on whether the building should go on the north end of the city in a new administrative center (on the site of the current building) or on the south end in an area bounded by Ninth, Washington, Figueroa, and Los Angeles streets, a rapidly expanding shopping and business district.

Council members Robert M. Allan and Othello P. Conaway voted against the resolution, arguing that the firm of landscape architects, Cook and Hall, had already been commissioned to lay out plans for a new civic center and should be allowed to complete their work and make recommendations on the location of new administrative buildings before any campaign to build a new city hall was launched.[25]

"I am firmly of the opinion that the location of the new city hall is a question which should be decided by all of the people and not by this council or any commission or other body appointed by this council, not by any self-appointed committee or organization," Criswell wrote in a statement.[26]

Wilbur D. Cook and George D. Hall presented their own tentative plan for a civic center to the council a week later. It showed a new city hall on a site on Spring Street, north of First Street, along with a new state building, a new county structure on the site of the courthouse, a new federal building, and

Los Angeles City Hall, Broadway, after the tower was shortened.

Los Angeles City Hall, Broadway, Council Chamber.

the new Hall of Justice. The plan called for the straightening of Spring Street through to Sunset Boulevard and the widening of Broadway by one hundred feet through to Ord Street.[27]

The civic center committee of the city planning commission, chaired by architect Sumner P. Hunt, unanimously agreed that the civic center should be located in the area bounded by First, Hill, and Los Angeles streets and Sunset Boulevard, believing "strongly" that it was where the new city hall should be built. Hunt suggested that placing the civic center in this location would provide a grouping of buildings "that will forever be a credit to Los Angeles."[28]

Although Cryer chose to support the municipal ownership of utilities in his 1923 re-election campaign, the *Los Angeles Times* continued to back him. "Mayor Cryer has made good and should be re-elected," the newspaper argued, as he faced off against the former president of the city council, Bert Farmer, in his bid for a second term. "In a half-hearted manner, other mayors have spoken of Los Angeles as having some day a new city hall, but next to his fight for a new city charter, the city hall problem has been nearest to the mayor's heart and desire, and he has worked to arouse the people to the point that now, on all sides, is heard the statement, 'Los Angeles must have a new city hall.'"[29]

Handily securing a new term, Cryer threw his support behind the city planning commission's report. In a statement, he appealed to voters:

> For the last two years I have been urging upon the people the necessity of providing a new and adequate City Hall. I hope that they will seize this opportunity to supply a long-felt want. The present building is shabby, antiquated, and poorly adapted to the business of a metropolitan city.
>
> It is now housing only about fourteen percent of the City business, and the other eighty-six percent of the City business is housed in scattered buildings, many of them poorly located, and not adapted to our needs. This makes for serious inconvenience to the public, and results in useless expense in rentals paid for outside buildings, and in waste in the public service.
>
> At the coming election the people are to have the opportunity of a site and the erection of a new City Hall, which will not only better the public service, but which will also arouse civic pride in its architectural beauty and setting.
>
> The City Planning Commission has recommended that the new City Hall be grouped with other public buildings north of First Street, thus forming an attractive administrative center.
>
> I am in accord with this recommendation.
>
> (Signed) GEORGE E. CRYER[30]

While support for the city's south-end location was mostly made up of nearby business owners, proponents of the north-end site included the board of directors of the Chamber of Commerce and the Business Owners' and Managers' Association, which argued that the site made financial sense, as fifty percent of the required land was already publicly owned and in close proximity to the county courthouse, Hall of Records, Hall of Justice, county jail, United States post office, and federal building.

As election day grew closer, the City Planning Association led a passionate campaign to avoid an "orphan" city hall, demanding "the economy, efficiency, and sightliness" that could be gained only through an "intelligent grouping in an administrative center."[31]

On the eve of the vote, the *Los Angeles Times* reported that the effort to locate the new city hall away from the administrative center north of First Street had "collapsed," in part, due to opposition from local property owners. "So it has resulted that the south-end business interests do not want a lonesome city hall in their district because they feel it would detract rather than add to the commercial development, and because by removing the city hall from the civic-center plans, the latter would go up in smoke," the newspaper reported.[32]

Among the other bond issues, voters were asked to approve $35 million for a power plant at Boulder Canyon (rejected) and $15 million for the development of Los Angeles Harbor (approved). Critics argued that the City of Los Angeles was bonding itself to excess.

"The need for every one of these bond issues can be recently traced to the city's growth," Councilman R.S. Sparks told the *Los Angeles Record* on the day before the vote. "If Los Angeles had not grown, we might have got along with the old city hall. It was big enough thirty-five years ago. . .. These improvements have to be made, if the city is to keep pace with population. There are only two ways to buy these things—one through direct taxation and the other through bond issues."[33]

As expected, the $7.5 million bond measure received resounding approval with 20,182 voting in favor and 2,819 against. The north-end site additionally gained overwhelming support with 11,600 in favor and 3,360 against. With the official green light from voters, the question now shifted to who would design the building.

George E. Cryer attributed his lack of a "tummy" to regular exercise.

GRAND
OLIVE
HILL
BROADWAY
COUNTY
COURTS
HALL OF
RECORDS
FIRST
SPRING

CHAPTER 3

CHOOSING AN ARCHITECT

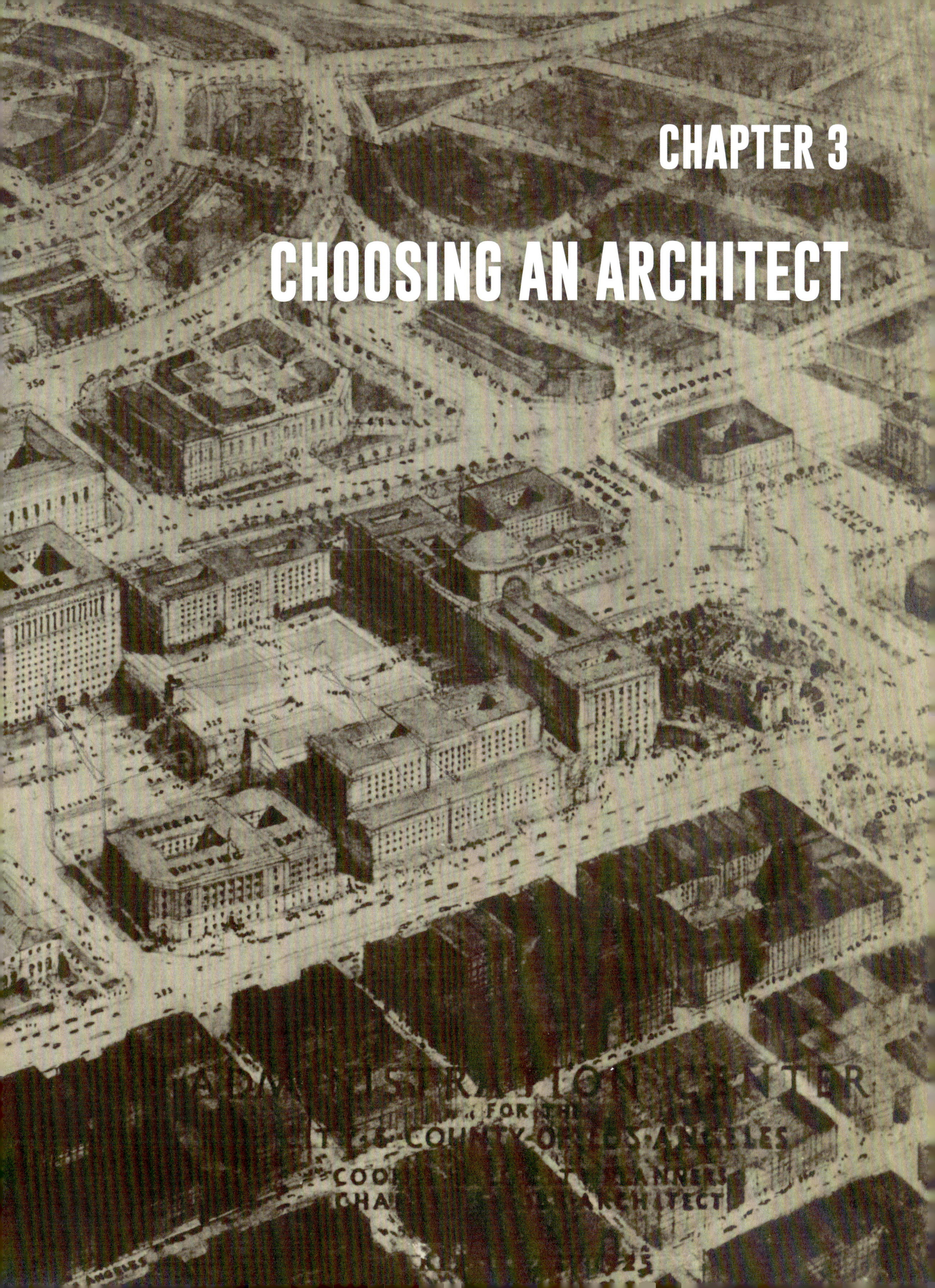

I recommend that every effort be made to settle as soon as possible existing controversy over details of our civic center project. . .. The money for the erection of the City Hall was voted nearly two years ago.

—Mayor George E. Cryer, January 2, 1925[1]

The effort to select an architect to design a new Los Angeles City Hall began with the best of intentions but quickly descended into an unprecedented power struggle between two competing forces, the City Council and the Board of Public Works. It culminated in a bitter legal conflict that significantly delayed the project and led to two rival teams of architects being commissioned for the same job.

"The new city hall will not be a monument of graft, such as have been other similar municipal buildings in other parts of the country," Councilman Miles S. Gregory told the council's civic center committee in November 1923. "The project should be clean and above board from the start."[2]

City leaders initially were unsure whether to hold an open competition for local architects or award the contract to the Los Angeles-based Allied Architects Association, a cooperative of local architects founded for "the purpose of providing architectural service for buildings built with the proceeds of public tax money."[3]

The organization, formed in 1921 with thirty-two licensed architects, believed it could "subordinate and submerge their individual interests" to secure the "best of architecture in public structures." Its members, including G. Edwin Bergstrom, Octavius Morgan, David C. Allison, and Elmer Grey, were responsible for the new Hall of Justice at Temple Street and Broadway. Individual architects had competed with one another to produce a design, and the resulting Beaux Arts concept had evolved out of thirty different designs submitted.

"By giving the architectural work to the Allied Architects Association," Councilman Robert M. Allan argued, "we shall be securing the service of ninety-five percent of the architects of Los Angeles."[4] Councilman Walter Mallard hit back, "Why shut out the other five percent? Let's have an open competition open to all Los Angeles architects, and then the Allied Architects can compete as well as any others who are not members of the association. . .. Then the people can never say that we handed the job to favored architects."[5]

When the council adopted a plan to invite all California architects to enter a competition, the Allied Architects Association warned against the idea. Nevertheless, the organization sought to keep doors open as a tug of war continued over who should design the new city hall.

The Board of Public Works produced a resolution outlining the terms of the competition. J.E. Allison and Harwood Hewitt agreed to represent the Allied Architects Association, while John C. Austin and John Parkinson would speak for architects outside the association. Together, they were to select a fifth member to help oversee the process.[6] While a number of independent architects, including Albert C. Martin and John C. Austin, publicly supported the idea of a competition, the Allied Architects made it known they preferred a proposal by the Community Development Association, which recommended the Allied Architects design all of the city's civic center buildings to ensure uniformity.

As the idea of an open competition lost momentum, knowledgeable observers predicted the work would go to either the Allied Architects Association or an independent trio of architects—Austin, Martin, and Parkinson—known as the Associate Architects.

Austin was a politically savvy designer, who today is best remembered for his work on Griffith Observatory and the Shrine Auditorium. Martin was an innovative architect and engineer who created St. Vincent's Catholic Church in Los Angeles and the Ventura County Courthouse. Parkinson was widely regarded as the dean of Southern California architects, whose many iconic structures include Bullock's Wilshire, Los Angeles Memorial Coliseum, and the Braly Block, the city's first skyscraper.

The Associate Architects had controversially lost out on a bid to design the Los Angeles Central Library the previous year to New York City architect Bertram Goodhue, much to the frustration of many city politicians, including the mayor, who had expressed a strong desire to see the job awarded to a locally based architect.[7] The prospect of a new city hall was no different.

"Every effort should be made to expedite the erection and completion of this much-needed building," Mayor Cryer proclaimed in his annual message delivered to the City Council on January 2, 1924. "If this is done, and a wise judgement [*sic*] is exercised in the selection of the design and plan of the building, the result should be a structure of which we may well be proud, and which will be adequate for the City's needs for many years to come."[8]

A year later, even though a large part of the site had been acquired through legal proceedings, no action had been taken to select an architect for the project. It was increasingly clear that a disagreement between the City Council and the Board of Public Works over whose responsibility it was to hire an architect potentially could get out of hand.

Frustrated by the lack of progress, the council decided to take control. In February 1925, it announced plans to appoint the firm of Curlett and Beelman as architects of the new building, much to the surprise of not only the Board of Public Works, but Curlett and Beelman themselves.

"We knew nothing of the city hall plan," Aleck Curlett told the *Los Angeles Times*, "until shortly before noon when we were notified our firm had been selected as architects. As a result we have no definite ideas on the structure and will not have until the proposition is given a thorough study. We had a general discussion with the council committee in the afternoon, but it will be several days before we can have even tentative plans."[9]

Left: Claud Beelman. *Right*: Aleck Curlett
Pages 32-33: Cook & Hall plan for administrative center, 1925.

One of the most respected firms in the city, Curlett and Beelman was responsible for the William M. Garland Building, Pershing Square Building, and Elks Temple. Aleck Curlett, born in San Francisco in 1881, had graduated with a degree in architecture from Columbia University in 1904. His partner, Claud Beelman, born in Bellefontaine, Ohio, in 1884, went to local public schools before earning the Harvard Scholarship in 1905 by the Architectural League of America. Arriving in California in 1921 from Omaha, Nebraska,[10] Beelman also worked in Cleveland, Detroit, Indianapolis, New Orleans, and Toledo over a career spanning twenty-five years.

Curlett told the *Times* he expected to meet with the Board of Public Works the following week and sign a contract shortly thereafter. He anticipated it would take thirty to sixty days to complete preliminary plans and an additional three months to produce the final design.

"We have no idea of erecting a city hall like is in San Francisco," he explained. "There is too much wasted space there and even $5,000,000 on such a proposed building [*sic*] we shall have to be conservative in our plans."[11]

Defending their surprise action, Council President Boyle Workman said council members were determined "to secure architects of standing who were not identified with either the Allied Architects Association or the so-called 'independents,' both of which groups had been active in the controversy over the planning of the city hall."[12]

On March 4, 1925, the City Council voted to prepare an ordinance directing the city attorney to employ Curlett and Beelman, despite the likelihood the Board of Public Works would not comply with the order. Mayor Cryer admitted to the press that he had heard "ugly rumors" about where the process was headed but refused to commit himself by openly taking sides.

Attorney Jess E. Stephens's opinion read: "The charter nowhere gives authority to the Board of Public Works, nor to any other administrative board to enter into the contract now in contemplation. While the Board of Public Works is given certain administrative authority in connection with the design and construction of public buildings, I find no inconsistency between the authority and the making of a contract by your honorable body for the employment of an architect for the drawing of plans etc. and while it would seem logical for the Board of Public Works to be authorized to enter into a contract for the employment of architects, there is nothing to require that the contract be executed by that board. It is therefore within your power to authorize the execution of such contract by any other appropriate office of the city, such as the Mayor, president of the council or city clerk."[13]

As expected, the city attorney's opinion only fueled the board's opposition. "As a member of the Board of Public Works," Arthur Eldridge insisted, "I shall never vote to approve a demand for payment for services as authorized by this contract by the City Council. I think it is not in accordance with the state law. I am very glad, however, that the city attorney has finally rendered an opinion about this matter, which has been hanging so many years; an opinion that really tells us where we stand."[14]

In the same month, Superior Court Judge Gavin W. Craig granted a temporary restraining order preventing the City Council from entering into a contract with Curlett and Beelman. The injunction, filed on behalf of private citizen Charles J. Casper, argued the council had no power to enter into such an agreement, and the Board of Public Works had sole authority on the matter. The board denied any knowledge of the action, however the injunction meant a court would now have to rule on whether the contract was valid.[15]

Meanwhile, the Board of Public Works, which had received bids from "several" local architects for the work, including Walker and Eisen, Lloyd L. Smith, and the Allied Architects Association, made its own move, selecting the Associate Architects for the job as the group had submitted "the lowest, regular bid of any responsible bidder."[16] On April 9, 1925, the board drafted a resolution authorizing a contract with the Associate Architects for the preparation of plans, stating their "combined ability and reputation" offered to the city "advantages which would be impossible to obtain except through their cooperation."[17]

When the council got wind of the action, President Workman called a secret conference in his office, and after an hour-long meeting, both groups emerged with unflinching support for their respective architects.[18] Although developments appeared to leave the Allied Architects Association on the sidelines, City Attorney Stephens gave them a glimmer of hope, explaining the law was unclear on who ultimately had authority.

George E. Cryer won his third term as mayor in May by defeating federal judge Benjamin Bledsoe, who was backed by Cryer's former allies at the *Los Angeles Times*. The newspaper sought to exploit Cryer's relationship with Kent Parrot, who by then had been accused of attempting to inappropriately influence the Harbor Commission and control members of the police department. "Los Angeles has outgrown Mayor Cryer and the clique of political wire-pullers that surround him," the newspaper stated in a front-page editorial to its readers.[19] The election had particular significance, as a new city charter meant the mayor's term would now be extended to four years from the previous two.

The new city charter, set to take effect in July, would make clear under the law that the Board of Public Works had the authority to hire architects for City projects. Board members quickly realized delaying the project until then using legal proceedings would be their best strategy.

A week after Cryer's re-election, Curlett and Beelman submitted an invoice for $10,000 to the City Council. The *Los Angeles Times* described the request as the latest of many moves in the comedy-drama of "Who is to build the city hall, and if so, when?"[20] City Auditor John S. Myers refused to issue any payment until it was determined if the contract was legal.[21] Four days later, Myers and City Treasurer Ned T. Powell and members of the City Council were served with copies of a temporary restraining order issued by Superior Court Judge Walter Guerin, instructing them to appear in court or to show cause as to why the Charles J. Casper injunction preventing payment to Curlett and Beelman should not be granted.[22]

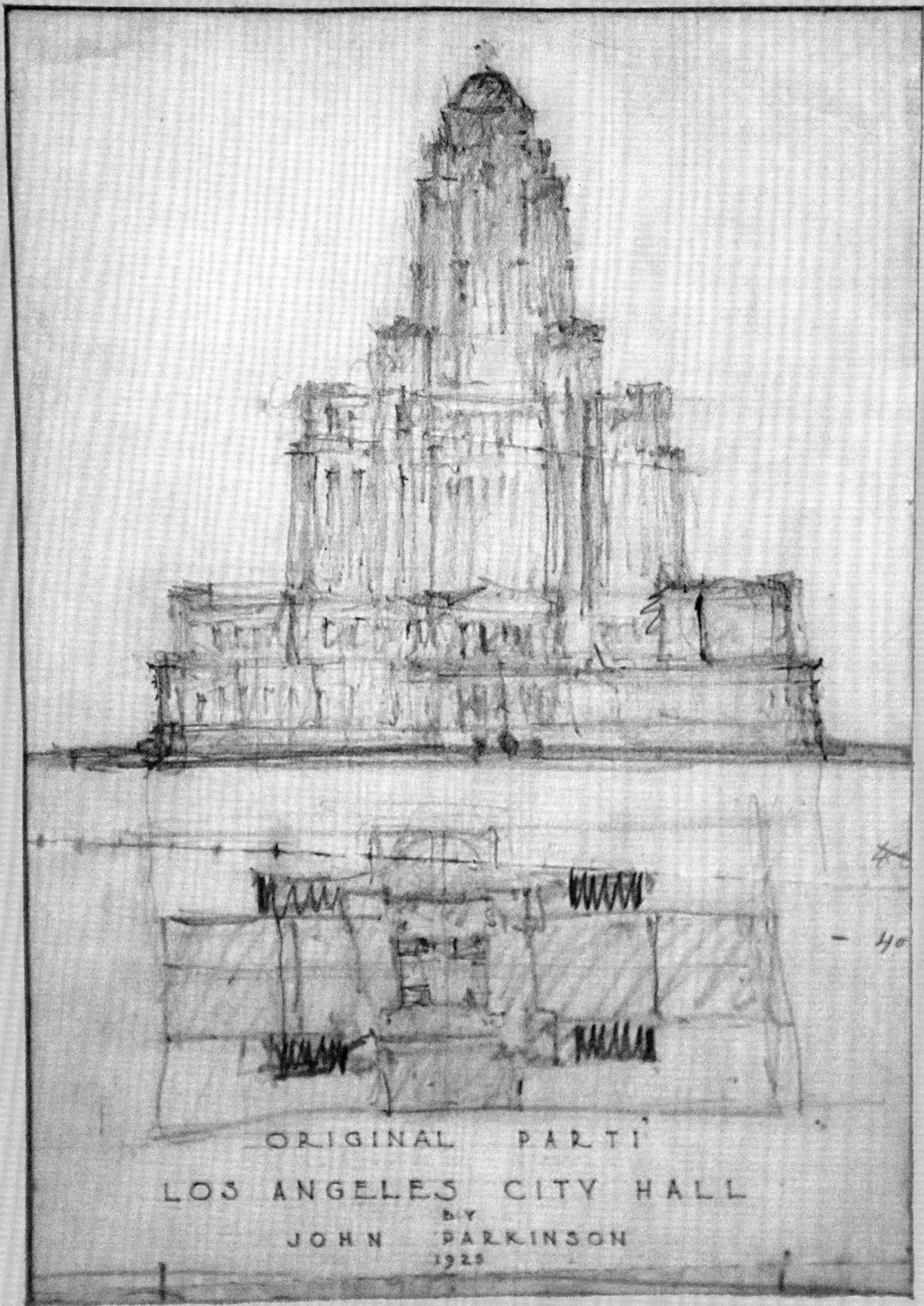

John Parkinson concept for Los Angeles City Hall

On July 27, 1925, Superior Court Judge Hartley Shaw ruled that under the new charter, the Board of Public Works had the right to hire an architect, and thus the contract between the City Council and Curlett and Beelman was invalid. Prior to the ruling, attorney Edward R. Young, representing Curlett and Beelman, had promised to appeal and take the matter to a higher court if Judge Shaw ruled against the validity of his client's agreement.[23]

That afternoon, a meeting of the City Hall committee was held in the mayor's office to discuss how to expedite construction of the building. Joining the committee were John C. Austin, Albert C. Martin, and Leslie R. Hewett, attorney for the Associate Architects. It was agreed going forward the entire matter would be handled in full by the Board of Public Works.[24]

Soon afterward and with the blessing of the mayor, the board formally re-awarded Austin, Martin, and Parkinson the contract to design a new city hall. Under the terms of the contract, the architects were to receive $270,000, or six percent of $4.5 million, for their services. Although the bond issue was set at $5 million, the contract amount was lowered to apportion $500,000 for contingencies.

In an effort to persuade Curlett and Beelman to drop their proposed legal action, Mayor Cryer called a conference in his office with City Attorney Stephens, Commissioner Dunn of the Board of Public Works, Commissioner Danburg of the city planning commission, as well as City Council President Workman and Councilmen Hall and Sparks. They agreed to meet with the architects to discuss what could be done.

Undeterred, Curlett and Beelman wrote to the City Council, advising them Claud Beelman had embarked on an "extensive trip through the principal cities of the country, for the purpose of securing information with respect to the plan and equipment for the proposed city hall building."[25]

For his part, City Attorney Stephens announced he planned to closely scrutinize the Board of Public Works contract with Austin, Martin, and Parkinson, though he admitted he would likely approve it with some minor changes.[26]

Nebraska State Capitol

Los Angeles City Hall Preliminary Perspective, Donald B. Parkinson

The *Los Angeles Times* reported Curlett and Beelman were considering a lawsuit seeking between $100,000 and $150,000 in damages, and that after several meetings with the architects, it became clear they had no intention of dropping their case.

The City Hall committee considered numerous compromise options, including cancelling all contracts and re-advertising the job. It was even suggested both groups of architects should get together and attempt to thrash out a compromise amongst themselves. Mayor Cryer favored continuing with the Associate Architects so as not to further delay the project.[27]

On August 11, 1925, Mayor Cryer received a telegram from New York architects Schultze and Weaver, who had designed Los Angeles's Biltmore Hotel and Subway Terminal Building and were now offering to design a new city hall, but no action was taken.

The following day, Mayor Cryer and the Board of Public Works agreed to a $50,000 bond to be given by Austin, Martin, and Parkinson to protect the City against potential damages from a successful lawsuit by Curlett and Beelman. At a meeting of the City Hall committee, City Attorney Stephens agreed to approve the board's contract with the Associate Architects, clearing the way for the trio to finally get to work on preliminary drawings for the structure.

The original concept for the building, created by John Parkinson, depicted an office tower rather than the traditional domed municipal building modeled after the U.S. Capitol in Washington, D.C. The plan he sketched showed a building organized into three distinct sections: a broad base and a mid-section dominated by a setback tower. The concept was further enhanced by his son and business partner, Donald Parkinson, to reveal a structure with striking similarities to Bertram Goodhue's 1920 design for the Nebraska State Capitol.

In Nebraska, Goodhue also abandoned notions of a domed municipal building and instead embraced the romantic age of the skyscraper. His ruthless determination to remove all unnecessary decoration in favor of an austere geometrical composition caused a sensation in the architectural community, and he further advanced the style with his 1924 design for the Los Angeles Central Library.

Similar to Goodhue's design for the Nebraska State Capitol and the Los Angeles Central Library, the preliminary plans submitted by the Associate Architects to the Board of Public Works on September 25, 1925, showed a cross-axial plan with a domed rotunda at the base of the tower. Like Goodhue's plan, there was also a dome atop the tower. The architects outlined their ideas in an accompanying report:

> In designing the building it has been necessary to exercise strict economy, and we believe we have accomplished this by the elimination of a large amount of ornament, relying on the size of the building for beauty. We have not followed the usual stereotyped design of city hall building [*sic*], but have adhered to the type of building that will give the maximum amount of floor space and the maximum amount of light, with minimum amount of expensive detail.
>
> Rather than follow closely any of the so-called "Styles of Architecture" of the past, the architects for the new city hall have adapted the details and forms, chiefly of the Italian Renaissance, to a modern steel-frame building. As with all good architecture, the exterior is a simple expression of the building's plan.
>
> Above the lower stories, which house the large public rooms of the city hall, the building is devoted to typical office floors which, due to the large shape of the building and its height, are unusually well lighted.
>
> Contrary to the usual type of City Hall building, in which only forty percent of the floor area is useful space, nothing of the efficiency has been sacrificed in this design to obtain an effect of dignity and beauty. The monumental character of the new Los Angeles City Hall will be obtained almost entirely by means of silhouette, structural form, and scale.[28]

The architects further explained they intended to confine decoration primarily to the lower stories on the exterior, where it could easily be appreciated by the public. On the interior, it would be limited primarily to "the main floor in the great central rotunda, the entrance areas, and the public audience rooms."[29] They confidently predicted the structural frame would be "the strongest in California."

The board praised the architects for the "excellent" appearance of the building and the speed with which they had delivered their plans. The architects, barring any unforeseen circumstances, projected the building would be completed within two years.

On September 30, 1925, a specially arranged meeting of the Los Angeles Municipal Art Commission was held in the office of the mayor to informally consider the merits of the architects' design. The meeting, attended by John C. Austin, Albert C. Martin, John and Donald Parkinson, and members of the commission, was a chance to discuss how the architects planned to address the future needs of the city. Austin spoke for the architects:

The Associate Architects considered an elaborate tiled roof.

> The architects were given a list of the departments, with the number of square feet desired by each, which set the size of the building. Then they were given the location and size of the land upon which the building was to set. In order to provide for the space asked and requirements for the next twenty years, they decided on a tower built 430 feet high. If they had adhered to the 150-foot limit, the building would have covered the area of the whole property. They wanted to leave park space for beautification of setting. Some time later the present court house would be removed, leaving that space as park area. For these reasons, they decided to go up in the air and build this size and shape to fit the needs of various departments.
>
> The 110-foot square for tower does not represent abutments at all; the wings are to be 63 feet x 100 feet. Across the front at the first story is to be an allegorical panel giving the history of Los Angeles. The materials of construction have not been decided upon. They hope to use granite for the first story and for the balance, terra cotta or limestone, according to funds allowed. An inner forecourt is at the base of the tower as one enters the building from Spring Street, also a courtyard about 40 feet x 60 feet.
>
> The building is to be placed 300 feet north of First Street and about 170 feet south of the Federal Building. This was considered necessary on account of a difference in grade of 20 feet between First Street and Temple Street, and for the reason that if the building were located near First Street, one would have to look up a hill about 20 feet to the park at the north end. A park is desired by all makers of Civic Centers. The architects kept at the upper end near the level of all other buildings in the Civic Center, above the street, and provided a 300-foot park between the building and First Street.[30]

Parkinson sought to assure the commission the high tower allowed for the best possible building that could be built with the funds available. The "comparatively low skyline" meant a taller structure was needed to make the necessary statement. The tower, the architects explained, would be "tapered on the abutments so it would not look top heavy, and tile was to be used on the steps at the top, making a sparkle

Los Angeles City Hall, Rendering

of light for the city from a distance." The structure's first story, Parkinson declared, would be "monumental in character."[31]

The architects insisted their plans were focused primarily on producing a functional office building and did not include funds for any costly sculptures. As Austin explained, they intended to contact noted sculptors for the work at a later stage. The explanation prompted Commissioner Arthur B. Benton to argue there "should be embodied in public buildings sculpture of the aspirations of our times" to inspire patriotism and encourage learning history.

When Benton pointed out that by building a new city hall, the City had embarked on the creation of a civic center without a formally agreed upon city center plan, Martin replied he had studied all the different civic center plans before deciding to place the structure "in the center of the plat between Temple and First streets" where it would fit "best with the group." In Paris, buildings were not placed symmetrically, he noted.

Mayor Cryer believed the civic center would develop with the new city hall "as an established fact in that locality." He added that the city attorney's office was studying the city charter to determine the legality of building above the established height limit. If it were not allowed, he suggested an amendment to the charter would be necessary.[32]

In October, the *Los Angeles Times* reported the City Council had denied a $54,000 payment due to the architects until a majority of its members were convinced a 430-foot structure could be built within the budget allowed.

"The building proposed by the architects is 430 feet high, or nearly three times the present building-height limit," Councilman Criswell argued. "This building cannot be built until the people of Los Angeles have amended the charter . . . I am told that a building of this size cannot be built for $4,500,000, but will cost nearly $8,000,000. If this is correct, then when the building is half built, the people of Los Angeles will be asked for another $4,000,000 or so to complete the building. I want the facts about this before I vote to give the board this money."[33]

The council voted to refer the request for payment to its civic center committee for further debate. Councilman Hall, the committee chairman, said he would welcome further explanation from the architects about their plans for the structure.[34]

The civic center committee gave its approval after the architects provided a statement outlining exactly how the money would be spent. Soon afterwards, the City Council voted unanimously to authorize the outstanding payment.

Adding some confusion to the project, in November 1925, the County Board of Supervisors formally adopted a civic center plan created by the Allied Architects Association. While it did not bind the board to any particular building plan, it was a significant step, with the County expected to invest as much as $50 million in new buildings in the next "few years."

The plan, which included locations for a new city hall, federal building, Union Station, and other structures, was at odds with the City's ambitions for the location of a new city hall. The City favored the location identified in the Cook and Hall plan that positioned the building fifty feet further north than the Allied Architects' suggestion.[35]

Councilman Mallard argued the Allied Architects' plan would leave the city hall "in a hole" compared to other structures and cost significantly more than the Cook and Hall plan. While local newspapers discussed whether a commission was needed to reconcile the differences, the Associate Architects continued with their existing plans.

In November 1926, the Associate Architects received an important letter from their attorney, Leslie R. Hewitt of the firm Hewitt, Ford, and Crump, informing them that the time limit for Curlett and Beelman to appeal the Superior Court ruling invalidating their contract with the City had now expired—officially ending the possibility of further legal action.

CHAPTER 4

ASSOCIATE ARCHITECTS

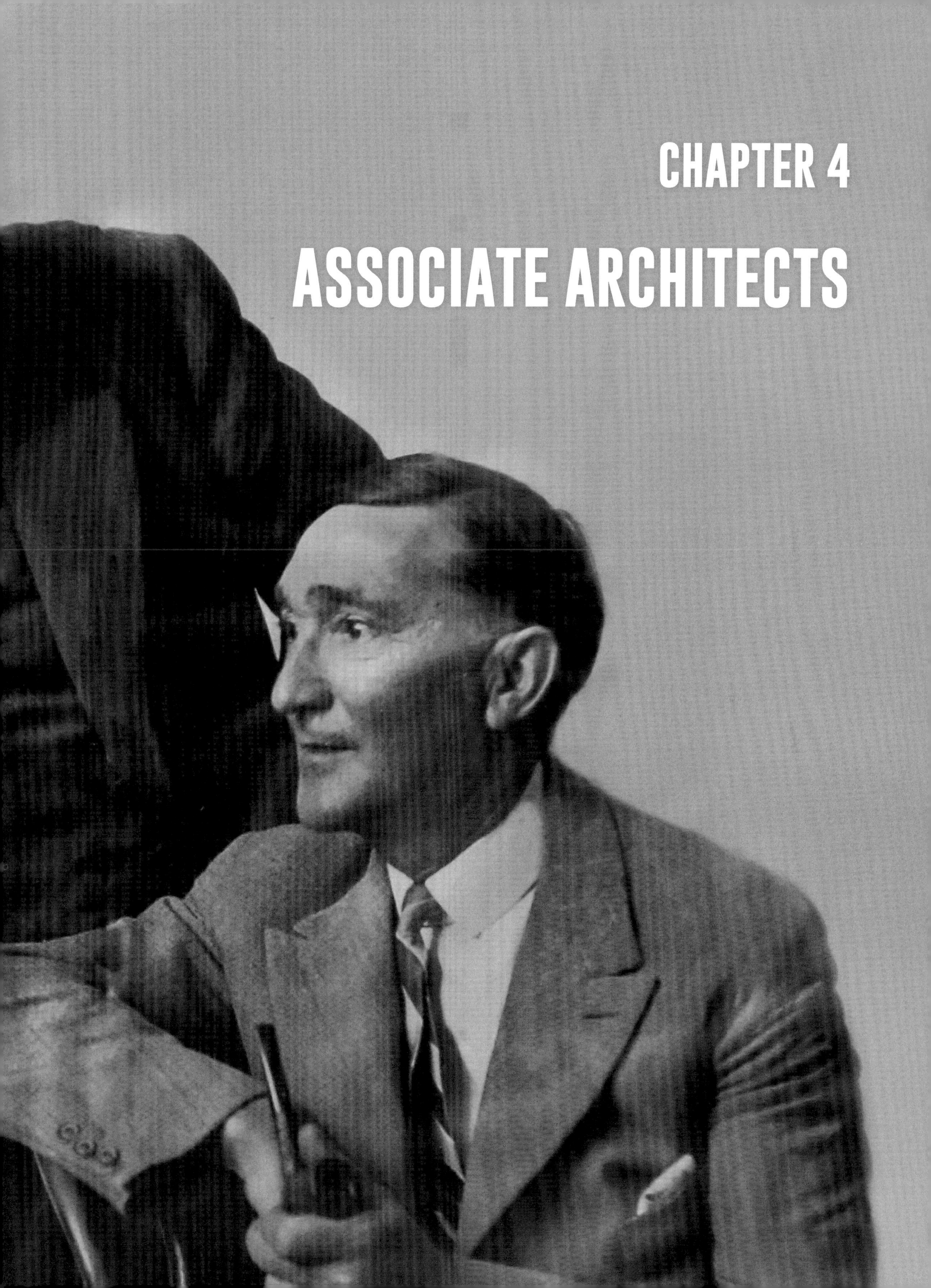

The commissioning of my father, along with John Parkinson and John C. Austin, was probably the highlight of my father's career. The three architects were unusual in their practice, and, as a team, they were quite formidable because of the many, many contacts that the three of them had.

—Albert C. Martin Jr.[1]

The Associate Architects were three of the most renowned architects in Los Angeles. Two Englishmen and an American, their partnership was rooted in a decades-long friendship enhanced by mutual respect for their complementary skills. Individually, they were responsible for some notable firsts in Los Angeles architecture, and each had a significant impact on the city's skyline. Collectively, they represented a formidable team with a strong sense of civic responsibility and passion for Los Angeles.

John C. Austin, Architect
Pages 44–45: John Parkinson, John C. Austin, Albert C. Martin, Associate Architects

JOHN C. AUSTIN

John C. Austin was the charismatic "politician" and "arranger" of the trio. A "suave" and "capable" designer,[2] his impressive list of architectural achievements is rivaled only by the enormity of his civic contribution. A larger-than-life, passionate champion of Los Angeles, he designed numerous iconic structures in the city, yet still managed to serve on a host of local, state, and national committees and as president of various prominent organizations.

Born John Corneley Wilson Austin in Bodicote, Oxfordshire, England, on February 13, 1870, the son of Richard Wilson and Jane Elizabeth Austin, he studied at local schools before beginning an architectural apprenticeship with William S. Barwick. In 1891, at the age of twenty-one, Austin headed to the United States looking for adventure. He found work in the Philadelphia office of British architect Benjamin Linfoot, and remained there for a year before returning to England, where he was once again hired by Barwick.[3]

After just three months at home, he set sail for a new life in California, where he went to work for the San Francisco office of architects William Mooser and Charles J. Devlin. He remained in the city for two-and-a-half years before heading south to Los Angeles, where he offered his services to various architects, including John Parkinson.

"Minus commissions, prospects, or capital, with pencil in hand, I stood behind the table, when in through the open door quietly walked John C. Austin, seeking work," Parkinson later reflected. "I liked his looks—a square face; firm mouth and good jaw; gray, intelligent eyes in which a twinkle hovered, a man to hold his ground and fight fair, asking nothing but opportunity, and, I was to learn, a man of wit, courage, and staying qualities.[4]

"We have been associate architects on several jobs, including the Chamber of Commerce Building, the City Hall at Los Angeles, and the Los Angeles Federal Building. He has worked hard and acquired wealth, but on that morning, over forty years ago, asking me for a job, neither of us had a nickel, not even a penny, but what did that matter? We were young—John was twenty-five and I was only thirty-two—and the world was ours."[5]

Austin would eventually find work in the offices of Morgan and Walls, then the prominent firm in the region. During the next two years, he worked for various architects before establishing his own practice. In 1922, he joined forces with Frederick M. Ashley, and the practice became John C. Austin and Frederick M. Ashley, later changing to Austin, Field, and Fry in 1937.

In addition to Griffith Observatory, the Shrine Auditorium, and the Chamber of Commerce Building, his long list of architectural credits includes St. Vincent's Hospital, the Wright and Callender Building, the Potter Hotel in Santa Barbara, and the Virginia Hotel in Long Beach.

He excelled in ecclesiastical architecture and designed St. Paul's Catholic Church, First Methodist Church, and a remodel of St. Vibiana's Cathedral on Main Street. During his career, he completed more than $25 million worth of school projects in Southern California, including Los Angeles High School, Monrovia High School, Ontario High School, Grand Avenue School, and Frank Wiggins Trade School,[6] and he was an important figure in the campaign to establish a state college in Los Angeles, now the University of California, Los Angeles (UCLA). Over the course of his career, his architectural imprint would spread as far east as Grand Rapids, Michigan, as well as Arizona, Washington, and British Columbia.[7]

Austin served as president of the Southern California chapter of the American Institute of Architects from 1912 to 1913.[8] He would also serve as president of the first state planning board and the State Board of Architectural Examiners.

In his personal life, Austin's first wife died shortly after they arrived in Los Angeles. In 1902, he married Hilda Violet Mytton, and together they had nine children, two of whom died in infancy. In 1931, he lost Hilda, who died after a long illness at their Pasadena home. "The funeral service for John C. Austin's wife was at a church on Grand Avenue and Twelfth Street," John Parkinson remembered. "As we passed out, John stood, a sturdy, pathetic figure, holding the hand of his little girl Dorothy."[9] Several years later, Austin would marry a third time, to Dorothy K. Bell in 1935. Described by his granddaughter Jacqueline Spaulding, Austin "was a proper, lovable man" who was good with children and a "well-liked mover and shaker" in the city.[10]

A member of numerous Los Angeles organizations, Austin served as president of the Jonathan Club from 1916 to 1917. A member of the Scribes, Mystic Shrine, Al Malaikah Temple, Lincoln Club, and Sierra Madre Club, he was also a thirty-second-degree Mason and president of the Los Angeles Humane Society.

In 1928, he was appointed by the City to a committee of seven, tasked with adjusting claims resulting from the failure of the San Francisquito Dam. In 1930, he became president of the Chamber of Commerce, where he championed the development of a larger water system in the city and a federal building program.[11]

Austin went on to help organize the Southern California chapter of President Hoover's Organization for Unemployment Relief in 1931.[12] He was elected vice-chairman of the citizens committee of the Metropolitan Water District of Southern California in 1932 and would later be recruited for President Roosevelt's Labor Mediation Board.

He was the organizer and first president of the Economic Council of Southern California and a member of the Motion Picture Panel of Arbitrators.[13] He chaired the State Legislative Advisory Committee on Defense and Employment during World War II.[14,15] He was appointed chairman of the California area of the National Architects Association to plan post-war construction.[16]

As John Parkinson conveyed in 1928, "As an architect, a man, and for his record, he has my admiration and esteem, and I have valued his friendship always since a lonesome English lad, thirty-three years ago, he asked me for work."[17]

ALBERT C. MARTIN

Albert C. Martin successfully combined the skills of a structural engineer and an architect to establish a stellar reputation in Los Angeles, where he was credited with a number of significant technological advances. He made important contributions to the design of Los Angeles City Hall and "covered the engineering aspects of the trio."[18]

Martin patented numerous reinforced concrete systems and was widely admired for his "close application to detail and originality of design."[19] As *Architect and Engineer* observed in 1926, he had "built up a clientele from all walks of life" and "never specialized in any one type of building."[20]

Born in LaSalle, Illinois, on September 16, 1879, Albert Carey Martin was the son of John Martin and Margaret (Carey) Martin, who ran a hardware store and also served as the local undertakers. As a young boy, Martin frequently drove the black horses that were used to pull the hearse.

In 1894, he graduated from St. Patrick's Parochial School in LaSalle before advancing to the University of Illinois to study architectural engineering.[21] "There was no question that he would be headed for university because of his IQ," his son Albert C. Martin Jr. recalled. "All through his life that was proven; in his most productive years, he was very inventive, very energetic."[22]

Albert C. Martin, Architect

At the time, architecture students at the University of Illinois were "greatly influenced" by the World's Columbian Exposition held in Chicago in 1893. As Martin Jr. explained, "History tells us there were some great architectural achievements in that fair and in the city of Chicago about that time, work by architect [*sic*] (Henry H.) Richardson and Louis Sullivan, and later on, Frank Lloyd Wright."[23]

Upon graduating in 1902, Martin was hired as a draftsman for Brown, Ketcham Iron Works of Indianapolis, where he worked for a year before joining the Pennsylvania Railroad Company as a steel inspector in Pittsburgh. There, he gained a thorough understanding of steel construction. He took this knowledge into his next position with the Cambria Steel Company, a branch of the United States Steel Corporation based in Johnstown, Pennsylvania.

Martin was encouraged to head to California by his brother, Father Joseph Martin, a Catholic Vincentian priest, who was living in the state. Martin arrived in Los Angeles on January 6, 1904. He found temporary employment working as a track coach at St. Vincent's College, having had experience as a low hurdler at the University of Illinois. His parents and other siblings would soon follow him west.

Martin was later employed by Carl Leonardt, one of the most successful contractors on the West Coast. A native of Lüdenscheid, Westphalia, Germany, Leonardt was an expert in cement and concrete construction and appreciated Martin's expertise. "He understood concrete like no one else in the construction industry here," Martin Jr. said of his father, "a reflection of his higher education at the university."[24]

Among the many projects Leonardt built in Los Angeles were the Orpheum Theatre, Los Angeles County Hospital, and the Los Angeles Hall of Records.[25] Martin supervised many important projects for his new boss, including the erection of the Pacific Electric and H.W. Hellman buildings.

Looking for new career opportunities, Martin approached the office of John Parkinson, who told him he didn't need a structural engineer. Instead, Martin was hired by Alfred F. Rosenheim, who was later commissioned to design the Hamburger Department Store (later the May Company building) on

Broadway at Eighth Street. When Rosenheim was fired from the project, Martin took over as architect and simultaneously established his own practice.

For the Hamburger store, Martin developed a system of reinforced concrete, which consisted of "building a skeleton frame for the pilings and beams out of reinforcing steel, which was strong enough, by its structural design, to suspend the forms for pouring the concrete."[26]

On October 15, 1907, at the age of twenty-eight, Martin married Carolyn Borchard, a "vivacious farm girl" and alumna of the Immaculate Heart Academy, at a ceremony at St. Clara's Church in Oxnard, California.[27] "He was a city feller, and he was thin, and they called him 'Bird Legs,'" Martin Jr. explained. "But he was a very charming man and the apple of my mother's eye, I presume."[28] The couple had six children: Albert C. Martin Jr., Evelyn, Margaret, Carolyn, Lucille, and J. Edward Martin.

His son, Albert C. Martin Jr., remembered his father's struggles with alcohol and his bouts with epilepsy, which developed after he contracted the flu in the 1918 pandemic. "I think the strongest influence on the children was the fear of his death, all through our lives," he recalled. "He used to collapse and fall on the floor, and you would think he was dying right there. And I think I lived perhaps my whole life in fear of his death. He lived to be eighty-one."[29]

Martin's wife, Carolyn, and her connections in Ventura County, led to commissions for private residences for a number of influential families in Ventura and Oxnard. He also designed the Ventura County Courthouse and the Chapel of St. Mary Magdalene for Adolph Camarillo in Camarillo, California.

Martin's mastery of concrete can also be seen in Grauman's Million Dollar Theatre at Third Street and Broadway, featuring a 104-foot poured-in-place concrete arch, then the largest such structure ever attempted. A shortage of structural steel during World War I had forced him to improvise.

While working on Los Angeles City Hall, Martin simultaneously designed and oversaw the construction of the Furnace Creek Inn in Death Valley and St. Vincent de Paul Catholic Church on West Adams Boulevard, a project paid for by oil baron Edward L. Doheny.

A member of the Architects and Engineers Society of Los Angeles and the Southern California chapter of the American Institute of Architects (AIA), he was also a member of Newman Club of Los Angeles and Knights of Columbus.

His grandson, architect Christopher Martin, remembered the advice given to him long ago. "My grandfather used to say, 'Never mind the awards. Just give the client a good floor and a good roof and the consequences of that will be made ample reward.'"[30]

Albert C. Martin developed a close friendship with John Parkinson, who gave him his first dog, an Airedale Terrier, a breed native to Yorkshire, England. The Martin family with their six children regularly enjoyed a weekend swim at Parkinson's home, named Woodacres, in Santa Monica.[31]

Although the firm Martin built struggled through the Great Depression of the 1930s, it survived and remains one of the most innovative architectural pioneers in modern Los Angeles.

JOHN PARKINSON

Praised by fellow architect Myron Hunt for his "splendid vitality, courage, and thoroughness,"[32] John Parkinson was, as the *Los Angeles Times* observed, the undisputed "dean of Southland architects."[33] The *Los Angeles Herald Express* went as far as championing him as "one of America's foremost architects."[34] He would exercise considerable influence over the design of Los Angeles City Hall and create the concept for the building.

The main focus of his architectural enterprise in Los Angeles was always commercial, industrial, and monumental buildings, and by the time he died in 1935, his firm had handled in excess of $200,000,000 worth of construction projects.

Included in his many contributions to the city are Bullock's Wilshire, an art deco cathedral of commerce; Los Angeles Memorial Coliseum, the main venue for the 1932, 1984, and 2028 Olympics; Hotel

Alexandria, the city's first world-class hotel; the Homer Laughlin Building (now better known as Grand Central Market), the city's first steel-frame structure; Union Station; and a number of important buildings on the University of Southern California campus, including the administration, science, law, and physical education buildings, as well as Bridge Hall and the foyer of the school's famed Town and Gown ballroom.

John Parkinson, Architect

The oldest of the Associate Architects trio, Parkinson counted such luminaries as Henry Ford and future President Herbert Hoover among his close associates. Like other friends and family, they knew him simply as "JP."

"He is known far and wide for his sterling integrity and unflinching fairness in the execution of his business," John C. Austin told the *Architectural Forum* in 1928. "John Parkinson has two aberrations, one being that he thinks he could play pool, the other being that he has the hope of becoming a golf champion. He has been actively identified with a good many civic activities."[35]

Like his fellow Associate Architects, Parkinson enjoyed a keen sense of civic responsibility, serving for many years as a member of the Los Angeles Municipal Art Commission, as well as contributing to various local and state government committees. He donated his time to successfully redesigning Los Angeles's Central Park (now Pershing Square) in 1911 and worked on Los Angeles Memorial Coliseum in the early 1920s without payment in an effort to ensure that the city had a modern stadium worthy of competing for the Olympic Games.

Parkinson's celebrated career in Los Angeles was in stark contrast to his humble upbringing. Born in a modest house in the English village of Scorton, Lancashire, on December 12, 1861, his father, Thomas, worked as an engineer at the local mill, while his mother, Mary Ann (Bibby), was a housewife.

In 1870, the family moved fifty miles south to Bolton. Parkinson left school at the age of thirteen and worked as an errand boy in a hardware store, and later as an office boy for the *Bolton Guardian* newspaper, before being apprenticed to a local contractor, John Roberts. During the next six years, he supplemented his practical experience with evening classes at the Bolton Mechanics Institute.

When his apprenticeship ended, he traveled to Winnipeg, Canada, looking for adventure, and later settled in Minneapolis, Minnesota, where he eventually became the foreman of a sawmill, building staircases. After two years, Parkinson returned home to England, but he quickly became frustrated by the lack of opportunity and returned to the United States.

He headed to San Francisco, where he responded to an advertisement for a foreman at the Enterprise Planing Mills in Napa, California. Here, he met his first wife, Meta Breckenfield, the daughter of German farmers, and got his first break as an architect. His landlord noticed the quality of plans he was designing for his own home and recommended Parkinson to his brother, who was looking for an architect to design an addition to a local bank. He completed the work, and energized by the opportunity, Parkinson headed to Seattle to pursue a career as an architect. After establishing his practice, he went on to design a number of notable buildings, including the Seattle National Bank, Pacific School, and Olympia Hotel.

Looking for more opportunity and with a drive to establish himself, Parkinson arrived in Los Angeles in March 1894 with his wife and a young daughter, Dorothea, to support. "Following the depression of 1893, business prospects in the spring of 1894 were not encouraging in Los Angeles, especially for an unknown stranger without friends or acquaintances amongst the banks or businessmen," he later reflected.[36]

After a brief partnership with architect J. Lee Burton, Parkinson established his own practice. In addition to his architectural enterprise, Parkinson was a keen inventor and held several patents on various elevator and locomotive innovations, as well as a speedometer for automobiles. While few of his advances generated significant income, they demonstrated his passion for embracing technology.

In 1905, Parkinson entered into a ten-year partnership with George Edwin Bergstrom, whom he first employed in 1902 as a draftsman. By the time their agreement ended in 1915, it was estimated the firm of John Parkinson and Edwin Bergstrom, Architects had designed eighty percent of the modern office buildings in Los Angeles. Parkinson would do business under his own name until 1920, when his son Donald, a graduate of the Massachusetts Institute of Technology (MIT), joined the firm, which then became John Parkinson and Donald B. Parkinson, Architects.

Born in Los Angeles on August 10, 1895, Donald Berthold Parkinson graduated from Los Angeles High School in the summer of 1913. His college education was disrupted by World War I, when he enlisted as a Flying Cadet, Aviation Section of the United States Signal Corps. "He was extremely intelligent, he was hard working, but he played hard, he drank too much, (and) he drove too fast. He could be wild,"[37] his granddaughter, Pamela Parkinson Kellogg, reflected.

The younger Parkinson would reinvigorate his father's practice and play an important, largely unheralded role in the design of Los Angeles City Hall. It was Donald Parkinson's name that appeared on early sketches of the buildings. He also frequently represented the Associate Architects at committee meetings with city politicians. "The business should pay in order to exist, and progress, but great profits are secondary to good work,"[38] the senior Parkinson wrote to his son in December 1926, acknowledging that Donald's professional advances had greatly impressed him.

After the death of his wife, Meta, in March 1922, John Parkinson developed a friendship with Florence Gumaer, a teller at the Bank of Santa Monica. They were married the following year in Pasadena on April 4, 1923.

"Your confidence in yourself is superb," architect John J. Donovan, who served with Parkinson on the State Board of Architecture, wrote to him in 1935. "You couldn't have gotten where you are, or accomplished the things you have done if it wasn't so. Self-confidence well placed is truly delightful; without it a man can get nowhere, and there is a vast difference between confidence and bragging."[39]

Donald B. Parkinson, Architect

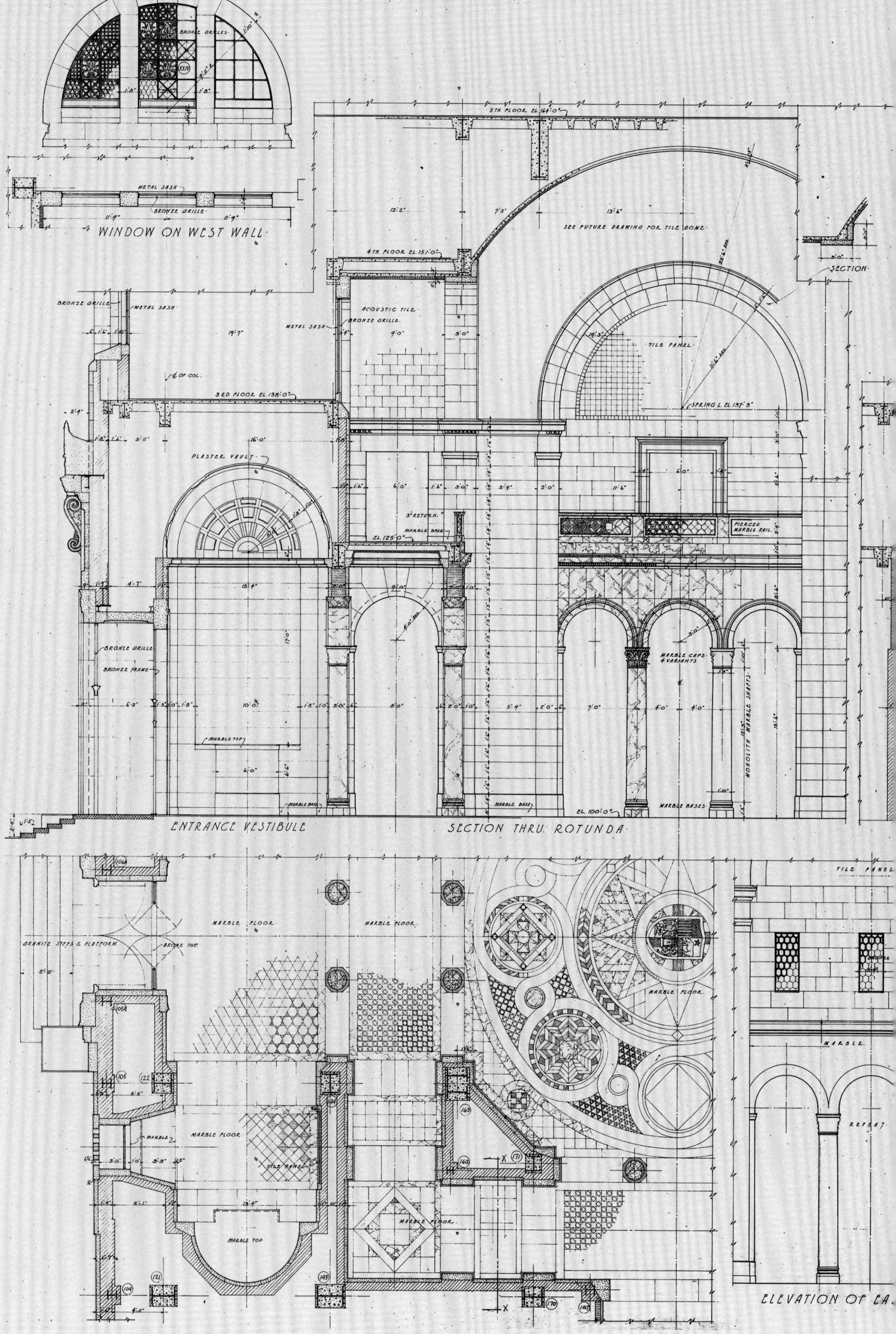
WINDOW ON WEST WALL
BRONZE GRILLES
METAL SASH
BRONZE GRILLE
5TH. FLOOR EL. 164'-0"
SEE FUTURE DRAWING FOR TILE DOME
4TH. FLOOR EL. 151'-0"
SECTION
BRONZE GRILLE
METAL SASH
ACOUSTIC TILE
TILE PANEL
SPRING L. EL. 137'-5"
3RD. FLOOR EL. 138'-0"
PLASTER VAULT
5" RETURN
MARBLE BASE
EL. 125'-0"
PIERCED MARBLE RAIL
MARBLE CAPS & VARIANTS
MONOLITH MARBLE SHAFTS
BRONZE FRAME
MARBLE TOP
MARBLE BASE
MARBLE BASES
EL. 100'-0"
ENTRANCE VESTIBULE
SECTION THRU ROTUNDA
GRANITE STEPS & PLATFORM
MARBLE FLOOR
TILE PANEL
MARBLE
REPEAT
ELEVATION OF EA.

Los Angeles City Hall, Entrance Vestibule and Rotunda

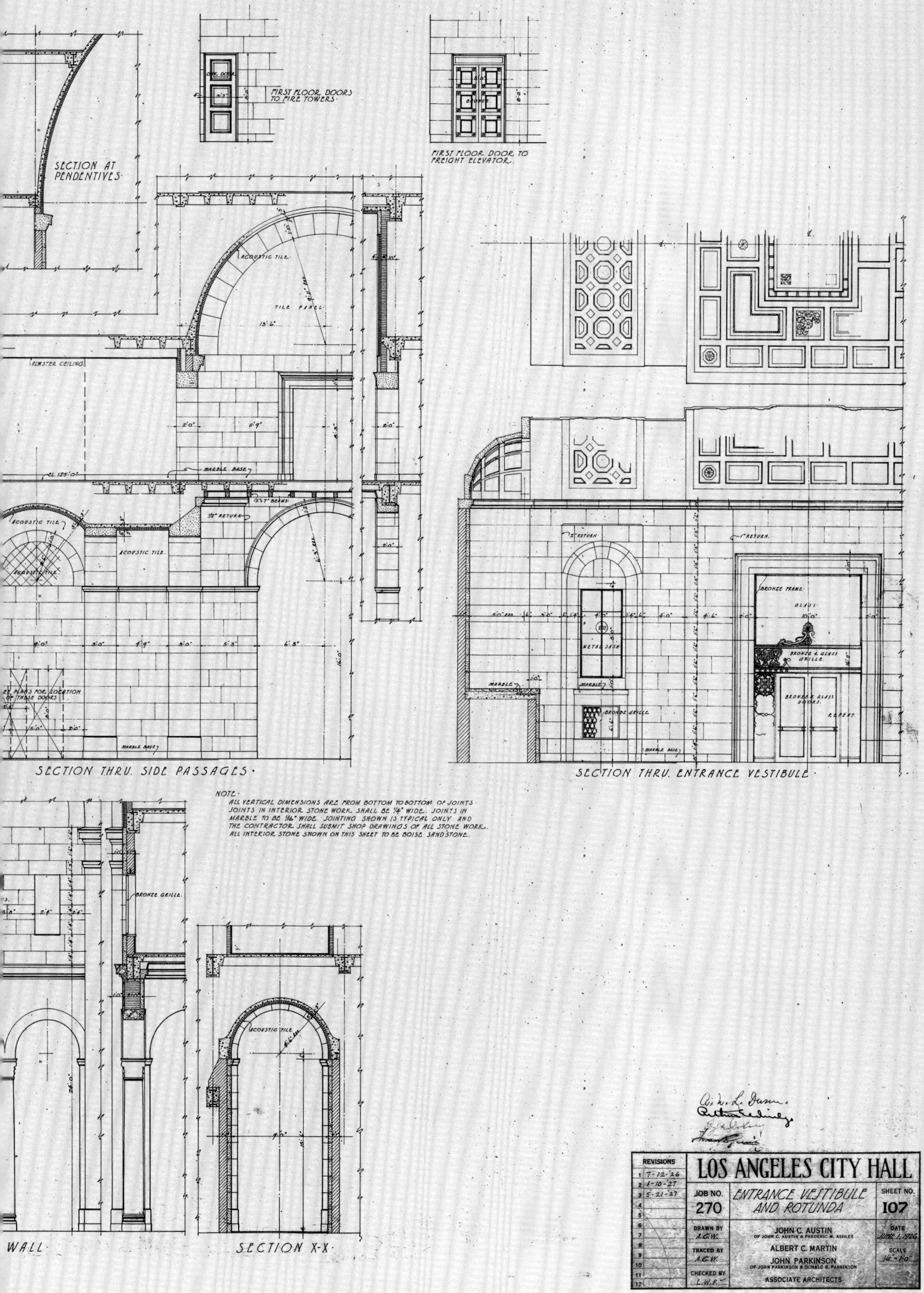

Los Angeles City Hall, Forecourt, Rendering

Los Angeles City Hall, Mayor's Office, Rendering

Los Angeles City Hall,
Council Chamber, Rendering

CHAPTER 5

MONUMENTAL SKYSCRAPER

If we do not build the new City Hall to twenty-eight stories, our children will.

—Albert C. Martin, Architect[1]

The Associate Architects imagined the new Los Angeles City Hall as a monumental structure dominated by a 452-foot tower. However, it would take a public vote and a court ruling to make it happen. Working through an ever-changing period of uncertainty, the architects were forced to re-evaluate their design and create plans for a radically shorter building in the event their effort to bypass the existing 150-foot height restriction proved unsuccessful.

While the architects considered their options, the task of securing the remaining real estate to build the structure was proving problematic. In October 1924, hearings were held about condemning thirty parcels to be acquired for the project. There were so many protests by property owners that referees hired to determine compensation estimated it would take at least a million dollars more than the $2.5 million already approved by voters to acquire the desired site. Several months would pass before all claims were settled.

In November 1925, a contract to demolish the City-owned Bullard Block was awarded to the Whiting-Mead Company. The firm was given forty days to raze the structure and remove salvage and refuse. The plan was to have the site cleared by March 4, 1926 so the Los Angeles Rock and Gravel Corporation could begin excavation of the block bounded by Spring, Main, Market, and Temple streets. "Already men and machines are panting in the work of destruction," the *Los Angeles Times* reported in January 1926 as the Bullard Block felt the "cruel bite of the crowbar and the smash of the hammer."[2]

Temple Block

Old timers lamented the impending destruction of the Temple Block, erected in 1856 at the junction of Temple, Spring, and Main streets. Long the center of city business, it had housed some of the city's first stores on the ground floor. In a corner room, Jacoby Brothers had opened Los Angeles's first dedicated men's apparel shop, while the Temple and Workman Bank had also been a tenant. Along with numerous other structures from "the north side of First Street to the south side of Temple and from the west side of Main to the east side of New High Street," the historic section was reduced to rubble.[3]

In all, more than forty buildings had to be cleared, including the Fisher Theatre, Phillips Building, and Equitable Bank Building[4] with some of the structures dating back more than half a century. Among the new properties constructed from the salvaged material were the Heinsbergen Decorating Company building on Beverly Boulevard completed in December 1928, and the Wolfer Printing Company building on the corner of Wall and Winston streets completed in April 1929, both of which still stand.[5]

"The architects are planning the building to be placed parallel with the new lines of Spring Street and desire that the west line of North Main Street be realigned and made parallel with the building and the east line of Spring Street," the city engineer reported in early February 1926.[6] Soon afterwards, the Board of Public Works announced it had awarded the Pennsylvania-based McClintic-Marshall Company two contracts, amounting to approximately $650,000, to provide an initial 6,600 tons of steel for the new building to be fabricated at the company's Los Angeles plant on Tenth Street and Central Avenue.

The McClintic-Marshall Company had supplied the structural steel for the new Hall of Justice, which held the distinction of having the largest amount of structural steel of any building in the city. The later City Hall contract was reported to represent the largest contract for steel ever awarded on the West Coast.[7] The Floyd L. Holser Company was awarded the contract to set it in place.

The McClintic-Marshall Company contract was described as a "serious blow" for organized labor, as the company operated an open-shop policy. Since Charles D. Marshall founded the enterprise in 1900 with his former Lehigh University classmate, Howard McClintic, it had grown to become the largest independent steel manufacturer in the country. Sixteen years before the contract was awarded, the company had almost been dynamited out of existence—literally—by the McNamara gang, who also targeted the *Los Angeles Times* building and the local Llewellyn Iron Works to protest declining union power.

"We have been open-shop ever since that time," Marshall recalled. "We pay our men as much or more than union men are paid, but we are open-shop, so that we can be free to carry on and develop our own business from union domination. If Los Angeles wishes to crucify its building industry, just let it go closed-shop, and the unions will do it."[8]

Los Angeles City Hall, Excavation

On March 4, 1926, beneath "threatening skies," a crowd of five thousand gathered "in a spray of falling mist" on open dirt where the Bullard Block once stood to witness Mayor Cryer turn the first spade of earth for the new Los Angeles City Hall.

At 3:25 p.m., the crowd cheered and a brass band played as the mayor stepped forward carrying a gold-plated shovel and dug into the soil where the monumental structure would rise. Cryer described the groundbreaking as the most important civic event to have taken place in the city for many years. "The present administration is working in harmony and unity to expedite construction of the building and to deliver it to the people of Los Angeles at the earliest possible moment," he proclaimed. "It is our greatest hope that we can give the City of Los Angeles an efficient city hall that will stand for years as a monument to the citizens of this community."[9]

The Associate Architects also addressed the crowd, with Albert C. Martin announcing plans for the structure were now eighty percent complete.[10] City Council President Boyle Workman told onlookers he had been present at the groundbreaking for the Los Angeles City Hall on Broadway back in 1888. "We were a small, inland city then, with about 30,000 population," he reminisced. "Some of our wildest dreamers looked forward to a city of possibly 150,000. No one dreamed of a magnificent municipality of 1,250,000 souls such as we now have."[11]

Former Councilman Walter Mallard told of how he had once hunted rabbits on the site, a spot where a post office and fruit store once stood fifty years before, a seemingly more innocent time when citizens rummaged through an old cigar box that held the mail, putting back that which was not addressed to them.[12]

Other speakers included former Councilwoman Estelle Lawton Lindsey, who received a rousing round of applause when she advocated that an advisory committee on furnishing the building be composed entirely of women, and City Attorney Jess Stephens, who promised there would soon be another groundbreaking for a Los Angeles Union Depot at the Plaza. "To attend this groundbreaking exercise, I was forced to ask to be excused from a meeting of the State Railroad Commission, where the City is carrying forward to victory a fight for another magnificent public building."[13] An exciting revelation to be sure, it would take yet another decade before that dream was realized.

Although city leaders had declared their intent to build a 452-foot, 28-story structure, whether they could legally exceed the city's 150-foot, 13-story height limit remained unclear. The restriction had its origins in a 1905 City ordinance, citing concerns over the "safety and durability of structural materials" in justifying a 130-foot ceiling. John C. Austin and John Parkinson had both been members of the commission that helped frame the building ordinance, drafted soon after the 1903 Iroquois Theatre fire in Chicago claimed more than six hundred lives. "The commission was wrestling with how to reduce

Los Angeles City Hall, Excavation

The Associate Architects considered alternative designs for the new City Hall that complied with existing height limits.

the fire hazard of Los Angeles to a minimum, thus averting the chances of a general conflagration, and how to make human life secure in places of public assemblance," Austin detailed.[14] The height limit was changed to 150 feet when voters approved an amendment to the city charter in 1911. The revised limit was adopted to ensure the city could grow "along broad and harmonious lines of beauty and symmetry,"[15] unlike the dark, intimidating East Coast cities many residents had abandoned to move west.

To resolve the issue, Mayor Cryer proposed asking voters in November 1926 to approve a charter amendment exempting the new city hall from the current ceiling. To gauge public sentiment, a non-binding "straw vote" proposition was included on an April 30 ballot. If an overwhelming number of citizens voted in favor of a taller structure, work would proceed as planned, assuming a charter amendment would be successful. Conversely, if it failed, the architects would adjust their plans to create a shorter structure.[16]

The Associate Architects were adamant their towering twenty-eight-story design was not only more economical, it was also essential to avoid being dwarfed by future federal, state, and county government buildings that were unbound by the same restriction, a legal gray area that caused contention. Nevertheless, should the charter amendment not succeed at the polls, they created a series of preliminary designs for a comparable structure with a truncated tower.

While several council members reported receiving angry protests from constituents and local newspapers published citizens' complaints, there was very little in the way of organized opposition to the proposed change.[17]

"The city should have a building of monumental character, but one hundred percent efficient," Albert C. Martin lobbied. "Our design enables us to use a small amount of granite close to the eye, with a cheaper stone above this base and below the fourth floor, and a still cheaper material such as terra cotta for the upper part."[18]

Asking voters to support the architects' plans, Mayor Cryer maintained they had designed a building that was a "rare combination of beauty and efficiency." He added, "Every requirement of the city is met in the design submitted by Architects John Parkinson, Albert C. Martin, and John C. Austin. They have designed a building which furnishes ample space for conducting business of city government, as well as a striking and beautiful architectural monument."[19]

Seeking to reassure doubters, Councilman A.J. Barnes told the *Los Angeles Express*, "Voters need not fear that favorable action toward the taller city hall plan will have any effect on the height limit restrictions for other buildings. . .While I am strongly in favor of our limit height ordinance, I am equally in favor of the plans for a city hall with a tower twenty-eight stories in height, a structure of beauty and dignity in which the people of Los Angeles will justly have deep civic pride."[20]

Councilman Robert M. Allan also expressed his support, "Misunderstanding of the design of the building is responsible for the objections raised on the score that such a tall building will darken surrounding streets and property. The proposed tower is but 100 feet square rising from a site containing 284,000 square feet."[21]

Hugh J. McGuire, president of the Board of Public Works, spoke to the practicality of the project.

"For the amount of money spent, more floor space will be available in the twenty-eight-story building than in a height-limit building. Therefore, the monumental City Hall as proposed will set alone be beautiful and worthy of our city, but will be more efficient with more office space and less corridor space than a 150-foot building."[22]

Martin told the *Los Angeles Express* he was aware of very little opposition to the architects' plan:

> The principal objection heard is that such a structure would be a cause of traffic congestion.
>
> This may be answered briefly. Our plan widens Spring Street to one hundred feet and provides garage space for four hundred cars, a parking space equivalent to two-thirds of a downtown city block . . .. The area of our entire building is equivalent to a two-story and basement building over the full lot, or less than one-fourth the work space were it occupied by a limit height structure. We must also remember that regardless of the height of the building, the flow of business remains the same. In this respect, the argument that applies to a height limit for office buildings does not apply to our City Hall.
>
> Another objection: high buildings darken adjacent property and streets. In our design we have a three- or four-story building set back from Spring Street 117 feet, 200 feet from the post office and about 350 feet from the nearest building on First Street. On Main Street we have a five-story building set back eleven feet from the property line, with a small portion of the building on this line extending up to the height limit. The balance of the building is set from sixty to ninety feet back from these lines. This objection, then does not apply here.[23]

Austin said he was confident any change to the city's existing height restrictions would not lead to taller privately owned buildings. "I would be one of the first to object to such a building if I believed it would endanger the existing restriction, for I am firmly convinced that Los Angeles owes much of its prosperity to the general equalization of real estate values effected by the height ordinance," he declared.[24]

Being in California, there were inevitable earthquake concerns over the building's potential vulnerability. Mayor Cryer told a meeting of Southern California retail grocers:

> Some people have talked about the danger of earthquakes, sometimes whispering it on the side, afraid to utter it aloud. But our architects assure us that the tall building is the safest structure in time of an earthquake. They are not afraid of them in San Francisco. They are preparing to build a building higher than that magnificent Pacific Telephone building and they have had a destructive earthquake up there . . .. Now why should the City of Los Angeles hesitate to allow the erection of this city hall? Our architects were given a certain amount of money, they were given certain space requirements. They assure us that the only way they can erect that structure for the money provided for that purpose, is by going up in the air . . .. I am very much interested in this matter, and I hope our people will go to the polls and vote in favor of the erection of this structure. I think we should have a place on top of that tower where we can take our visitors to view the city. There is no such place in the city of Los Angeles today. That tower will be visible for many miles around. I believe that we will make a mistake if we do not authorize it.[25]

A number of influential groups, including the Central Business District Association, West Wilshire Development Association, Chamber of Commerce, Municipal League, and Commercial Board of Los Angeles, all supported an exception to the existing height limit.

"The preponderance of written and spoke favorable expressions over those declaring in opposition to or an uncertainty in respect to the plan" made the outcome of the straw vote on the height of the new city hall "reasonably certain," the *Illustrated Daily News* predicted.[26] As the vote approached, the *Los Angeles Record* reported a "hot row" had broken out between the county's Board of Supervisors and the city's Building and Safety Commission over whether the County would be forced to abide by city building laws.

City Attorney Stephens argued the new charter would, in fact, force the County to comply with City building rules, in direct contradiction to the county's legal team, which argued otherwise. The city's building inspector, J.J. Backus, predicted the unresolved matter would wind up in the courts, as the newly constructed Hall of Justice already exceeded the height limit allowed by the charter.[27]

Observers predicted the "violent clashes of opinion on several measures on the ballot" would lead to a significant turnout at the polls.[28] Proposition 7 asked voters: "Do you favor the City Hall plan proposed by the City's architects which provides for a height of 28 stories for a portion of such building?"

On the morning of April 30, 1926, some 1,331 polling places across the city opened at 6 a.m., and according to City Clerk Robert Dominguez, 337,448 voters were registered for the special election.[29] After the polls closed at 7 p.m., results revealed 112,507 had voted in favor of the charter amendment with only 45,496 against.

The resounding victory confirmed what city leaders had expected. But even still, it represented an energizing boost to the project. On May 7, work began on the foundations. The tower foundation was poured on June 14 and 15. More than 2,800 yards of concrete were poured in one continuous thirty-hour-long process. Contractors Lange and Bergstrom, Inc. required more than four thousand barrels of cement to create a slab almost twelve thousand square feet in size.[30]

In early July, the Board of Public Works announced it had awarded the general contract for the new City Hall to the C.J. Kubach Company with a bid of $2,852,700. Kubach was a highly respected contractor in the city and worked on numerous Los Angeles-area landmarks, including the Merchants' National Bank Building, Stimson residence, and Alexandria Hotel Annex, as well as First National Bank of Riverside and buildings in Pasadena, Redlands, San Diego, and Santa Barbara. During World War I, he built structures for the balloon training facility at Rose Field in Arcadia, California.

C.J. Kubach

Born in Germany in 1855, Kubach was well known to the City Hall architects and lived in an impressive John Parkinson-designed Italian Renaissance Revival home on the southwest corner of Alvarado and Twelfth streets. His firm had built the Parkinson-designed Brownstein-Louis Building and the Austin-designed Wright-Callender Building. He would later work with both Parkinson and Austin on the new Chamber of Commerce building.

The son of a contractor, Kubach grew up near Heidelberg and first arrived in the United States in 1873, traveling to Pittsburgh, Pennsylvania, to stay with an uncle. He later moved to San Francisco before working as a millwright in Virginia City, Nevada, during the deep-mining frenzy that followed the Comstock-Lode silver ore discovery. He traveled around Southern California and Mexico before settling in Los Angeles in 1878, where he opened an office on East First Street. Five years later, he married Sophia Wetteraner, and they would later welcome two daughters, Rose and Sophia.

A Republican, Kubach had a keen interest in civic affairs and local politics, and served a term on the Los Angeles school board in 1896. The C.J. Kubach Company was formed in 1903 with Kubach's nephew, George Schneider, acting as secretary, treasurer, and superintendent.[31] Kubach was also vice-president of the K. & K. Brick Company.[32]

The C.J. Kubach Company had submitted two bids for the new city hall. The accepted bid would substitute California granite for limestone on the exterior of the first four floors; the remaining twenty-four floors would feature a terra cotta exterior. Although more expensive, it was hoped the granite exterior would produce a more impressive building.

Kubach immediately faced questions over whether he planned to ignore the so-called American-plan policy of refusing to negotiate with unions. "I will not discriminate between union and nonunion men," he told the *Los Angeles Times*. "It is not true that I will employ only union men. They can work side by

A view of the partially completed Los Angeles City Hall.

side, and if they don't like to do it that way, they can quit. That's what I call the American plan."[33]

To clarify how tall of a structure he would be building, Kubach appealed to the State Supreme Court for a writ of mandate after Hugh J. McGuire, president of the Board of Public Works, symbolically refused to sign a contract with the C.J. Kubach Company on the grounds it was in violation of city charter building restrictions. It was hoped the writ of mandate would settle if the 150-foot height limit did not apply to public structures.

In all practicality, McGuire described the action as a friendly suit to resolve the matter quickly. "As the charter provides for the 150-foot maximum height, and the plans and contract call for 400-foot structure, the City and Kubach Company have become parties, by mutual agreement to this action for the purpose of definitely deciding the matter," he wrote in a statement. "It was with this prearranged plan in mind that I refused to sign the contract warrants of the Kubach Company, the latter appealing to the Supreme Court for a decision to protect its interests. The question for the court to decide is whether the charter provision applies to public as well as private buildings."[34]

McGuire predicted little delay, if any, would result from the suit. Since the earlier straw vote was not legally binding, it was expected if the Supreme Court did not resolve the matter, the November election would.

A decision from the state tribunal could typically take up to sixty days; however, an answer came just a week later when the high court authorized the 452-foot structure. City Attorney Stephens, who handled the proceedings, called the decision a triumph for the city.

"The court's action will speed up the building of the twenty-eight-story city hall, for now the contracts can be signed," he advised. "Had the decision been against us, then there would have been uncertainty as to the legality of the twenty-eight-story city hall until a charter amendment had been approved at the November election."[35]

The steel frame nears completion.

With the major obstacles cleared, construction now proceeded at a rapid pace. The Floyd L. Holser Company began erecting the steel frame on July 24, and as soon as it was completed, Kubach got to work finishing the building.

The McClintic-Marshall Company, struggling to keep pace on their promise to deliver fifty tons of steel daily, was forced to sublet a portion of the fabrication of structural steel to the Baker Iron Works.[36] The same firm would also provide the elevators for the building.

"We wish to report that the McClintic-Marshall Company, contractors for the furnishing of the structural steel for the above mentioned building, are not living up to the terms of the contract regarding the delivery of fabricated steel," the Associate Architects wrote to the Board of Public Works in August. "According to the terms of their contract with you, a definite time was set for the completion of certain parts of the steel structure, as well as the completion of the entire steel frame, and it is our opinion that they are carrying the work along so slowly that at least one month's time will be lost in the completion of the building."[37]

In response, the McClintic-Marshall Company promised to "immediately accelerate to the fullest extent the delivery of fabricated steel."[38] More than one hundred steel workers labored to hoist huge beams and girders into place. For locals, the sound of pneumatic riveters was incessant. By October, the structure's massive steel frame was almost halfway complete. Soon, workers would turn their attention to the outside walls surfaced with granite and terra cotta and the concrete floors.

As Albert C. Martin Jr. recounted, safety standards then were much different from what would be expected today, and several workers were killed during construction. "In the corner of the tower, there are elevator shafts, and at the top of the city hall there's kind of a gallery," he described. "And the elevator shaft in the southeast corner was, during construction, an open shaft, and one of the workmen thought the elevator was there and took his wheelbarrow and himself and walked right into the hole and (the fall) killed him."[39]

In November, City Research Engineer George L. Rogers wrote to the Board of Public Works, urging its members to allow the Board of Park Commissioners to proceed with landscaping around the structure. "This park should emphasize the advantages of Southern California. Flowers blooming and leaves on the trees in January with oranges glistening in the sunshine when the East and Middle West are thirty feet deep in snow. Plenty of evergreen trees and effective shrubs with blossoms always in abundance."[40]

By late January 1927, steel was being put into place on the twenty-fifth floor, and in early February, Rogers reported the final 187 of the full 8,167 tons of steel to be used for the structure were on site and ready to go into the top of the tower. The first two floors were completed, and the third was nearly sixty percent finished. The granite for the ground floor above the terrace was in place on the south end of the structure and along the west façade up to the Spring Street entrance.

Bids for the marble were now being accepted, and crews were almost ready to begin pouring the

A view of City Hall construction from across Main Street.

dome in the rotunda with the supporting pillars already completed.[41]

On February 26, the last of the new building's massive steel frame was put into place, the milestone moment captured by the sight of the Stars and Stripes flying high from a temporary mast at the peak of the structure.

"This contractor deserves a great deal of credit for the way he handled his part of the work," George L. Rogers wrote in a report to Mayor Cryer in March. "He has cheerfully cooperated with everyone and has steadily shoved steel skyward at the rate of one thousand tons a month and better. He will also guarantee every rivet that has been placed in the structure." Rogers reported the sixth floor was half finished, and the seventh about one-third complete, while some 13,000 out of an estimated 90,000 cubic feet of granite had been laid.[42]

By May, construction activity was in full gear with more than eight hundred workers reportedly on site. Some 1,600 window frames had arrived ready for installation, while 16,000 cubic feet of French limestone had been unloaded at the harbor, ready to be fabricated by the Raymond Granite Company to be used for interior decoration.[43] Confident the building work was progressing on schedule, plans were made for a ceremony to lay the cornerstone.

At 1:15 p.m. on the afternoon of June 22, 1927, Mayor Cryer had sent a car to pick up California Governor Clement Calhoun Young to join the parade beginning at the old city hall on Broadway. Escorted by the Los Angeles Fire Department Band and local police, the procession made its way past the courthouse and Hall of Records, where county officials joined the celebration. From there, they traveled down Temple Street to Spring Street and the new Los Angeles City Hall.

There a platform holding two thousand seats for distinguished guests had been constructed at the main entrance. Several thousand spectators gathered to watch the proceedings broadcast live on loudspeakers. The historic ceremony began at 2 p.m. and was conducted by the Native Sons of the Golden West and presided over by the organization's Grand President Charles A. Thompson. When his moment arrived, Mayor Cryer took center stage to deliver the opening address, drawing attention to an article published in *Harper's Monthly* in December 1883.

> The City of the Angels is in general effect, another San Jose, only upon a more hilly site. Its population must be about 14,000. Long thoroughfare of Main Street proceeds from the depot, at first through a shabby Spanish quarter, locally known as Sonora, consisting of one-story, white-washed adobe houses. But presently, after passing a small Spanish plaza, set out with sharp-pointed cypresses, and the principal hotel—the Pico House—it is lined with excellent buildings of modern pattern, and becomes the principal street of the town.

Workers labor on the new City Hall forecourt.

> [He continued in his own words:] When we think of the changes which a few short years have wrought, changes which have transformed the little semi-Spanish and Mexican city, described by the author, into the great throbbing metropolis of today—when we think of our marvelous growth from a city of 14,000 to one of almost 1,400,000, a growth perhaps unequaled in rapidity in the history of the world—we may well hesitate to hazard a prediction as to what changes the next fifty years will bring forth.[44]

Governor Young, who had developed a severe cold prior to his arrival in Los Angeles, kept his remarks brief, congratulating Los Angeles on its impressive new city hall. Also introduced to the crowd were architects Austin, Martin, and Parkinson, who had poured their talent and toil into giving the city a monumental structure of which all could be proud.

A time capsule of sorts, a small copper box, was placed inside a specially carved crypt shortly before the cornerstone, measuring four feet long, two-and-a-half feet high, and one-and-a-half feet thick, was lowered into position. The program for the day's event lists the contents of the box: a history of the City Hall site by Joseph Mesmer; the "Charter of the City of Los Angeles;" a historical record of the Pioneer Society of Los Angeles County; the Annual Message of Mayor Cryer; the Annual Report of the Controller of the City of Los Angeles; the Budget of the City of Los Angeles for fiscal year 1927–1928; a history of the Los Angeles Chamber of Commerce, with photographs of its officers; an account of the discovery of gold in California by Rev. Eugene Sugranes, CMF; photographs of a drawing of the completed building; a composite photograph of the structural steelwork of the building; a photograph of the building taken on June 15, 1927; a list of judges and officers of the Superior Court of the County of Los Angeles; signatures of the personnel of the mayor's office; the names of employees of Raymond Granite Company who cut and carved the cornerstone; a parchment scroll containing the signatures of all those who aided in the preparation of plans and papers for the building; the pen used for these signatures; *El Camino Real, The King's Highway* by Rev. Eugene Sugranes, CMF; three gold nuggets from Los Angeles County; the poem, *Gold* by Clark B. Stocking; "To Our Pioneers;" a copy of the song, "The Golden State," by Violet Estelle Barter; a copy of the song, "California," by Silverwood; a Los Angeles telephone directory; an autographed photo of Mayor Cryer; a copy of the day's event invitation; a copy of the day's event brochure, with program; a copy of the "Constitution of Native Sons of the Golden West;" a copy of "Grizzly Bear," the official organ of the Native Sons of the Golden West; copies of the following Los Angeles newspapers: the *Times*, the *Examiner*, the *Daily News*, the *Express*, the *Herald*, the *Record*, and the *Searchlight*; a new Lindbergh airmail stamp; and progress charts of structural steel and concrete in the building.[45] Sand from every county in California, cement from every state cement mill, and water from each of the California missions were mixed to make the mortar to secure the stone in place.

In July 1927, Norman W. Kelch, superintendent of construction, declared that with the exception of the twenty-seventh floor, the tower was now covered in terra cotta. Gladding, McBean and Company provided three thousand tons of terra cotta for the building, claiming it to be the most ever used in a single Southern California structure. "The terra cotta work is eighty percent completed, the granite setting is ninety percent finished, the plastering ten percent, plumbing roughing-in one hundred percent, and electric wiring rough work, ninety percent," Kelch detailed.[46]

By November, the building was 98 percent finished, according to George L. Rogers, with the majority of work left to be done in the rotunda and forecourt. The Weber Showcase and Fixture Company promised to have all of the counters, partitions, and other fixtures installed by the end of the month. Meanwhile, Gladding, McBean and Company confirmed the building's tiles, fired at their Glendale plant, were ready to be set in place on the dome of the rotunda and the forecourt.[47]

The contractors were given until January 1, 1928, to complete the construction work. The very next morning, the first employees of the Superior Court of Los Angeles County moved in. By early April 1928, almost all of the City

Los Angeles City Hall, Construction

New Los Angeles City Hall
C.J. KUBACH CO
GENERAL CONTRACTORS
Los Angeles, California

departments had taken up residence in their new home, which was so large, a twenty-six-page directory was produced to help locate the different departments.

All around the premises, decorators rushed to complete the new city hall. In the Council Chamber, workers accidentally painted over the acoustic holes in the ceiling tiles and had to cover them with acoustical felt and redecorate.

In the end, the final cost to acquire the site was $3,512,500, while the total cost of the building came to $5,542,976. Demolition of the previous structures on the site totaled $76,195.88; furnishings and equipment, $300,000; and decorations and incidentals, $295,165.[48]

The first City Council session in the new Council Chamber was held on April 16. A large crowd gathered as the Associate Architects, John C. Austin, Albert C. Martin, and John Parkinson were presented and heartily congratulated for their efforts.

Los Angeles City Hall, Cornerstone Ceremony, June 22, 1927.

Below: John and Donald B. Parkinson seated in the newly completed Council Chamber.
Opposite: Angelenos gather for cornerstone ceremony.

The handling of this undertaking, quite as much as the design of the structure and the working out of all the intricate and interesting details in construction and design, reflects great credit upon the architects who planned it.

—*Architectural Forum*, July 1928[1]

CHAPTER 6

MODERN CLASSIC

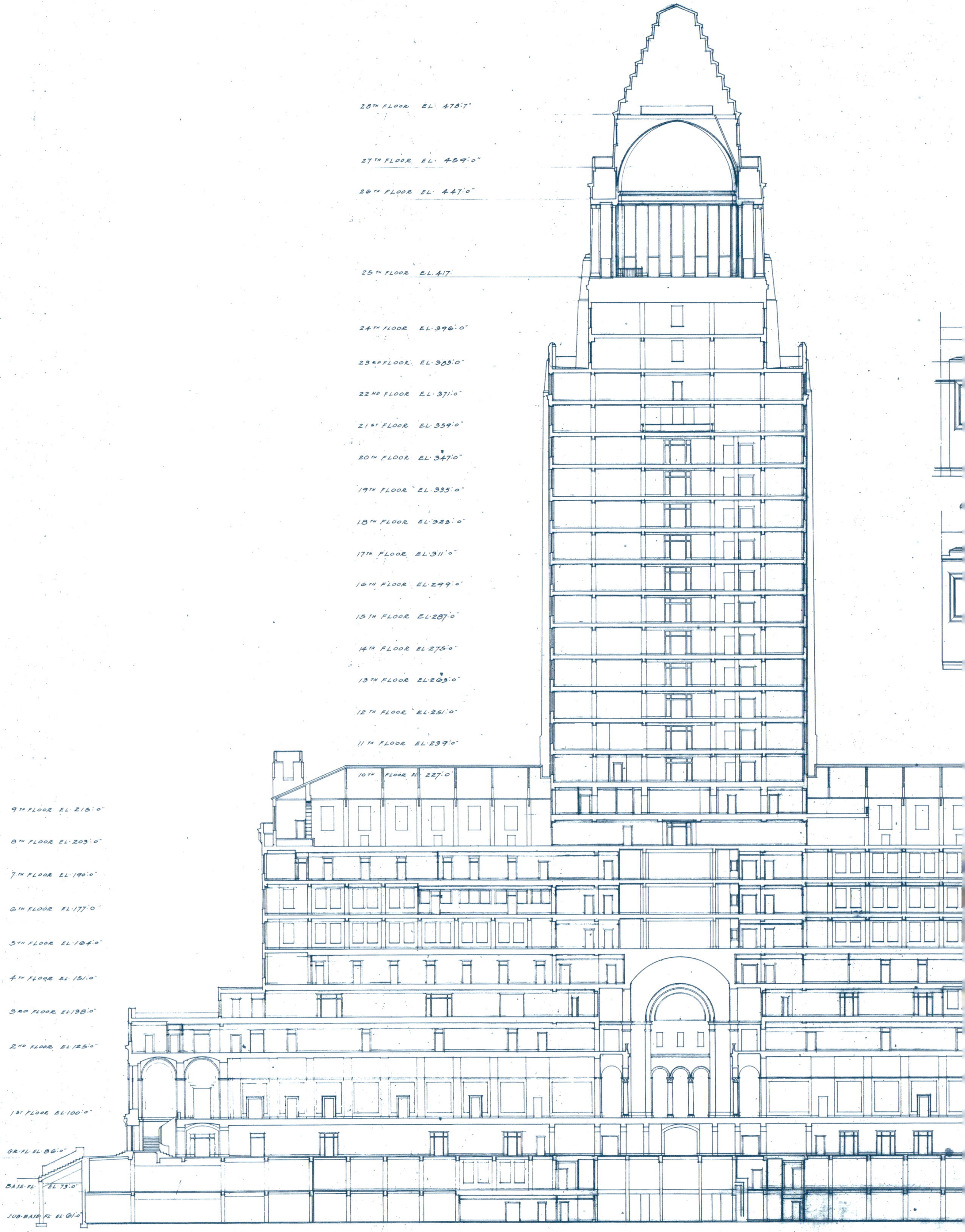

SECTION ON NORTH-SOUTH AXIS LOOKING EAST
SCALE 1/16" = 1'0"

THE BUILDING Los Angeles city leaders wanted a bold and modern city hall that looked to the future. Architects John C. Austin, Albert C. Martin, and John Parkinson responded, delivering something altogether unique to the area, a gleaming monumental structure in the form of a neoclassical skyscraper, bounded by four streets and consuming an entire city block.

Constructed and occupied in less than two years, it was divided into three distinct sections: the base, encompassing all the building from the basement to the third story and measuring 250 feet wide and 476 feet long; the 452-foot tall, twenty-eight-story, gleaming terra cotta-clad central tower, one hundred square feet from the base narrowing at the twenty-third floor; and the north and south flanking wings measuring 64 feet wide, 113 feet long, and 150 feet high with roofs covered by Gladding, McBean's Granada clay tiles, shaded in burnt red, old gold, and brown.

The gross floor area of the building totaled 856,000 square feet, or approximately twenty acres, of which 94,888 square feet were rented to the County of Los Angeles for the superior courts and other purposes, while the gross volume amounted to twelve million cubic feet and the dead weight, ninety-five-thousand tons.[2]

The structure's skeleton contained 8,167 tons of structural steel, 900,000 rivets, and four hundred columns. More than 129 miles of wire were used in a building that boasted the largest light-and-power switchboard on the West Coast and a telephone switchboard with the capacity of two thousand phone lines.[3]

The architects designed entrances to the building on three different levels. On the lowest level, there was access, via ramps, to a parking structure with room for more than five hundred automobiles.

The new Los Angeles City Hall was so large, it required a team of 184 people just to maintain it.

Pages 72-73: A view of the new Los Angeles City Hall.

Opposite: An aerial view of City Hall taken on November 3, 1927.

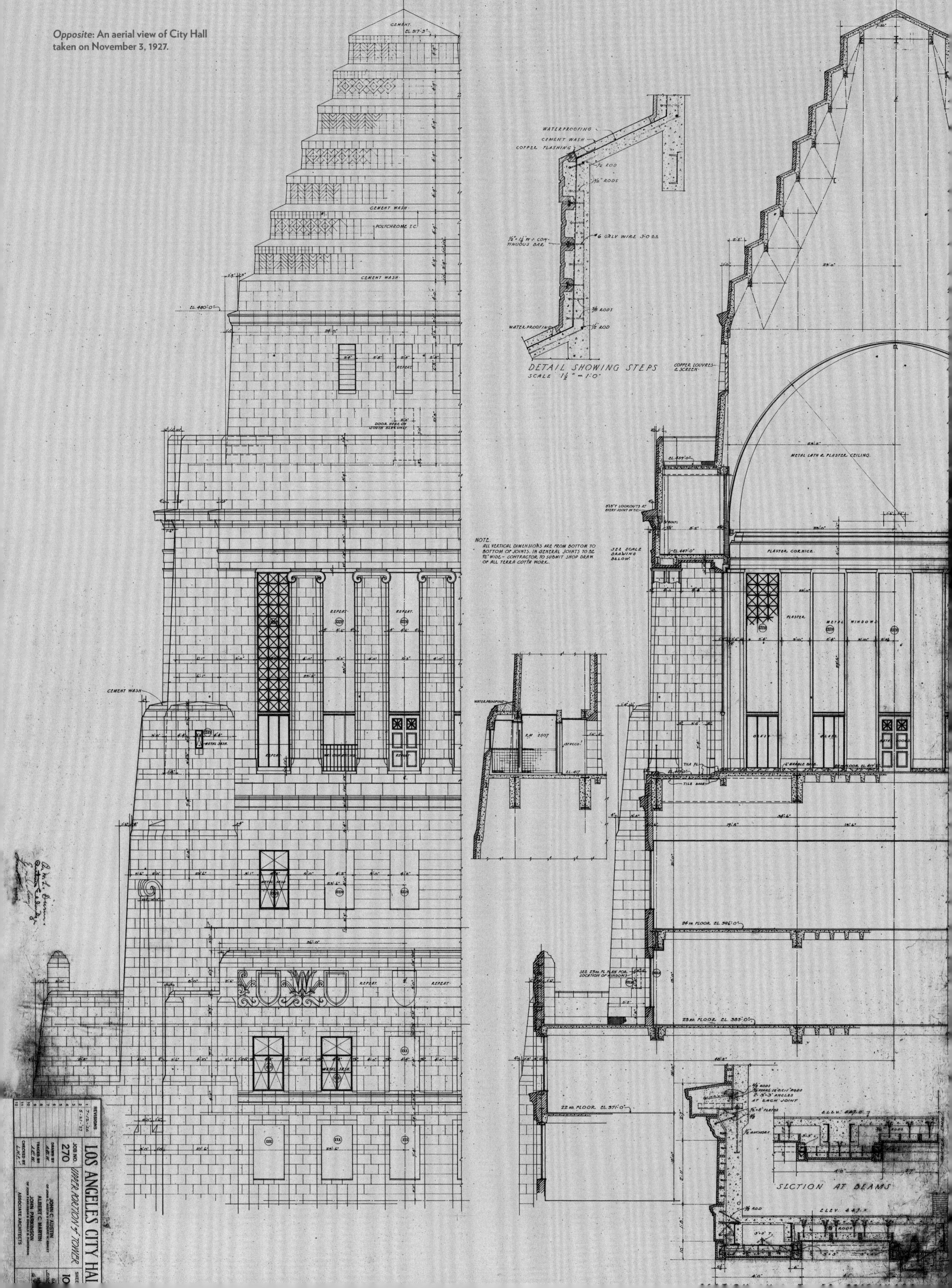

THE STYLE Unlike the Beaux Arts city halls of San Francisco and Chicago built a decade earlier, Los Angeles's new municipal home was an ambitious blend of both historical and contemporary inspiration. "In their preliminary consideration of the problem, the architects determined not to confine themselves to any particular style of architecture in the general design of the building, and the completed structure shows this determination was carried into effect," John C. Austin elucidated shortly after the building opened.

"Grecian detail was adopted for the main entrance, while Romanesque was used in the arcades of the forecourt, rotunda, Council Chamber, and the Board of Public Works room. The tower and the flanking wings may be regarded as 'modern American,' influenced by the present-day set-back style so widely adopted in other parts of the country."[4] The architects, according to Albert C. Martin, designed a building "appropriate to the climate and the traditions of California."[5]

As anticipated, architectural embellishment was restricted to the substructure where California light gray granite was used for facing the exterior walls. All other walls, including those extending to the pinnacle of the tower, were covered with a light cream enamel-finish terra cotta flecked with black, designed to harmonize with the granite. As Albert C. Martin pointed out, "expensive materials" were used "only where they will be seen and their beauty appreciated."[6]

For the interior design, the Associate Architects relied heavily on Austin Whittlesey. The son of architect Charles F. Whittlesey, he had gained valuable early experience in his father's San Francisco practice before moving to New York City, at the age of twenty, in hopes of finding work with famed architect Bertram Goodhue. It took two years before he convinced Goodhue to hire him, all the while picking up work at various firms in New York and Cleveland, Ohio.[7]

In 1916, Whittlesey won the Le Brun Traveling Scholarship, which normally would have him traveling to Europe, France, and Italy. But with war engulfing much of Europe, he headed to Spain and North Africa instead, where he was exposed to many Moorish, Renaissance, and Gothic influences.

He returned to Goodhue's practice and would later work as a delineator of interior and exterior renderings for the Nebraska State Capitol, an experience that would prove invaluable to his work in Los Angeles. Whittlesey designated Los Angeles City Hall's architecture as "Modern Classic" and demanded, "None of the traditional styles would be acceptable."[8]

The Associate Architects also relied on assisting architect George P. Hales, who represented their interests at numerous meetings with city officials. Hales had previously been employed by the United States Navy, where he designed the Naval Academy in Annapolis and the Marine Base and Training Station in San Diego. He also served as president of the Architectural Club of Los Angeles and later wrote a celebratory booklet providing a comprehensive description of Los Angeles City Hall for the Board of Public Works.

THE TOWER The building was dominated by its tower, symbolizing "the indomitable spirit of the citizens that made it possible," assisting architect George P. Hales wrote.[9] "The framing of the tower is designed as an independent structure, with braced bents in both directions, anchored to a solid mat of reinforced concrete resting on stiff blue clay," he detailed. "In the tower, an elastic joint is provided in the outer wall at each story to allow for expansion, contraction, and oscillation."[10]

At its apex, early sketches revealed a domed roof comparable to that of the Nebraska State Capitol. However, as the design evolved, the architects imagined a stepped pyramidical roof, a modern reference to the Mausoleum at Halicarnassus (now Bodrum, Turkey), designed by Greek architects Satyros and Pythius of Priene around 350 B.C. The change also reflected a heightened interest during the 1920s in ancient forms and geometrically based design that had only intensified with the 1922 discovery of King Tutankhamun's tomb in Egypt. Alternative designs also revealed that the architects considered covering the roof with decorative tile.

"In drawing up plans, we took into consideration the value of the high elevation of the tower as a means of advertising Los Angeles," Albert C. Martin explained.[11] Atop the roof was placed an airway beacon dedicated to Colonel Charles A. Lindbergh, a modern hero to Angelenos and people around the world—and a way to shine a spotlight on Los Angeles's embrace of the burgeoning aviation industry.

FORECOURT ENTRANCE, STATUES AND FRIEZE

The west entrance on Spring Street was reached via granite steps that arrived at a forecourt measuring 76 feet wide by 117 feet long with colonnaded passages on three sides.

The architects anticipated a world-renowned sculptor would eventually create two "heroic" statuary groups on granite pedestals to be placed on each side of the entrance, along with a 75-foot long by 9.5-foot high frieze to be carved in deep bas-relief above the colonnade, but the funds never materialized.

Donald Parkinson later urged the Municipal Art Commission to consider a proposal from sculptor William Zorach for the frieze, showing the development of civilization in California from "primitive man" to the "modern family." Although the *New York Times* described Zorach's design as "powerful" and "beautifully drawn," it was never commissioned.[12]

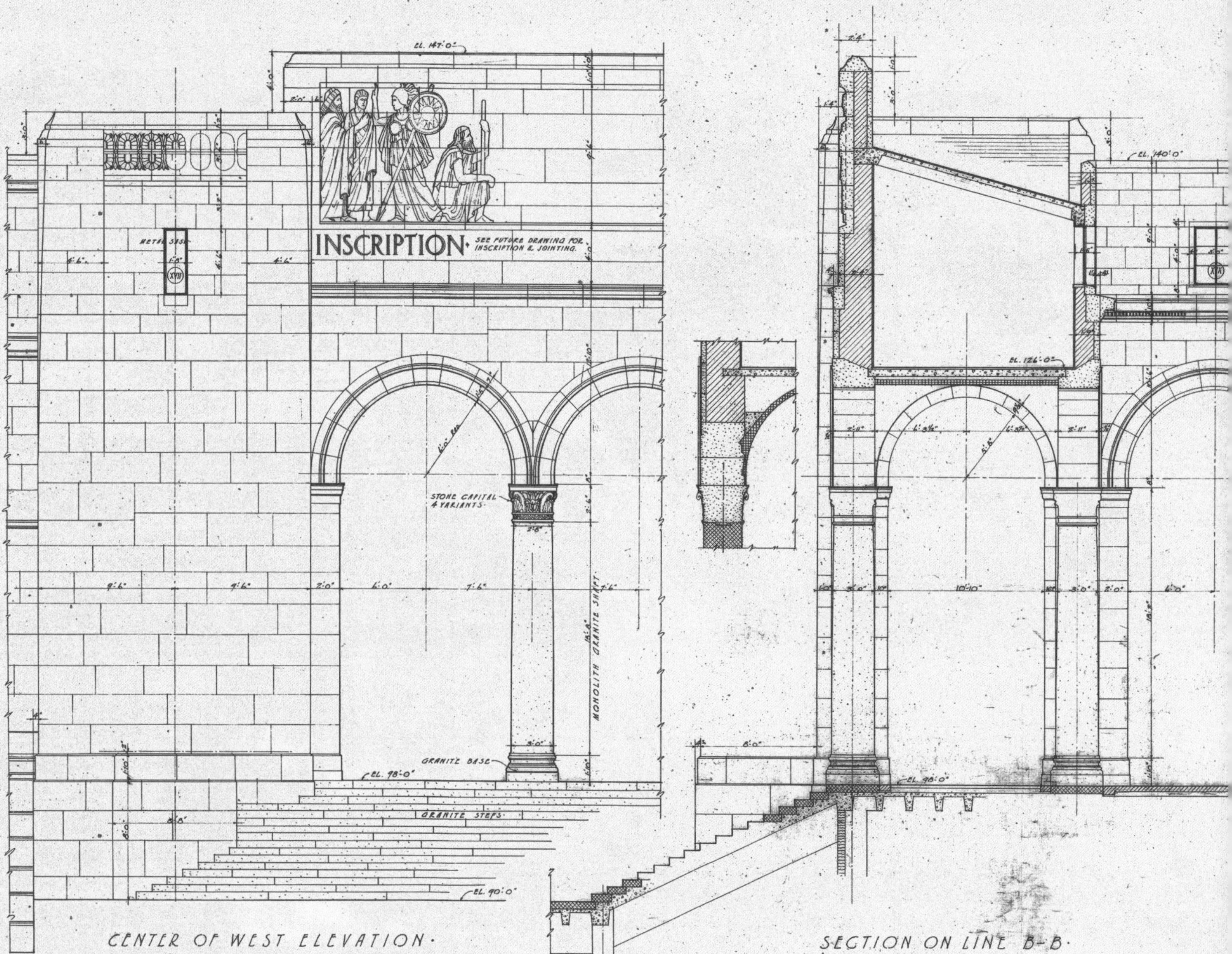
EL. 147'-0"
INSCRIPTION·
SEE FUTURE DRAWING FOR INSCRIPTION & JOINTING.
STONE CAPITAL 4 VARIANTS
MONOLITH GRANITE SHAFT
GRANITE BASE
EL. 98'-0"
GRANITE STEPS
EL. 90'-0"
EL. 140'-0"
EL. 126'-0"
CENTER OF WEST ELEVATION·
SECTION ON LINE B-B·

ROBERT PAINE In 1940, the City Council voted to award local artist Robert Paine the honor of creating a decorative panel for the forecourt entrance, but Mayor Fletcher Bowron vetoed the project. The model for Paine's work, titled *The Immemorial Migrations and Commingling of People are the Root Flowering in the Highest that Man has Become,* was temporarily placed above the Spring Street entrance as part of Art Week in November 1941.[13]

IN·THE·HIGHEST·THAT·MAN·HAS

FORECOURT The forecourt, featuring monolithic columns with embellished capitals, provided passages on both sides leading to alternative entrances into the building. The ceilings featured tiled groined arches and walls adorned with tiled panels crafted by Gladding, McBean and Company at their Glendale, California plant. Dominated by "delicate blue-greens," the panels portrayed many of the city's leading industries, including aviation, automotive, building, machinery, motion pictures, oil production, printing, and shipping.

The arcade floor was covered in Gladding, McBean's Promenade tile, and the court was paved in brick. Almost all of the materials used in the construction of the forecourt—the granite, brick, tile, and cement—were produced in California.

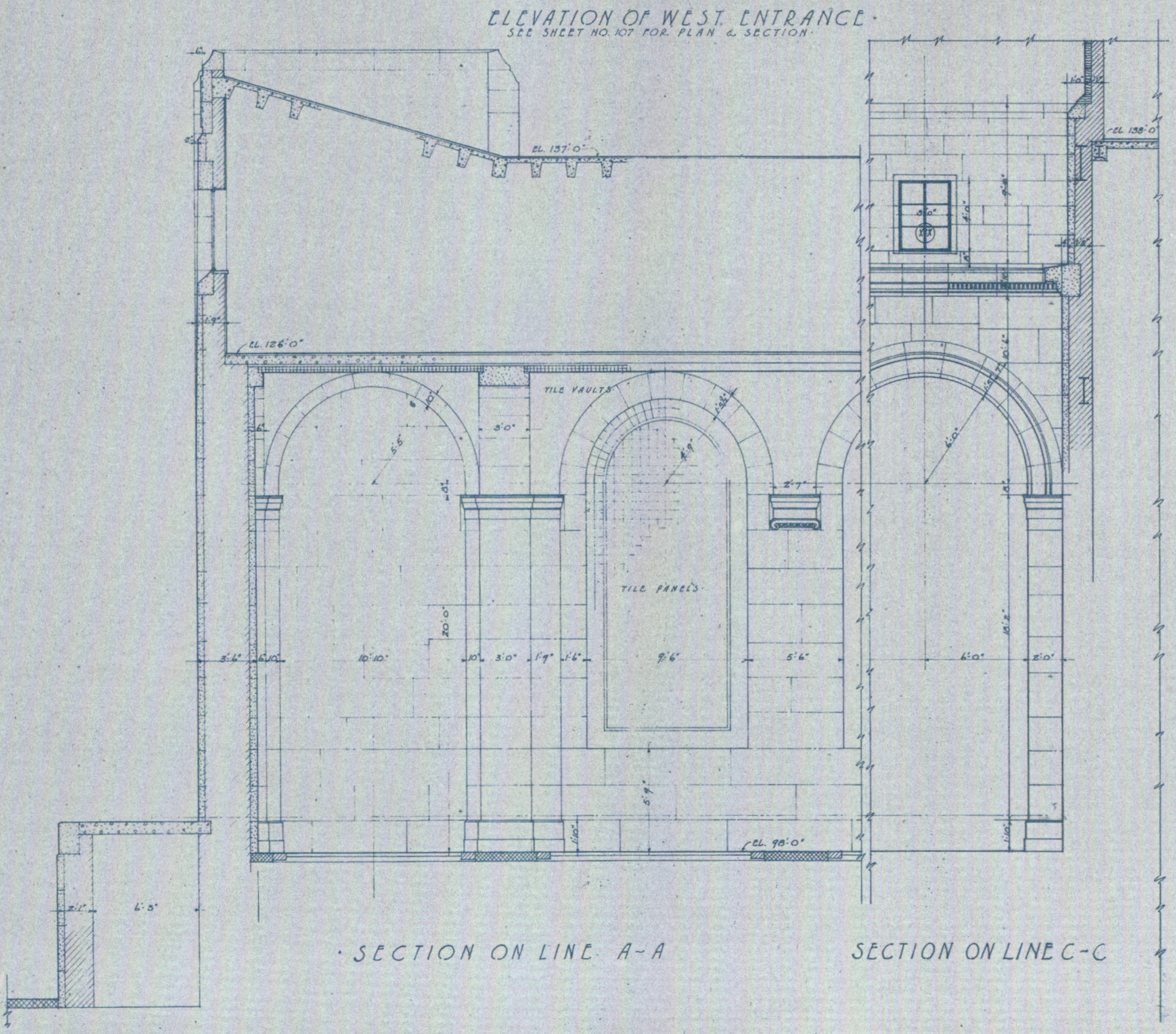

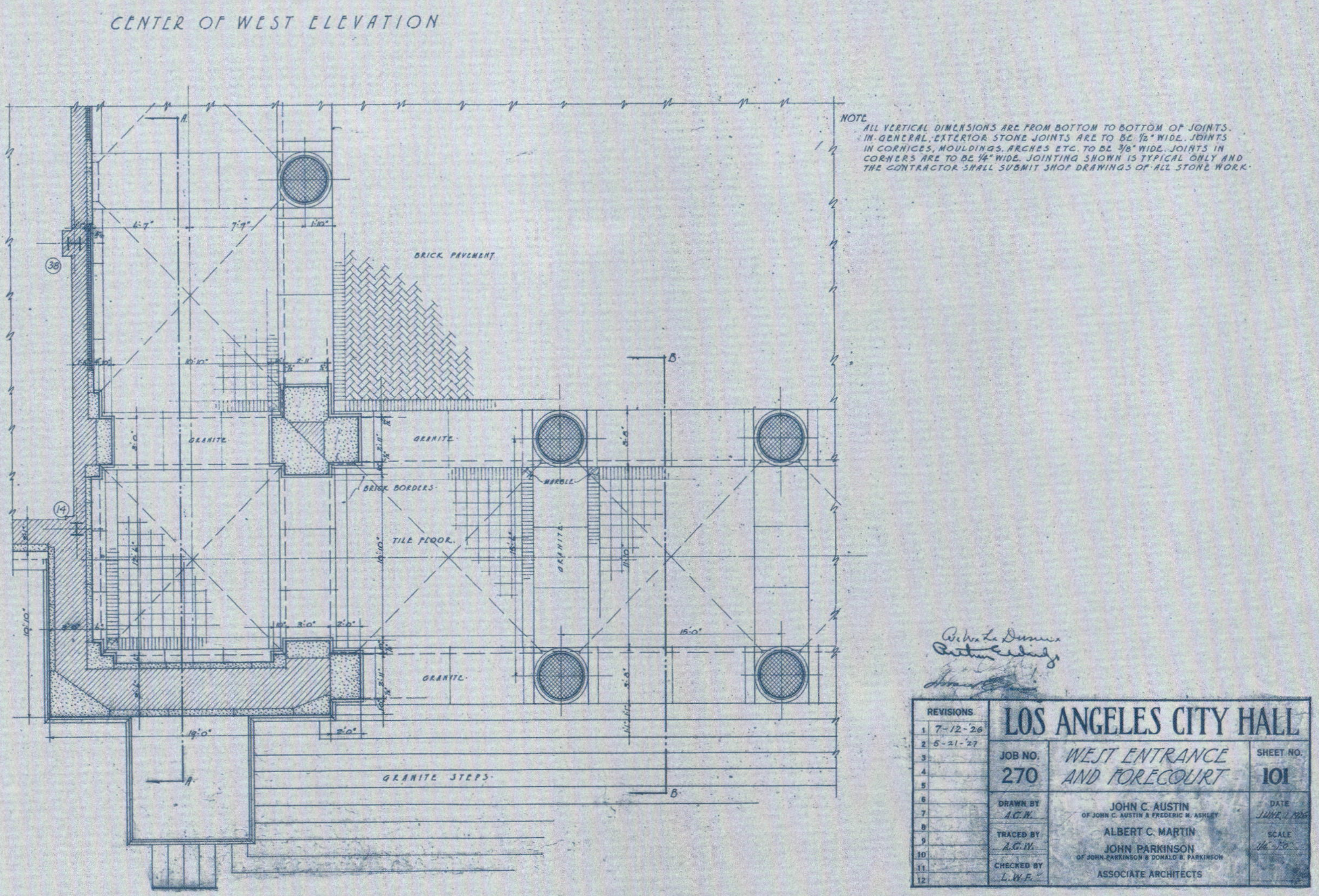
CENTER OF WEST ELEVATION
NOTE
ALL VERTICAL DIMENSIONS ARE FROM BOTTOM TO BOTTOM OF JOINTS.
IN GENERAL, EXTERIOR STONE JOINTS ARE TO BE ½" WIDE. JOINTS
IN CORNICES, MOULDINGS, ARCHES ETC. TO BE ⅜" WIDE. JOINTS IN
CORNERS ARE TO BE ¼" WIDE. JOINTING SHOWN IS TYPICAL ONLY AND
THE CONTRACTOR SHALL SUBMIT SHOP DRAWINGS OF ALL STONE WORK.
BRICK PAVEMENT
GRANITE
BRICK BORDERS
TILE FLOOR
MARBLE
GRANITE STEPS
REVISIONS
1 7-12-'26
2 5-21-'27
LOS ANGELES CITY HALL
JOB NO.
270
WEST ENTRANCE
AND FORECOURT
SHEET NO.
101
DRAWN BY
A.C.W.
TRACED BY
A.C.W.
CHECKED BY
L.W.F.
JOHN C. AUSTIN
OF JOHN C. AUSTIN & FREDERIC M. ASHLEY
ALBERT C. MARTIN
JOHN PARKINSON
OF JOHN PARKINSON & DONALD B. PARKINSON
ASSOCIATE ARCHITECTS
DATE
JUNE 1 1926

LIGHT FIXTURES

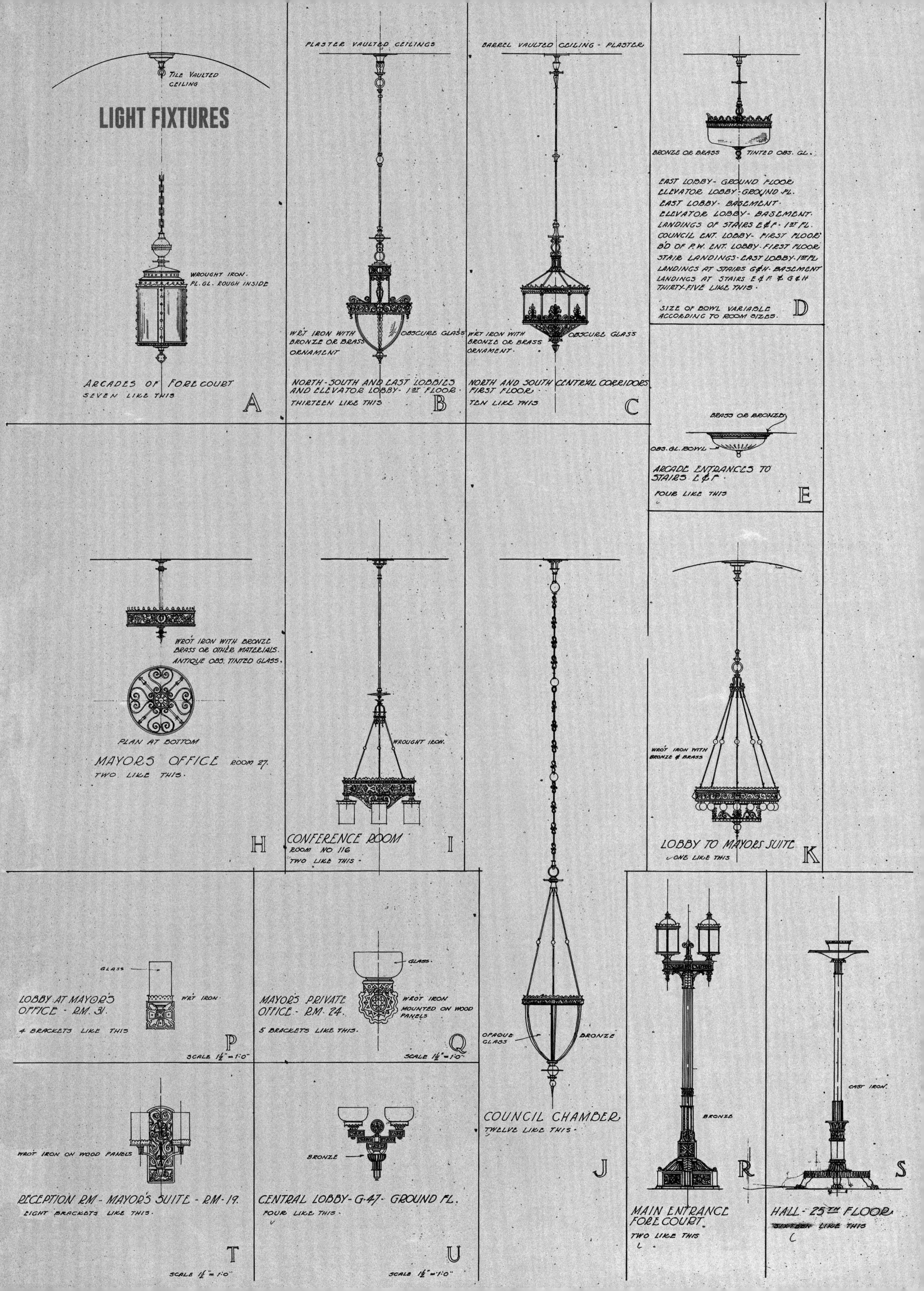

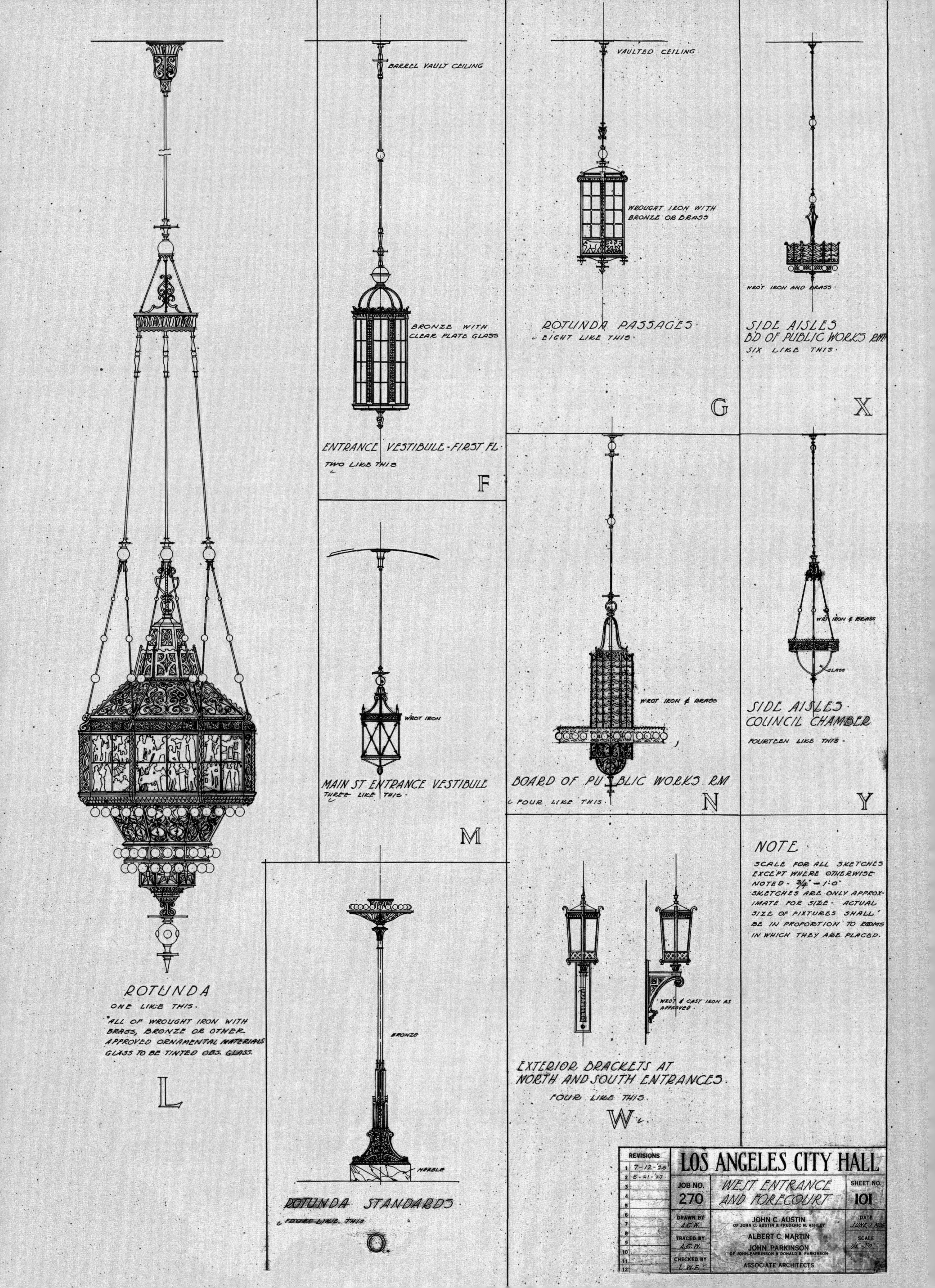
ROTUNDA
ONE LIKE THIS
ALL OF WROUGHT IRON WITH BRASS, BRONZE OR OTHER APPROVED ORNAMENTAL MATERIALS GLASS TO BE TINTED OBS. GLASS.
L
BARREL VAULT CEILING
BRONZE WITH CLEAR PLATE GLASS
ENTRANCE VESTIBULE - FIRST FL
TWO LIKE THIS
F
VAULTED CEILING
WROUGHT IRON WITH BRONZE OR BRASS
ROTUNDA PASSAGES
EIGHT LIKE THIS
G
WROT IRON AND BRASS
SIDE AISLES
BD OF PUBLIC WORKS RM
SIX LIKE THIS
X
WROT IRON
MAIN ST ENTRANCE VESTIBULE
THREE LIKE THIS
M
WROT IRON & BRASS
BOARD OF PUBLIC WORKS RM
FOUR LIKE THIS
N
WROT IRON & BRASS
GLASS
SIDE AISLES
COUNCIL CHAMBER
FOURTEEN LIKE THIS
Y
BRONZE
MARBLE
ROTUNDA STANDARDS
FOUR LIKE THIS
O
WROT & CAST IRON AS APPROVED
EXTERIOR BRACKETS AT NORTH AND SOUTH ENTRANCES
FOUR LIKE THIS
W
NOTE
SCALE FOR ALL SKETCHES EXCEPT WHERE OTHERWISE NOTED - 3/4" = 1'-0"
SKETCHES ARE ONLY APPROXIMATE FOR SIZE - ACTUAL SIZE OF FIXTURES SHALL BE IN PROPORTION TO ROOMS IN WHICH THEY ARE PLACED.
REVISIONS
1 7-12-26
2 5-21-27
LOS ANGELES CITY HALL
JOB NO. 270
WEST ENTRANCE AND FORECOURT
SHEET NO. 101
DRAWN BY A.C.W.
TRACED BY A.C.W.
CHECKED BY L.W.F.
JOHN C. AUSTIN
OF JOHN C. AUSTIN & FREDERIC M. ASHLEY
ALBERT C. MARTIN
JOHN PARKINSON
OF JOHN PARKINSON & DONALD B. PARKINSON
ASSOCIATE ARCHITECTS
DATE JUNE 1, 1926
SCALE 1/4" = 1'-0"

INSCRIPTIONS The question of how to select the symbolism and inscriptions for the city hall was an important one, but it proved problematic for the design team. John C. Austin encouraged Mayor Cryer and the Board of Public Works to recruit noted philosopher Hartley Burr Alexander, who created the sculptural scheme, inscriptions, and symbolism (executed by Lee Lawrie) for the Nebraska State Capitol and Los Angeles Central Library.[14] For both structures, Alexander envisioned a series of ideological inscriptions that served as a running commentary on the purpose of the building. It was agreed a similar approach should be adopted for Los Angeles City Hall.

Struggling to come up with a solution, the Municipal Art Commission considered presenting the problem to architecture students at the University of Southern California (USC) as a class project or possibly asking the school's president, Dr. Rufus B. von KleinSmid, for suggestions. The Board of Public Works also reached out to Robert A. Millikan, president of the California Institute of Technology (CalTech), for ideas, while the architects wrote to Orra E. Monnette, president of the Los Angeles Public Library Board of Commissioners, hoping his experience working on the city's new Central Library might help.[15] "There are a number of splendid inscriptions in the interior of the Library in San Francisco," the architects wrote to the Board of Public Works. "We hope that we shall have inscriptions equally appropriate."[16]

Ultimately, the Board of Public Works assembled a committee chaired by Dr. Ernest C. Moore, who served as president of the Los Angeles State Normal School and later president and provost of UCLA, who was joined by Susan M. Dorsey, superintendent of schools; von KleinSmid; Reverend Father Marshall Winne of the Los Angeles Seminary; Frederick W. Blanchard, president of the Municipal Art Commission; and John C. Austin. The committee's list of inscriptions, approved by the art commission on March 8, 1927, was as follows:

1. For the mantel in the mayor's reception room: "The execution of laws is more important than the making of them" —Thomas Jefferson (later changed to "Fidelity is the Foundation of Justice" —Cicero)
2. Over the door in the Council Chamber: "Law is reason without passion" —Aristotle
3. Over the east entrance: "A people cannot have the consciousness of being self-governed unless they attend themselves to the things over against their own doors" —Benjamin Ide Wheeler
4. Over the south entrance: "He that violates his oath profanes the divinity of faith itself" —Cicero
5. Over the north entrance: "The highest of all sciences and services—the government" —James Russell Lowell
6. Over the west entrance: "Let us have faith that right makes might" —Abraham Lincoln
7. Under the bas-relief over the west entrance: "Righteousness exalteth a people" —Solomon
8. Under the bas-relief panel over the west entrance: "Though free they are not absolutely free for they have a master over them, the law" —Herodotus (never executed)[17]

"LET US HAVE FAITH THAT RIGHT MAKES MIGHT"
LINCOLN
"RIGHTEOUSNESS EXALTETH A PEOPLE" SOLOMON

MODELING AND STONE CARVING In October 1926, the Board of Public Works reviewed bids for the modeling and stone carving and awarded contracts to local artists Casper Gruenfeld and Joseph Conradi.

Working from his Los Angeles studio at 209 East Thirty-first St., Gruenfeld created the models for the pediment crowning the west entrance and the capitals for the columns that formed the court at the Spring Street entrance. Born John Caspar Lache Gruenfeld on December 29, 1872, in Holzminden, Germany, he developed his craft in Chicago while working with renowned Danish sculptor Johannes Gelert.[18] Later in his career, having settled in Los Angeles, John Parkinson recruited him to create the eight stone figures, representing the *Progress of Civilization*, which adorned the USC Administration Building. They also collaborated on the iconic fountain at the center of Parkinson's 1911 celebrated redesign of Los Angeles Central Park (later known as Pershing Square).[19] Gruenfeld was aided by sculptor Carlo Gerrone. Together, they were allowed four months to complete their work on City Hall, which included modeling much of the ornamental iron and bronze work for the building as well.

Joseph Conradi is known for his work on the Library of Congress, the Los Angeles Times Building, and USC's Doheny Memorial Library. Born in Switzerland in 1867, he immigrated to the United States in 1887. In Los Angeles, he worked with Albert C. Martin on a number of projects, including St. Vincent de Paul Catholic Church. "The time for the completion of all the work in Mr. Conradi's contract should be set for not later than twelve months from the date of the award, with provision that he must work in conjunction with the granite contractor and have his work prepared so that the granite contractor will not be delayed in setting the stone," the architects advised the Board of Public Works.[20]

Gruenfeld (*right*) produced two wax-and-clay models of City Hall. One was temporarily displayed in the Broadway department store; the other was shown in the Robertson Company department store on Hollywood Boulevard.

WEST ENTRANCE The architects' design for the west entrance included plans for a never-realized frieze above the main doors that was intended to complement a nearby larger panel above the front of the forecourt arcade that also was never completed.

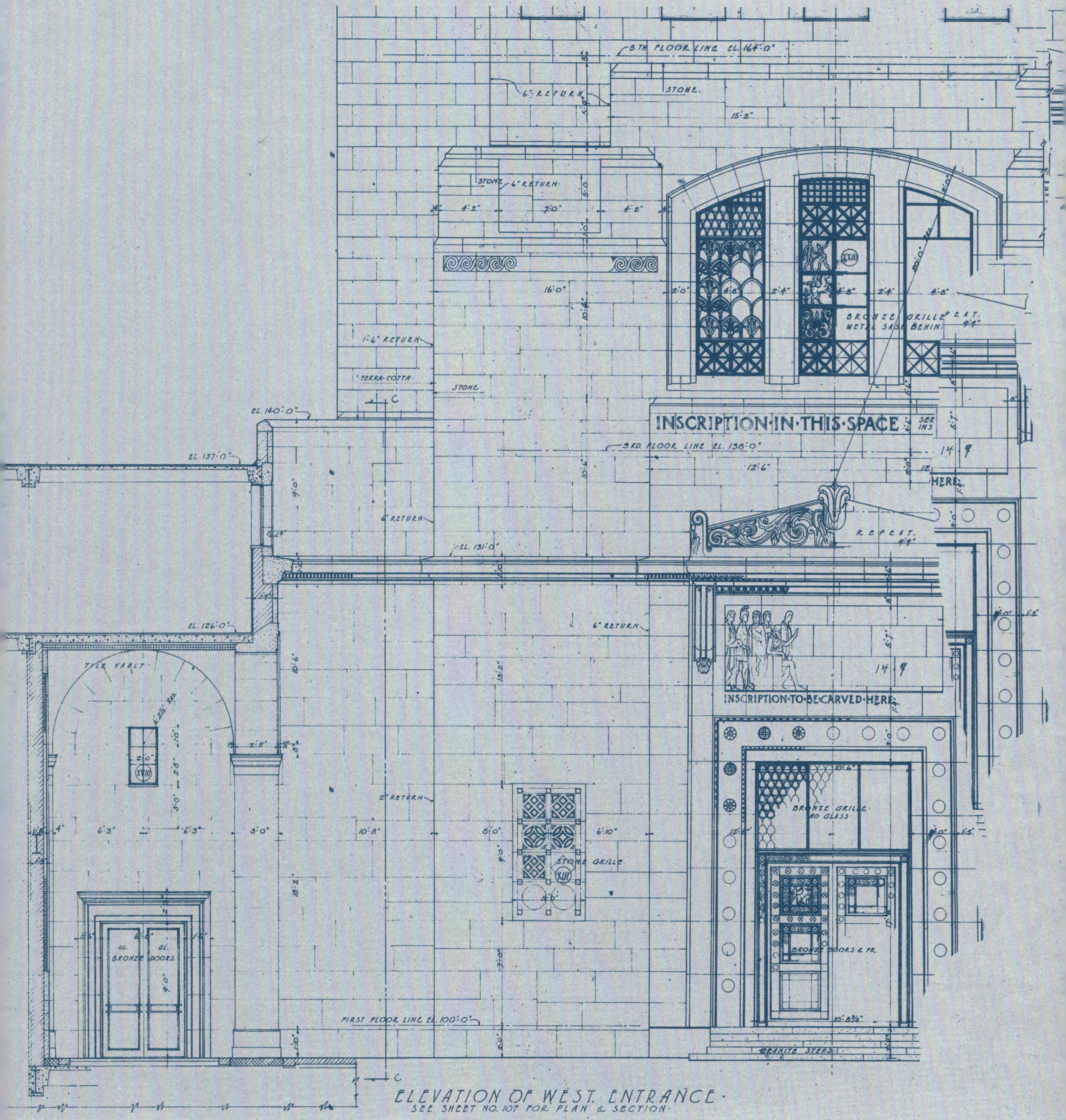

GRILLE OVER WEST ENTRANCE

Above the west entrance was an elaborate grilled window that included details from the Coat of Arms of the City of Los Angeles. The Castle of Castile from the Arms of Spain represented Los Angeles under Spanish control from 1542 to 1821; an eagle holding a serpent from the Arms of Mexico represented the period of Mexican rule from 1822 to 1846; the Bear and Star represented the Bear Flag of the California Republic of 1846; while a bald eagle replaced the Stars and Stripes, representing the shield of the United States.

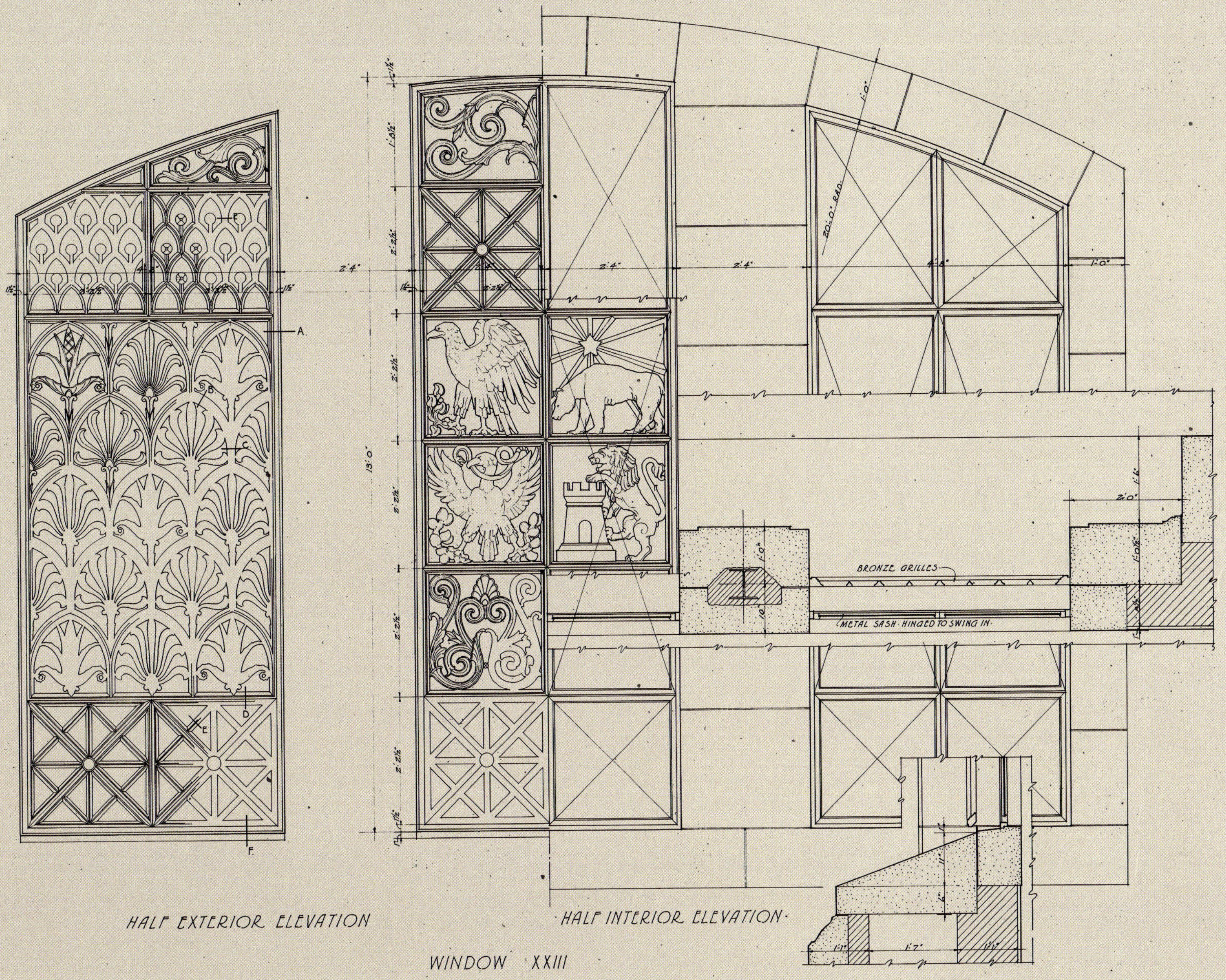

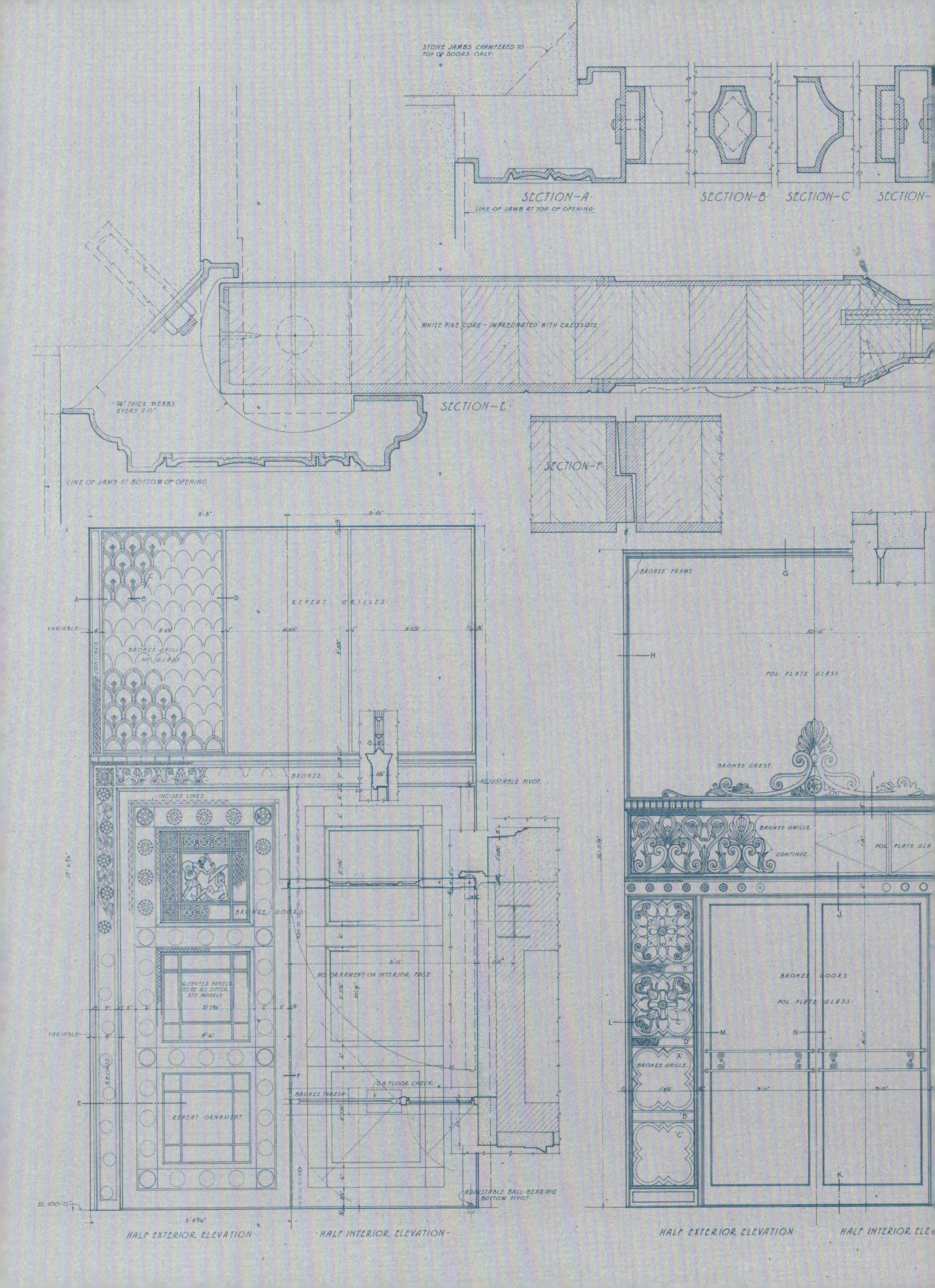
STONE JAMBS CHAMFERED TO TOP OF DOORS ONLY
SECTION-A
LINE OF JAMB AT TOP OF OPENING
SECTION-B
SECTION-C
SECTION-
WHITE PINE CORE - IMPREGNATED WITH CREOSOTE
¼" THICK WEBBS EVERY 2'0"
SECTION-E
SECTION-F
LINE OF JAMB AT BOTTOM OF OPENING
REPEAT GRILLES
BRONZE GRILLE NO GLASS
BRONZE
ADJUSTABLE PIVOT
INCISED LINES
BRONZE DOORS
4 CENTER PANELS TO BE ALL DIFFER. SEE MODELS
NO ORNAMENT ON INTERIOR FACE
REPEAT ORNAMENT
BRONZE THRESH
D.A. FLOOR CHECK
ADJUSTABLE BALL-BEARING BOTTOM PIVOT
BRONZE FRAME
POL. PLATE GLASS
BRONZE CREST
BRONZE GRILLE
CONTINUE
BRONZE DOORS
POL. PLATE GLASS
BRONZE GRILLE
EL. 100'0"
HALF EXTERIOR ELEVATION
HALF INTERIOR ELEVATION
HALF EXTERIOR ELEVATION
HALF INTERIOR ELE

ENTRANCE DOORS AND GRILLES

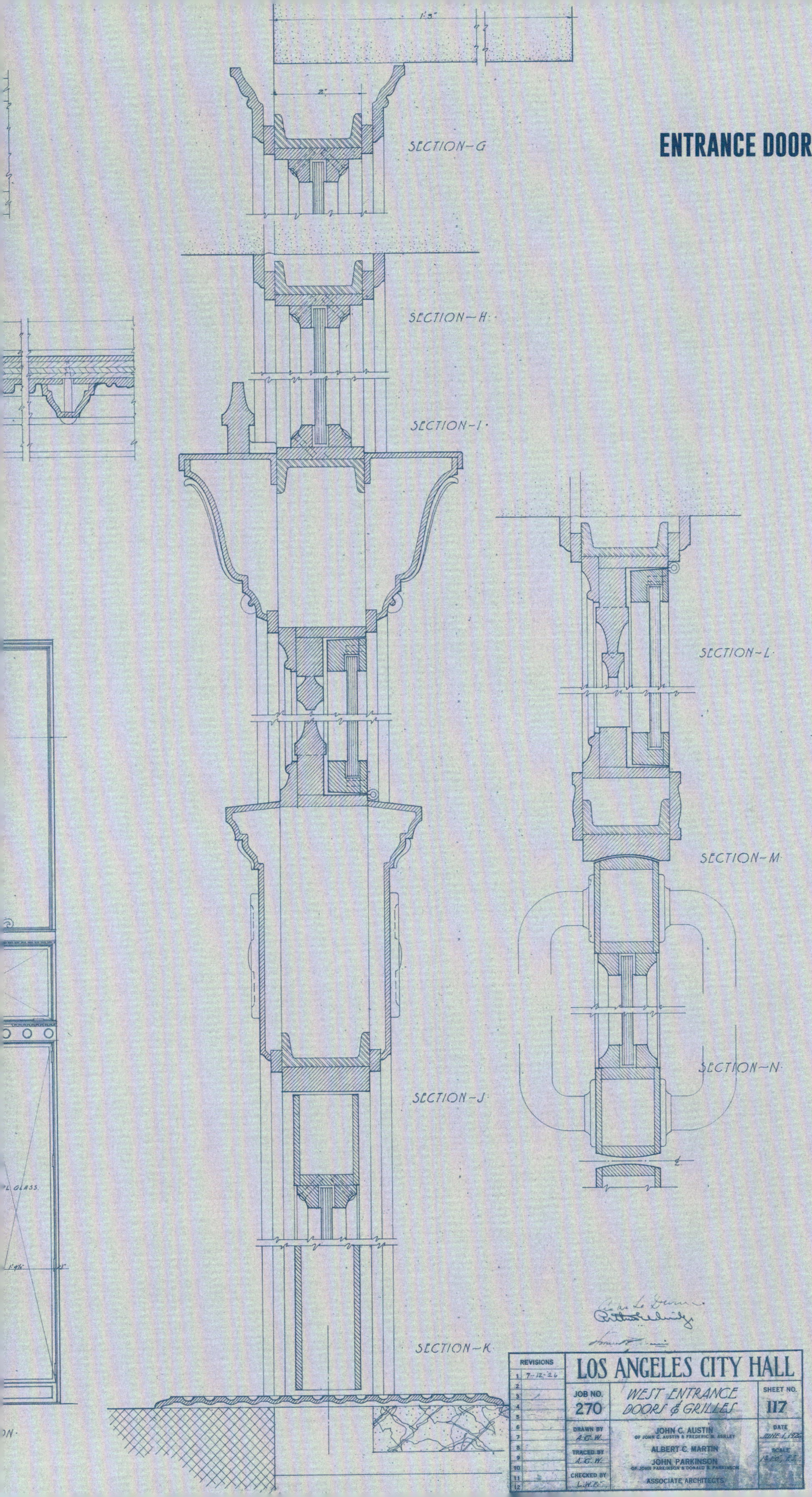

ENTRANCE DOORS Entering the building through the Spring Street forecourt, visitors arrived at two imposing cast-bronze doors with a verde antique finish. Each door featured three panels with bas-reliefs symbolizing the growth and history of California created by sculptor Henry Lion.

The architects' early plans had revealed a gladiator in each of the panels in anticipation of a final design. Arthur B. Benton, vice-president of the Municipal Art Commission, championed the idea that the panels should feature significant events in the city's history.[21] Born in Peoria, Illinois, Benton was an architect who, in addition to designing noted residences, possessed a keen interest in history and helped restore many California missions. He worked with the arts commission to produce a preliminary list of subjects for the panels, which included, "The visit of the first expedition to the site of the present city; the founding of the pueblo of Los Angeles by Gov. Felipe de Neve, September 4, 1781; the bringing of the news of the admission of California and the carrying of the charter of statehood, October 18 and 19, 1850; the building of the harbor 1896–1897; the building of the aqueduct 1906–1907; and the Olympic Games."[22]

The commission recommended "an artist of known ability in portraiture, such as Max Wieczorch, be employed to prepare cartoons upon which bids may be obtained."[23] After further deliberation, it was decided the sixth panel should represent education rather than the Olympic Games, in case the anticipated 1932 games were not held in the city. Artist Norman Kennedy submitted speculative designs for two panels, while Casper Gruenfeld produced a series of models that Benton observed were "incorrect historically" and would lead to the commission being "very justly criticized" if used.[24]

Benton favored hiring artist William A. Sharp to produce six full-size cartoons. Sharp developed an initial sketch titled *Discovery of L.A.*, which Art Commission President Frederick W. Blanchard presented, along with photographs of Gruenfeld's models, to the Associate Architects, who instead requested the work be awarded to Henry Lion.

Born on August 11, 1900, in Fresno, California, Lion had grown up on a farm. He attended Fresno High School and, during his senior year, won a scholarship to the California School of Fine Arts. After graduation, he headed to Los Angeles to study at the Otis Art Institute. In 1917, he began training under sculptor Julia B. Wendt, who believed he was "destined for great achievement in his art."[25,26]

His many credits include the *Fountain of Honor* at the Wilshire Ebell Club, the Felipe de Neve statue in the Plaza, and the sculpture of Juan Rodriguez Cabrillo at Cabrillo Beach.

"He has exceptional skill in modeling," critic Arthur Millier wrote of Lion, "the clay never goes on in niggling fashion but always largely related to the main form."[27]

By January 1928, Lion's models were complete; however, there was a growing controversy over the date on two of the panels. The Municipal Art Commission received word from local history groups suggesting the dates for the discovery of Los Angeles of 1770 and American occupation of 1847 be changed to 1769 and 1846, respectively.[28] Lion said he had been given the dates by Arthur Benton, who had since passed away following a long illness.[29]

The commission asked Walter S. Hertzog, director of American historical research for the city schools, to investigate the matter. He agreed 1770 should be changed to 1769 but suggested 1847 remain, "as the 1846 occupation was temporary."[30] The commission later overruled him.

The history department of the Los Angeles Public Library also confirmed 1769 as correct, based upon the diary of Spanish missionary Father Juan Crespi.[31]

The final list was as follows:

1. *Finding and Naming the Site, 1769*—Governor Gaspar de Portolà and his expedition camped near the Los Angeles River and held a religious service, August 1, 1769
2. *Founding, 1781*—Governor Felipe de Neve reads instructions to settlers who found the Pueblo de Nuestra Señora la Reina de los Ángeles, September 4, 1781
3. *American Occupation, 1846*—Commodore Robert Field Stockton and Major John Charles Fremont enter the city and raise the American flag, August 13, 1846
4. *Public School, Founded 1853*—The first ordinance authorizing establishment of public schools was passed by the council, July 25, 1853
5. *Opening Aqueduct Headgate*—William Mulholland opens the headgates releasing water into the aqueduct, February 13, 1913
6. *Placing Last Stone of Breakwater*—An engineer supervising the placing of the last stone on the breakwater giving the city its harbor, September 30, 1915[32]

Opposite: Henry Lion at work on the models for the west entrance doors.

ENTRANCE VESTIBULE

The entrance doors Henry Lion designed opened into a vestibule with vaulted ceilings, where the architects imagined niches capable of displaying "statuary of heroic size," although none were commissioned.[33] The walls of the vestibule were faced with Crazannes Anteor stone from France.[34]

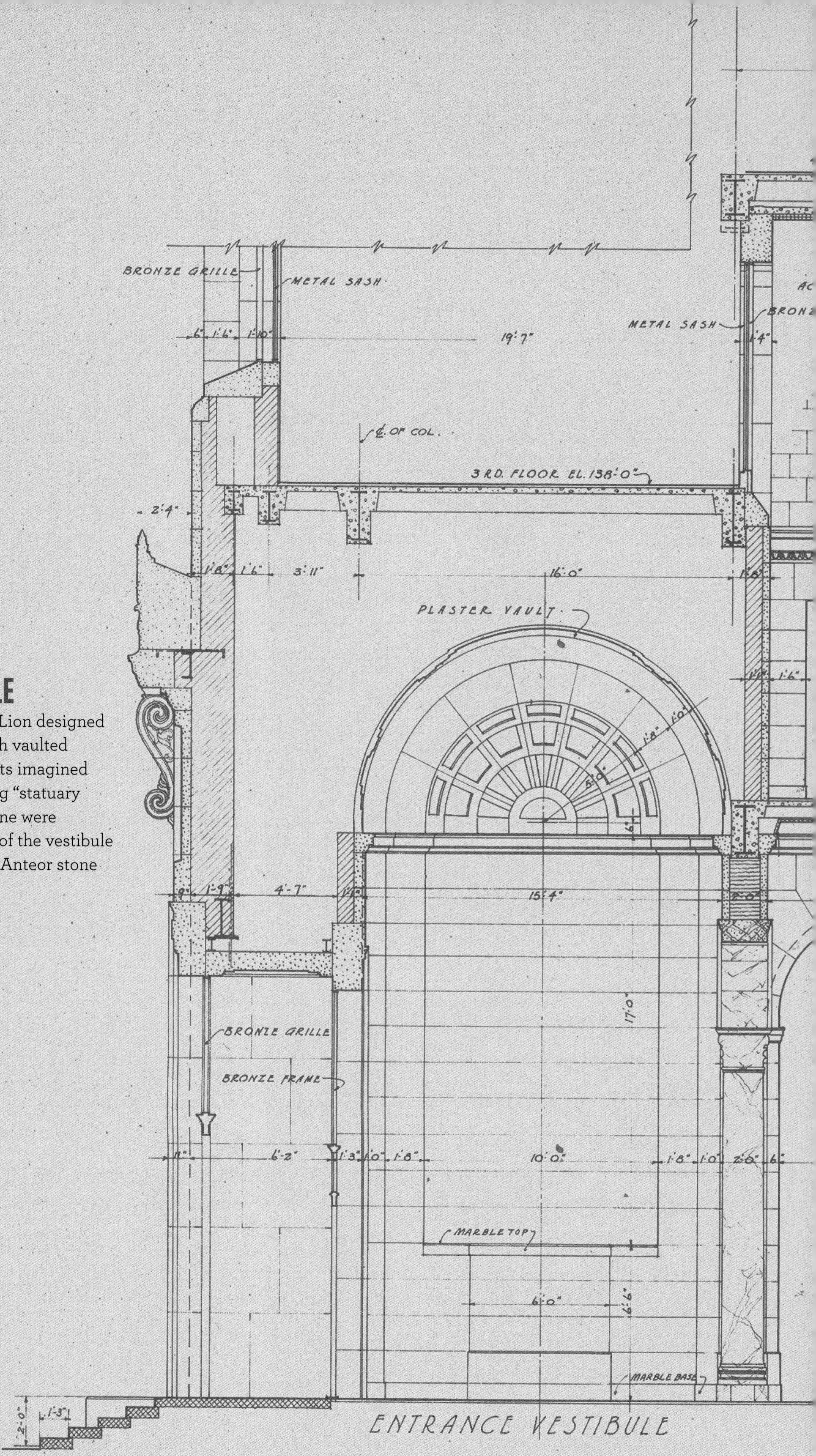

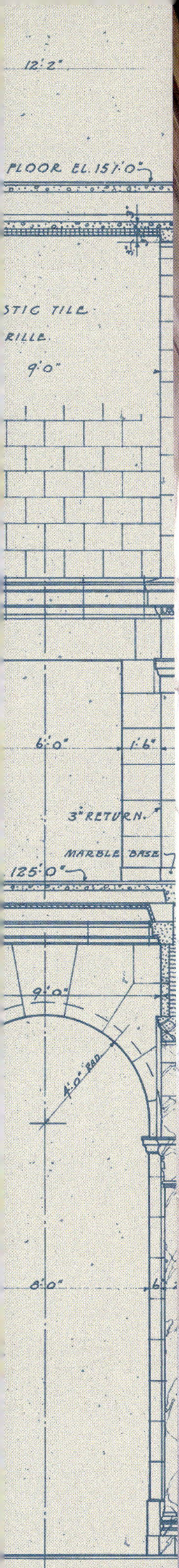
12'2"
FLOOR EL. 157'-0"
STIC TILE
RILLE
9'0"
6'0"
1'6"
3" RETURN.
MARBLE BASE
125'0"
9'0"
4'0" RAD
8'0"

TORCH OF XXIIIRD OLYMPIAD
LOS ANGELES 1984
GAMES OF THE XXIIIRD OLYMPIAD
LOS ANGELES 1984
TORCH CARRIED TO CITY HALL
MAURICE M. MATHEWS
OLYMPIC TORCH ARRIVED
SATURDAY JULY 21, 1984 4:20

ENTRANCE VESTIBULE, LIGHT FIXTURE

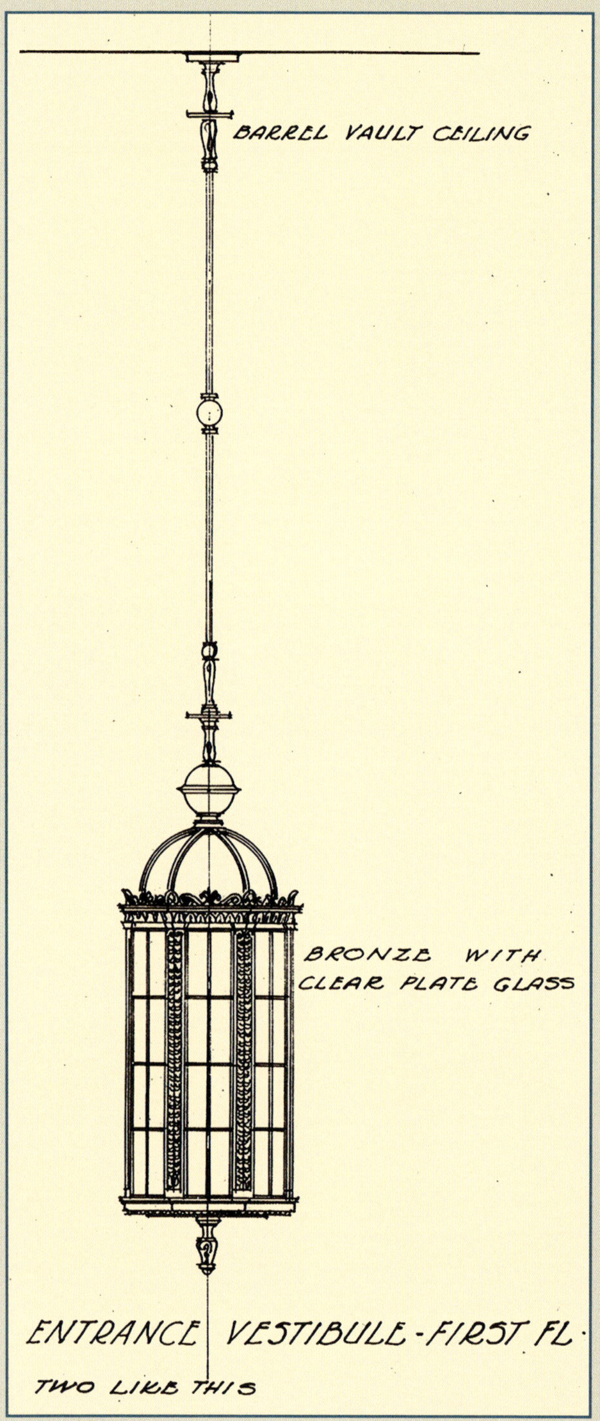

ENTRANCE VESTIBULE PANEL

Inside the vestibule were two faience tile panels burned by Malibu Potteries, one with the names of City Council members in 1927, and the other, the names of Mayor Cryer, members of the Board of Public Works, the Associate Architects, and the general contractor, C.J. Kubach Company.

ENTRANCE VESTIBULE, CEILING

"The barrel vaulted ceiling of the vestibule is paneled and coffered," George P. Hales wrote in *Pacific Coast Architect*. "Rich in color, with its dull reds and golds, softened with touches of blues and greens, this ceiling is appropriately decorated. Symbolic figures, rendered in monotones on dark background, portray Law, Justice, Charity, and Kindred subjects."[35] He added, "Emphasis is given to the symbolical group representing the City of Los Angeles, surrounded by Nature's bounteous gifts, depicted by the ball of golden sunlight, the sea at its shores, and an abundance of fruits of the soil."[36]

MALIBU POTTERIES PANELS

Malibu Potteries created twenty-three large decorative panels designed by J. Donald Prouty for the building. "The Associate Architects, Austin, Martin, and Parkinson, had a field office on the job site and furnished me with office space there," Prouty later wrote. "I spent three or four days a week there designing the tile work assigned to Malibu Potters. This consisted of arched top panels and lunettes in each monumental stair hall at the north and south ends of the City Hall (and in the east lobby). There also were two dedicatory panels. . .in the narthex (entry vestibule) on the west side of the building, and another decorative panel in the City Council Chambers. Each panel had to be individually designed to exactly fit the recesses in the marble walls furnished by other contractors."[37]

FLOOR PLAN The architects were determined that the areas most used by the public, including the Council Chamber and Board of Public Works Session Room, should be within easy reach of the principal Spring Street entrance. Another feature the architects considered was the amount of daylight that reached interior spaces. Within the walls of the structure's base, the architects designed four light courts to provide natural light to the surrounding rooms facing inwards.

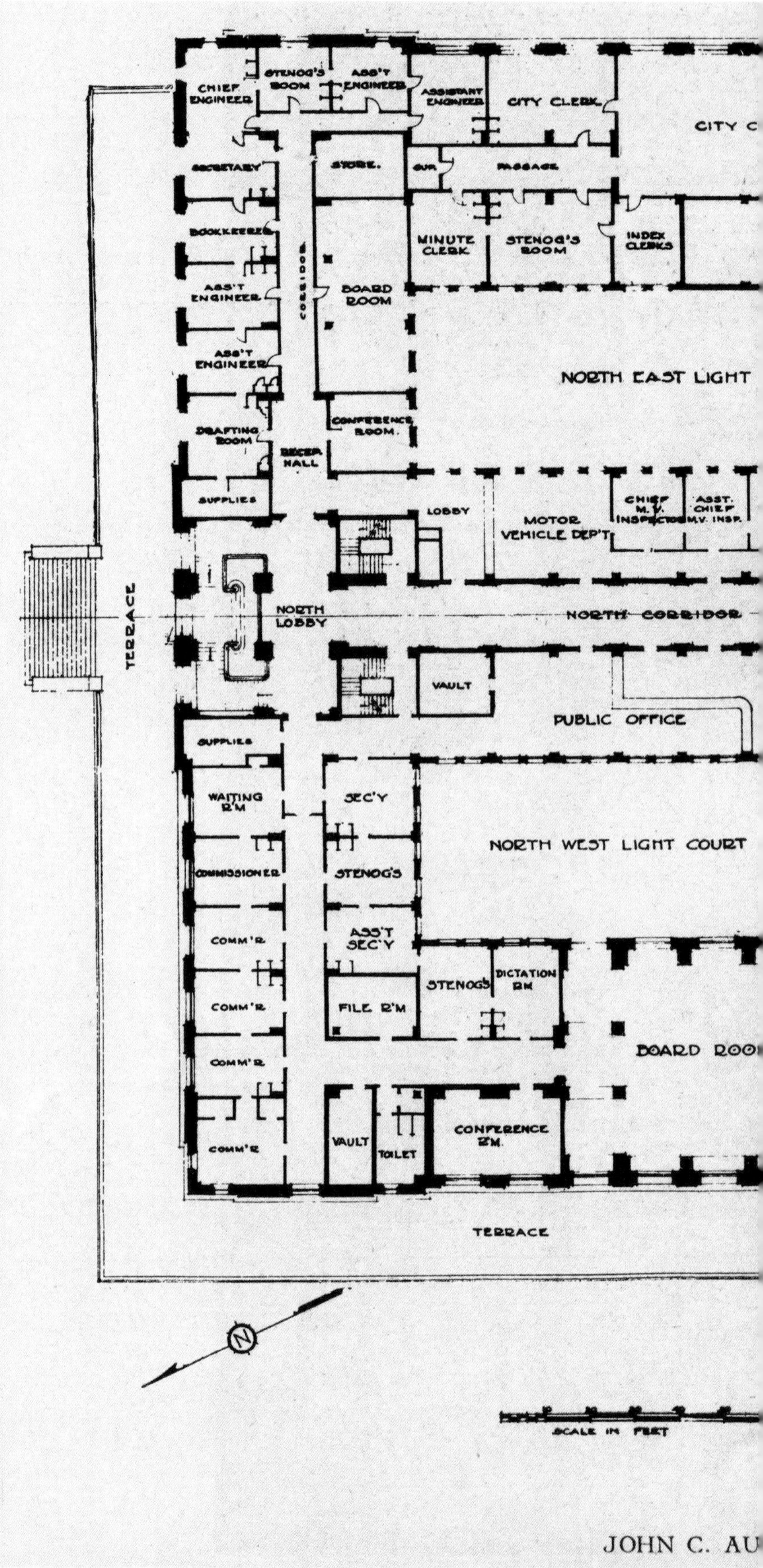

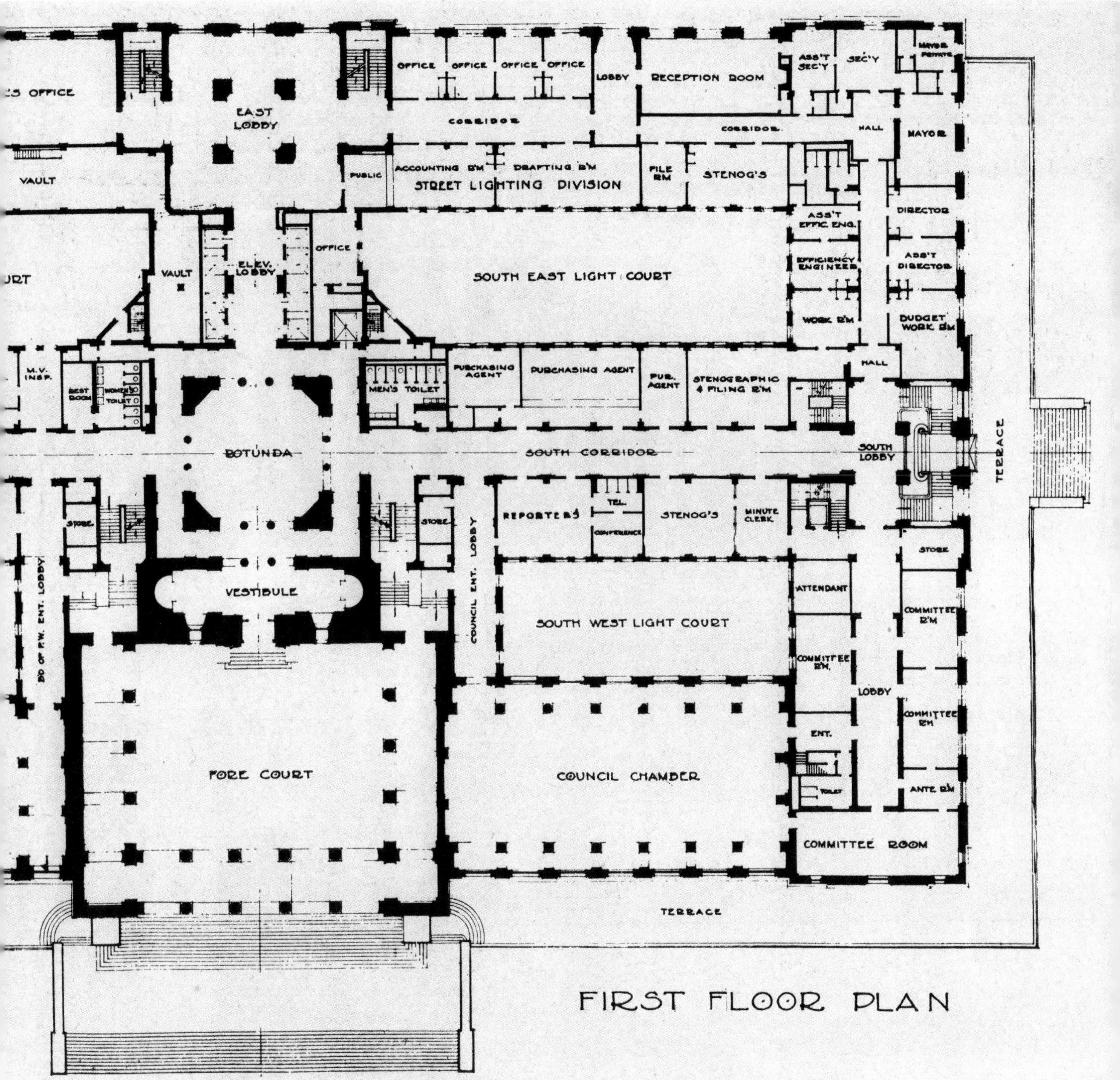

FIRST FLOOR PLAN

CITY HALL, LOS ANGELES, CALIFORNIA

IN, ALBERT C. MARTIN, JOHN PARKINSON, ASSOCIATED ARCHITECTS

ROTUNDA The architects envisioned the rotunda of City Hall to be the architectural tour de force of the building. Visitors stood in awe as they gazed around the majestic sixty-foot square space spanning three stories, filled with Byzantine and Romanesque influences and surmounted by a spectacular domed ceiling measuring more than thirty-eight feet in diameter.

"In the plan, the rotunda is square, except for the splayed angles, and is completely surrounded by generous passages connecting with the main longitudinal corridors, the elevator lobby and secondary passages to the angle stairways and adjacent light courts," John C. Austin laid out.[38]

ROTUNDA PASSAGES The grand beamed ceilings of the passages around the rotunda were made from treated California redwood.

ROTUNDA PASSAGES, LIGHT FIXTURE

ROTUNDA FLOOR The floor of the rotunda, passages, and vestibule featured multiple kinds of marble laid in geometrical patterns that formed a scheme made up of a series of circular designs. "The outer circlets are separated from each other by geometrical figures, and the whole scheme is of so complicated a nature that one is immediately sensible of the skill required of the artisans who fashioned this marble pavement," the journal *Through the Ages*, dedicated to the use of marble, proclaimed in 1929. There were approximately 25,000 individual pieces of marble in the floor design, including Yellow Numidian from Africa and Hauteville from France, although the bulk of space was covered by Asbury Pink Tennessee.[39] The building's different hallways and rooms were decorated with forty-eight different types of marble[40] from Algeria, Belgium, Italy, France, Germany, Greece, and five American states: Minnesota, Missouri, Pennsylvania, Tennessee, and Vermont.[41]

At the center of the rotunda floor was a cast-bronze insert of an old Spanish caravel surrounded by marble to represent the sky and the ocean. Early plans revealed the architects anticipated the city's crest to be the central symbol.

ROTUNDA COLUMNS At the sides of the rotunda, ten columns in various colors, each with elaborately carved marble capitals, supported an overlooking gallery. As *Through the Ages* reported, "Each of the columns is, without exception, of a different kind of marble; the pair on the north a Premier Campan Griotte, from Cahors, in France, and Premier Vert Campan Melange, from Hautes-Pyrenees, France; the eastern pair are Premier Vert Campan Melange and Premier Rose Corail Claire, also from France; the south pair are Premier Rouge Acajou, from Cierp, Haute-Gironde, and Premier Rouge de Rance, from Rance, Hainaut, Belgium; and the four on the west are of Premier Emerald Curly Green, Premier Purple Levanto, Premier Red Levanto (these three from Italy), and Tinos, from the island of that name in the Grecian Archipelago."[42]

ROTUNDA CEILING The domed ceiling of the rotunda was faced with tan acoustical tile, produced by Gladding, McBean and Company, and inlaid with patterns of glazed tile and figures, symbolizing important aspects of government: art, public service, government, protection, trust, education, health, and the law.

"The rotunda is the chief interior feature of the building, and the architects enriched it with special opulence," wrote Edward F. O'Day, editor of Gladding, McBean's journal *Shapes of Clay*. "For the dome, they chose a tile treatment archaic Greek in design, and Greek in color—ivory, golden buff, pink-tan, and deep crimson terra cotta. The effect is surprising loveliness, and the student is delighted to preserve the adaptability of old world beauty to a building that will forever be the newest of New World cities. It might be said in passing that this dome of decorative tile is the most important achievement in that medium thus far credited to Gladding, McBean, and Company."[43]

SYMBOLICAL CHARACTERS ON ROTUNDA CEILING

LUNETTES A similar treatment was given to the three barrel vaults and the tiled lunettes containing figures portraying Justice, Government, and Our Lady, Queen of Angels, patron saint of the city.

"For the rotunda and side arches, and also for the main panels in the Council chamber and in the meeting-room of the Board of Public Works, Gladding, McBean and Company, produced an acoustic tile," *Shapes of Clay* reported. "It was manufactured specially for this building. It is all-clay and fireproof, cellular in texture, its weight one-fourth that of ordinary clay tile, and may be in colors to match any terra-cotta or stone."[44]

ROTUNDA CHANDELIER The rotunda received light from a grilled window and an elaborate cast-bronze chandelier designed by Henry Lion that was suspended from the center of the domed ceiling. It was decorated with geometric patterns and silhouetted figures portraying Spanish explorer Vasco Núñez de Balboa, the first European to reach the Pacific on September 29, 1513; Juan Rodriguez Cabrillo, the first European to navigate to present-day California in 1542; Father Junipero Serra, who established the first missions in California in 1769; Explorer Juan Bautista de Anza, who arrived in San Gabriel, California, in 1774; Governor Felipe de Neve, founder of the Pueblo of Los Angeles in 1781; Jedediah Strong Smith, the first American to arrive in California cross-country from the East Coast, who visited Los Angeles in January 1827; and Commodore John Drake Sloat, who raised the United States flag at Monterey on July 7, 1846. The fixture had a capacity of five thousand watts, and the intensity of light was controlled by mirror reflectors that produced a soft, even glow.

EXIT

ROTUNDA STANDARDS

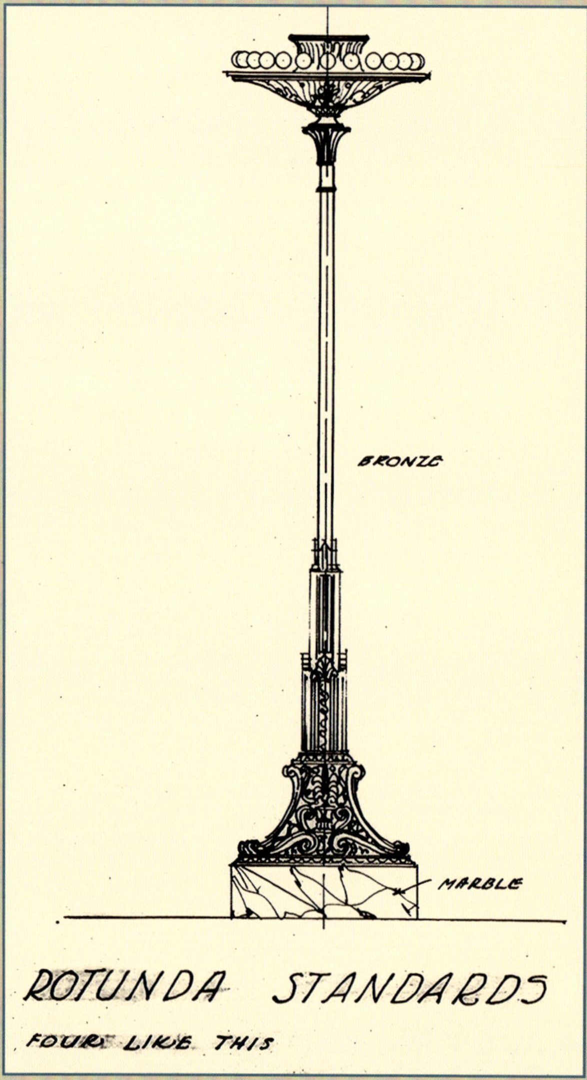

ANTHONY HEINSBERGEN The responsibility for decorating the ceilings was divided between teams led by master painters Anthony Heinsbergen and Herman Sachs.

Heinsbergen's canvases adorned ceilings and walls in some 750 of the most extravagant theaters in the country, as well as important civic buildings. "At the height of our busiest period, we had twenty theaters on the go all at one time," Heinsbergen recollected. "I once spent fifty-seven consecutive days on trains crisscrossing this country."[45] He also decorated the Interstate Commerce and Labor Buildings in Washington, D.C.; California Club in Los Angeles; Hollywood Roosevelt Hotel; California State Capitol Rotunda in Sacramento; and numerous hotels, including the Sir Francis Drake in San Francisco.

Born in Holland in 1894, Heinsbergen was introduced to art by his father, who on three Sundays of every month, took him to see the work of Frans Hals in the Hals Museum in Haarlem. On the fourth Sunday, they made the journey to Amsterdam to view Rembrandts.

Heinsbergen started working when he was ten as an apprentice to a local artist and restorer. In 1906, along with his father, he left Holland to begin a new life in California. They settled in Los Angeles, where Heinsbergen was hired by the Parker Decorating Company, which specialized in interiors. He stayed with the company for five years, working at night so he could obtain his high school diploma.[46]

His big break came when, as a nineteen-year-old, he caught the attention of Alexander Pantages, who commissioned him to paint the proscenium arch of the Pantages Theatres in Portland, Oregon, and Seattle. Impressed by the young man's work, Pantages commissioned Heinsbergen to work on twenty other theaters in the United States and Canada.

The same year Heinsbergen was recruited to work on Los Angeles City Hall, he also worked on another city icon, the Wiltern Theatre, at the corner of Wilshire Boulevard and Western Avenue.

As *Los Angeles Times* art critic William Wilson later wrote of Heinsbergen's designs, "They are a delightful mish-mash of byzantine sumptuousness, Art Deco cubism, and pure kitsch, perfect for the timeless and vulgar opulence of movie-going."[47]

An early concept for the ceiling of the north lobby.

HERMAN SACHS Master painter Herman Sachs was born in Romania in 1889. He began his career working with his father, Martin Sachs, a noted muralist who created frescoes in the Balasha Cathedral in Bucharest and the Royal Palace in Cotroceni, Romania.

Upon graduating from the Royal Academy in Bucharest, Sachs continued his education in Vienna, Budapest, Berlin, Munich, Paris, and London before returning to work with his father in Bucharest while also taking on independent commissions.[48]

After relocating to the United States in the early 1920s, he established the short-lived Chicago Industrial Art School and later became the director of the Dayton (Ohio) Art School. After moving to Los Angeles, he served as the director of the Creative Art Students League.[49]

He was well known to John and Donald Parkinson, having collaborated with them on numerous local buildings, including Los Angeles's Title Insurance Building and Los Angeles Gas Company Building, San Diego's Spreckels Building, and First National Bank in Santa Ana.

Sachs would also later work with the Parkinson firm on the Federal Reserve Bank of San Francisco, Los Angeles branch; the Chamber of Commerce Building (with John C. Austin); Bullock's Wilshire; and Union Station.

"I believe that if the decoration in the principal rooms were given to Mr. Sachs he would contribute more to the building in a creative and constructive way than any other decorator you could employ," Donald Parkinson wrote to the Engineering Committee for Union Station in 1937.[50]

Below, Herman Sachs's crew poses for a group photo in the forecourt. Right, workers prepare designs in Sachs's temporary studio on Flower Street. Above right, Sachs's design for a barrel-vaulted ceiling in the Council Chamber.

Below: Herman Sachs's crew poses for a group photo in the forecourt. *Opposite:* Workers prepare designs in Sachs's temporary studio on Flower Street. *Opposite top:* Sachs's design for a barrel-vaulted ceiling in the Council Chamber.

ELEVATOR LOBBY Anthony Heinsbergen and his colleagues brought to life the ceiling of the elevator lobby adjacent to the rotunda, with a central panel adorned with mythical characters to symbolize the "courage, perseverance, progressiveness, and energy of the people of Los Angeles."[51] Other panels represented agriculture, commerce, industry, motion pictures, and art.

In the elevator lobby were two banks of four elevators. "The elevator entrance doors, of ornate design, are of cast bronze framed with Red Verona marble," George P. Hales wrote. "Marble pilasters of French Pink and walls of Saint Genevieve Rose, extending to the spring line of the vaulted ceiling, form an appropriate finish of the wall surfaces."[52]

THE MASTERS OF EDVCATION HOLD IN THEIR HANDS THE FVTVRE OF THE WORLD
WATER

CENTRAL PANEL, EAST LOBBY CEILING

The ceiling of the east lobby consisted of a series of vaults with a stunning central dome. Decorated by Anthony Heinsbergen, the dome featured a star-shaped medallion ringed by the signs of the zodiac and an inscription reading, "The Masters of Education Hold in Their Hands the Future of the World." The pendentives in the dome featured a series of murals portraying earth, wind, water, and fire. Other nearby panels highlighted commerce, civil engineering, science, and other themes. The work earned enthusiastic praise from the Municipal Art Commission.

CENTRAL CORRIDOR The rotunda served as a hub with corridors extending outwards; the main corridor running north and south, linking offices, lobbies, and stairways, was described by the architects as "simple and restrained." The corridor featured an unbroken 24-foot barrel-vaulted ceiling decorated with designs portraying animals, including bears, buffalo, and deer, as well as human virtues such as courage and good over evil. Near the rotunda were murals representing art, architecture, sculpture, and poetry. The walls were embellished by Saint Genevieve, Napoleon Gray, and Bottico marble.[53]

COUNCIL CHAMBER On the south side of the central corridor was a passage connecting to the Council Chamber, measuring 54 feet wide by 104 feet long by 34 feet high. Basilica architecture was chosen for the space, which Albert C. Martin described as "simple and restrained in its architectural treatment, the note color being brought out in the decorative ceiling and arcades with tile patterns."[54]

As George P. Hales elucidated, "The twelve marble columns are monolithic, with varying characteristics of the three [*sic*] kinds used, viz.: Escallette, Breche, Opal, and Breccia Buchet. The column capitals, of Champville marble, are carved in typical Romanesque designs. The panels on each of the four sides of every capital contain designs emblematic of several states of the Union. California is thus represented by the Grizzly Bear, Texas by the Star, Massachusetts by the Codfish, and the remaining states by similarly accepted emblems."[55]

Attention in the Council Chamber was drawn to the south end of the chamber, where an arched canopy supported by two monolithic Rouge Acajou marble columns was capped by a carved oak cresting. The columns and the canopy surrounded a glazed Malibu Potteries-designed decorative faience tile panel burned in various shades of green.

The architects decided on benches rather than chairs for the public, to reduce noise, and selected rubber tile for the floor for the same reason. "Every precaution has been taken to assure the room's proper acoustic properties," Martin assured.[56] To illuminate the chamber, they envisioned two lines of seven lanterns, thirteen large windows, and a series of smaller windows above.

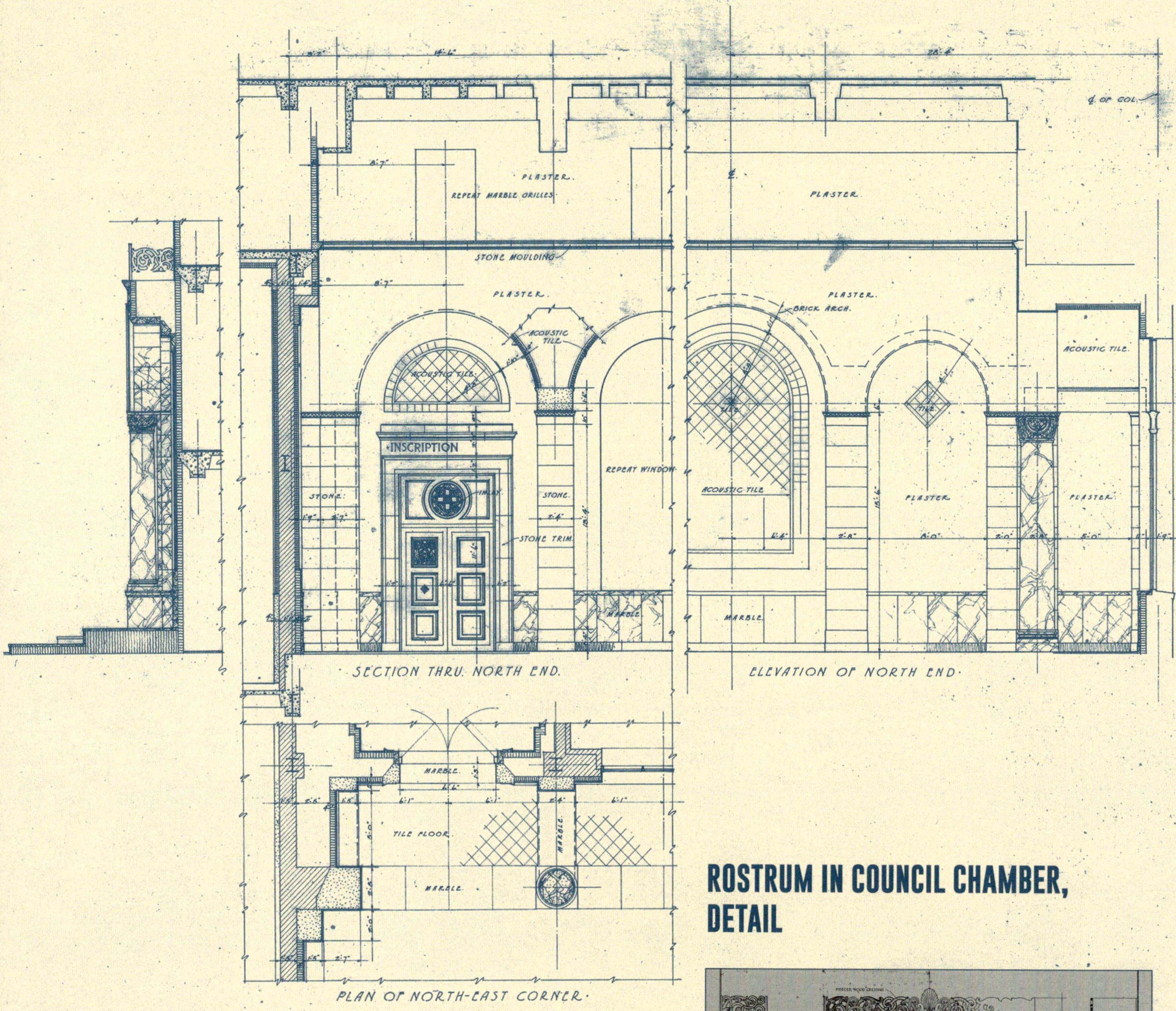

INTERIOR DETAILS OF COUNCIL CHAMBER

ROSTRUM IN COUNCIL CHAMBER, DETAIL

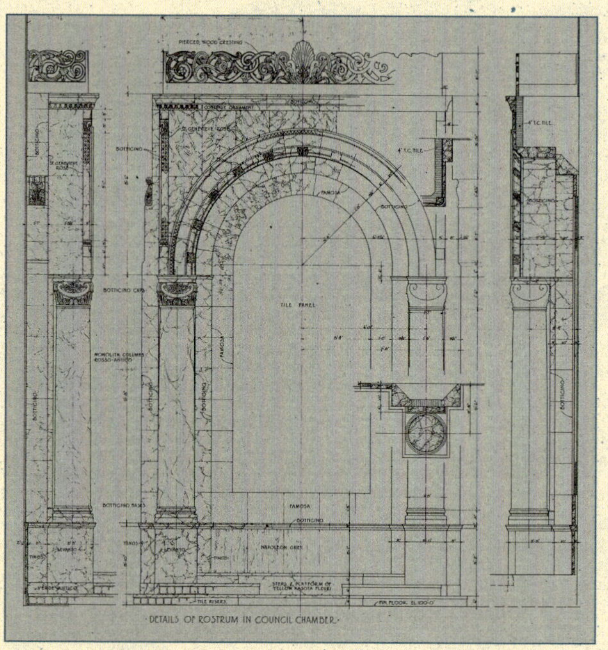

COUNCIL CHAMBER CEILING, LIGHT FIXTURES

The Council Chamber's central ceiling, decorated by Herman Sachs, was made of beamed cast concrete painted to resemble wood and decorated with gold, deep red, and blue tones contrasted with bold greens and vermillion. Four areas on the ceiling were decorated with signs of the zodiac and figures representing Apollo, Eros, Jupiter, Mars, Mercury, Neptune, Vulcan, and Venus.

The barrel-vaulted ceilings of the Council Chamber aisles featured elaborate murals representing themes of art, architecture, drama, law, music, medicine, poetry, and science.

Enhancing Sach's intricate artwork are light fixtures whose designs were included in the Associate Architects' detailed plan.

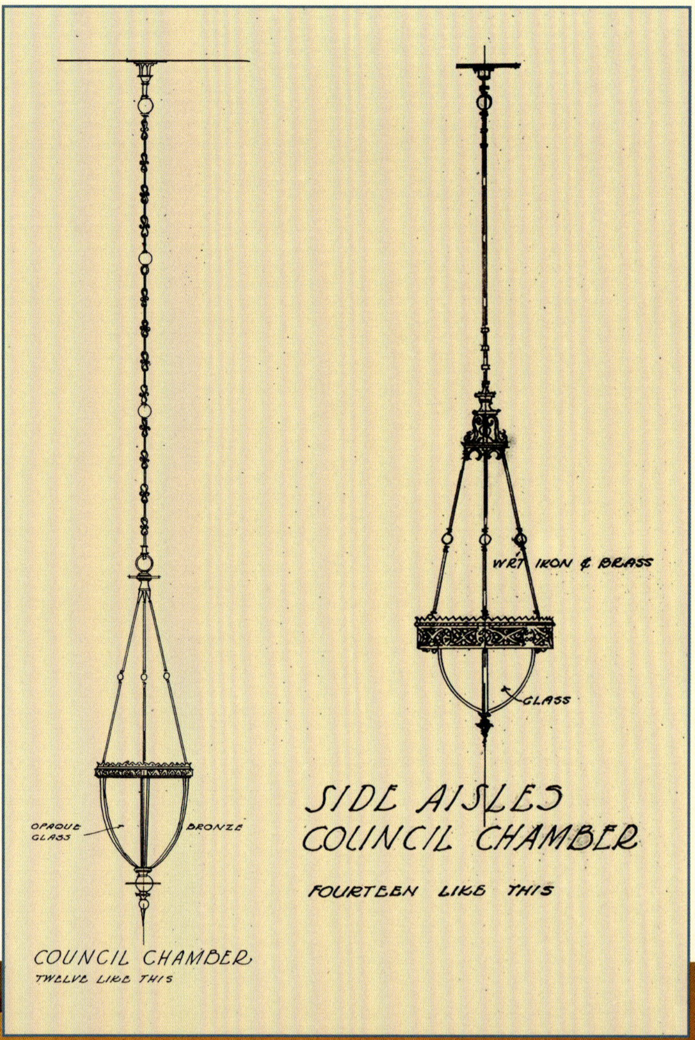

BOARD OF PUBLIC WORKS SESSION ROOM

The architects conceived the Board of Public Works Session Room as an almost square space, with arcades at the north and south sides, and arches supported by Escalette and Rouge Campan Melange marble columns that framed the windows.[57]

To reach the room, visitors passed through a corridor with a vaulted ceiling where decorated beams displayed images of historical figures, including Juan Bautista Alvarado, Vasco Núñez de Balboa, Juan Rodriguez Cabrillo, Christopher Columbus, Hernán Cortéz, José Figueroa, Father Junipero Serra, and Gaspar de Portolà.

CITY OF LOS ANGELES
FOUNDED 1781

BOARD OF PUBLIC WORKS SESSION ROOM, CEILING

Herman Sachs decorated the beams of the Board of Public Works Session Room ceiling in gold, blue, and green to focus attention on the centerpiece, the official seal of the city. The ceilings of the arcades also featured elaborate patterns created by Sachs.

BOARD OF PUBLIC WORKS SESSION ROOM, LIGHT FIXTURES

INTERIOR DETAILS OF BOARD OF PUBLIC WORKS ROOM

NORTH AND SOUTH ENTRANCE LOBBIES

The architects used a very similar approach for the north and south entrance lobbies; both were entered via outside terraces through bronze doors, both featured decorative faience tile panels designed by Malibu Potteries, and both had Pink Kasota stone balustrades on the stairways. The primary difference was the color of the ceilings, both decorated by Heinsbergen. The south lobby was treated in a deep blue, with brilliant medallions, while the north lobby was treated in mulberry tones.

EXTERIOR BRACKETS AT NORTH AND SOUTH ENTRANCES

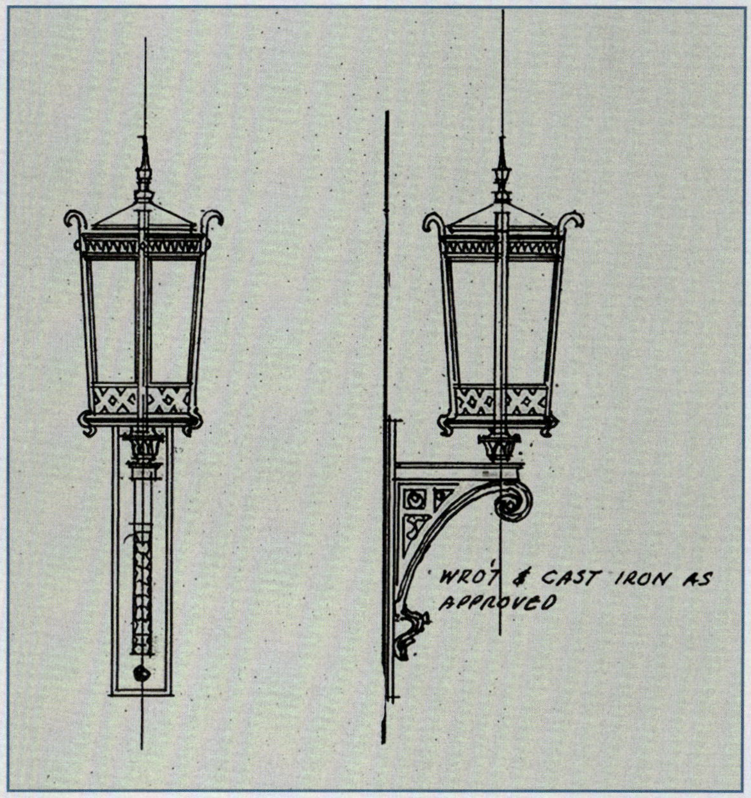

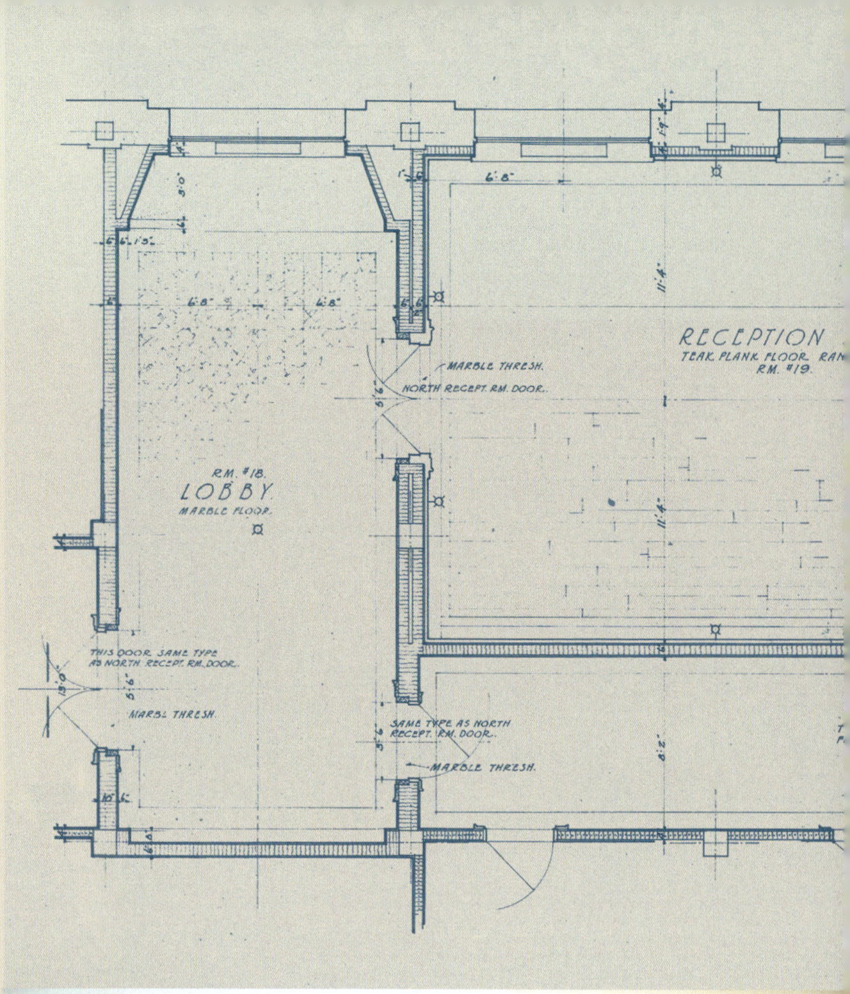

MAYOR'S SUITE The architects positioned the mayor's suite at the southeast corner of the main floor, as it offered an "attractive outlook over the park or garden, on the south, the exposure to many hours of sunshine and to a cooling summer breeze rendering its occupancy pleasant and comfortable at all seasons of the year,"[58] John C. Austin reasoned.

Reached by way of a corridor extending from the east lobby, the suite included a waiting room with a barrel-vaulted ceiling and checkered-marble floor, as well as a reception room with a teak floor and walnut dowels, a beamed redwood ceiling decorated with various coats of arms and emblems, and a fireplace and mantel.[58] Adjoining the mayor's office was a "retiring room" and bathroom including shower. Also located in the suite were offices for the mayor's secretary and assistant secretary.

MAYOR'S SUITE, RECEPTION ROOM, FIREPLACE

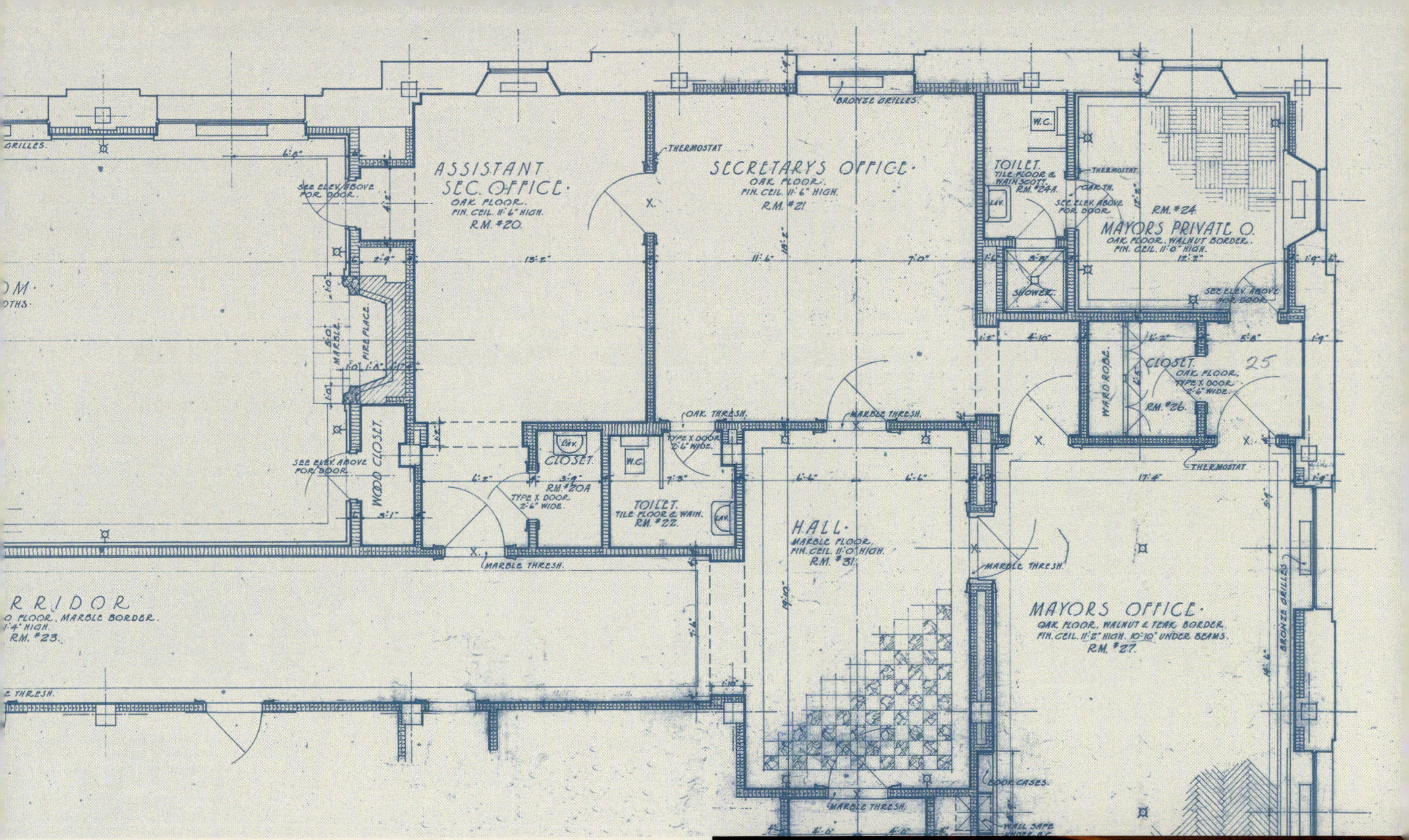

MAYOR'S SUITE, RECEPTION ROOM, LIGHT FIXTURE

MODERN CLASSIC

MAYOR'S OFFICE

ANTHONY HEINSBERGEN CONCEPT, CEILING, MAYOR'S OFFICE

MAIN STREET ENTRANCE LOGGIA

The architects anticipated the Main Street entrance would be the most heavily trafficked of all the entrances. Inside, they positioned the main bank of passenger elevators in this area to add to the "efficiency of this entrance."[59]

MAIN STREET ENTRANCE LOGGIA, LIGHT FIXTURE

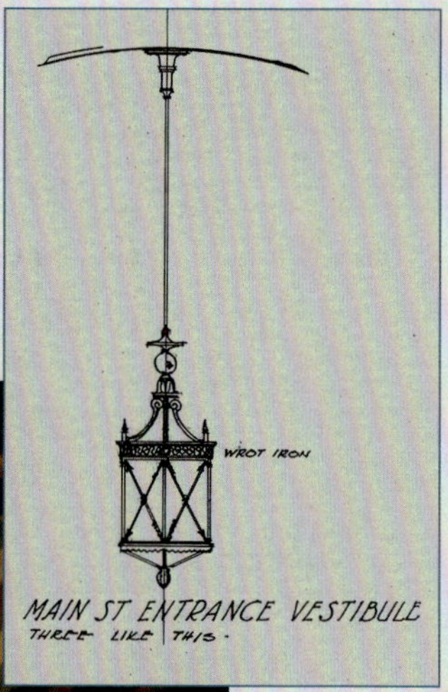

OBSERVATION ROOM As John C. Austin described, the only other room "treated more or less pretentiously from an architectural standpoint" was the whole of the twenty-seventh floor, where he observed, "one can enjoy an unobstructed panoramic view of the city and surroundings, reaching from the Sierra Madre range of mountains to Santa Catalina Island and the sea, and to Mt. San Jacinto on the east."[60]

The architects designed a square space, forty-five feet on each side with a fifty-foot ceiling and pilasters framing its tall windows. Each of the four walls carried a quote in gold lettering to be read by generations of visitors:

"The city came into being to preserve life, it came for the good life"—Aristotle
"With written laws, the humblest in the state is sure of equal justice with the great"—Euripides
"No government demands so much from the citizens as democracy and none gives so much back" —James Bryce
"That government is the strongest of which every man feels himself a part"—Thomas Jefferson[61]

CITY·HALL·ERECTED·M·D·CCCC·XX·VII
LOS·ANGELES·FOUNDED
ANNO·D

OBSERVATION ROOM, CEILING

Herman Sachs submitted a proposal (*left*) to decorate the ceiling of the observation room, although the responsibility to embellish it was awarded to Anthony Heinsbergen, who decorated the acoustical tiles with octagonal patterns, contrasting the lighter-colored beams with precise interwoven lines. Below, Heinsbergen's concept.

Heinsbergen's concept.

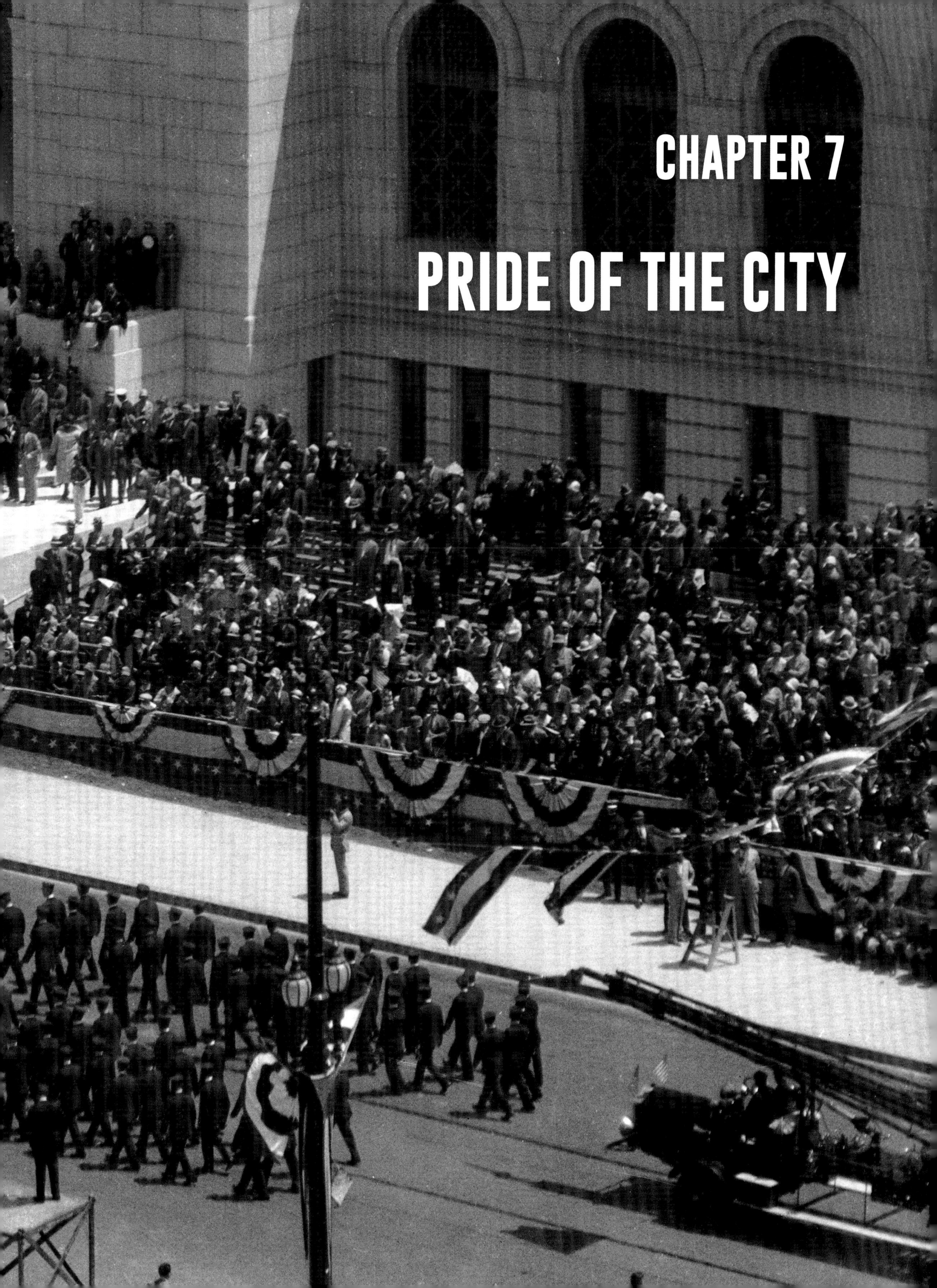

CHAPTER 7

PRIDE OF THE CITY

Last night, silhouetted against the star-flecked heavens, the towering white granite monolith seemed like a living, breathing thing. It was as though the structure sensed the honor and importance of the occasion, which had turned the day into joyous holiday revelling.

—*Los Angeles Evening Express*, April 27, 1928[1]

There was no more exhilarating way to experience the majesty of Los Angeles's new municipal headquarters than from the air, high above. On the morning of April 10, 1928, Mayor Cryer boarded the *Spirit of Los Angeles* at Rogers Field, an unpaved runway at the northwest corner of Wilshire Boulevard and Fairfax Avenue, to get a bird's-eye view of the structure he had so championed for the city.

Moments earlier, Cryer had christened the aircraft, built at Benjamin F. Mahoney's San Diego factory, by affixing the golden seal of the City of Los Angeles on its bow. The plane, piloted by Jack Laas, would take Cryer and Arthur Eldridge, president of the Board of Public Works, eight thousand feet above the building. "The City Hall tower and the Lindbergh Beacon will tell flying tourists during the coming century of their arrival in Los Angeles," the mayor proudly proclaimed as he took in the spectacular view.[2]

Three days later, the same aircraft took off carrying invitations from the mayor and Joseph M. Schenck, the film studio executive and chairman of the Citizens City Hall Dedication Committee, to Mayor James Rolph of San Francisco and other dignitaries in Oakland, Stockton, Sacramento, and Fresno, welcoming them to attend the formal dedication of Los Angeles City Hall in less than two weeks.

More than 200,000 visitors were expected to attend the three-day celebration, and special trains were arranged to bring guests from Northern California. On April 24, Mayor Cryer issued a proclamation urging City departments and local businesses to treat the City Hall Dedication Day as a public holiday and allow as many employees as possible to enjoy the commemoration. The proclamation read in part,

> . . .Today the City of Los Angeles has an estimated population of 1,416,000. We have completed the construction of a City Hall that is in keeping with its present size and prospective development: and I believe that in beauty, in efficiency, and in sincerity of construction it is second to none in America.
>
> Its completion and dedication should be fittingly observed, and arrangements to that end are being made by a committee of citizens.[3]

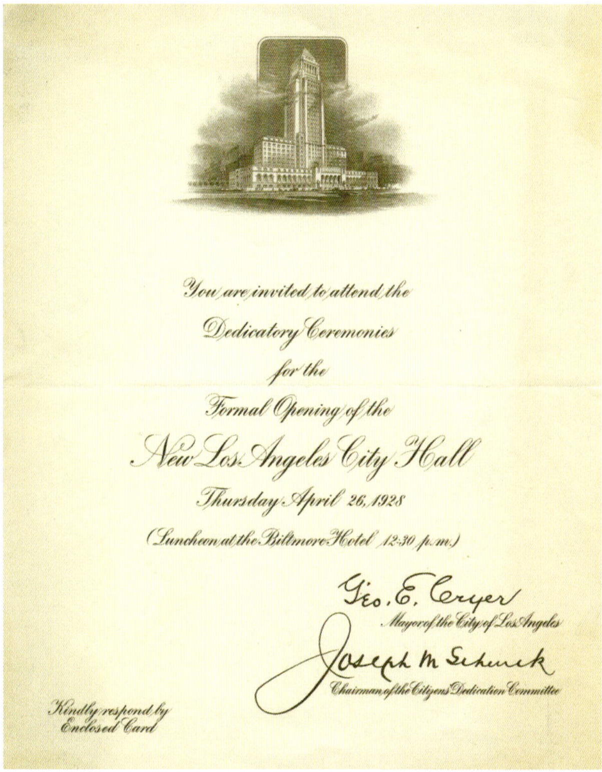

You are invited to attend the
Dedicatory Ceremonies
for the
Formal Opening of the
New Los Angeles City Hall
Thursday April 26, 1928
(Luncheon at the Biltmore Hotel 12:30 p.m.)

Geo. E. Cryer
Mayor of the City of Los Angeles

Joseph M. Schenck
Chairman of the Citizens Dedication Committee

Kindly respond by Enclosed Card

Los Angeles City Hall, Dedication, Invitation
Pages 158–159: Dedication Parade

Long before sunrise in the early morning hours of April 26, crowds began to gather along the route of the Opening Day parade, with onlookers eager to secure a good vantage point to witness what city leaders confidently predicted would be the largest civic celebration ever held in any city west of Chicago.

Packed Pacific Electric and Los Angeles Railway streetcars brought thousands into the downtown area, and hours before the 10 a.m. start time, sidewalks were almost impassable. By the time the parade began on Hill Street between Sixteenth Street and Washington Boulevard, more than a half-million spectators had converged on the city.[4] Los Angeles Police Chief James E. Davis and his battalion of more than eight hundred officers were ready for a busy day ahead.

The parade featured 32,000 marchers, thirty-four bands, and close to 150 decorated floats, all divided into four divisions. It took more than ninety minutes to travel along Pico Boulevard east to Broadway and north to First Street before passing a viewing stand in front of the Spring Street entrance of the new building.

"As the first units of the parade approached, silence would fall briefly over sections of the crowd, to be followed by waves of cheering," the *Evening Herald* reported. "Sixteen long blocks of humanity cheered and cheered as the long cortege passed, and when the last float had disappeared from view, there was hardly a cheer left in the happily aching throats."[5]

Leading the parade was an official delegation that included Mayor Cryer, Mayor Rolph of San Francisco, members of the City Council and Board of Public Works, and other civic leaders, as well as Desea Pico Todd and Cathalina Pico Bell, granddaughters of Pio Pico, the last California governor under Spanish rule.

A bird's-eye view of the dedication parade.

Onlookers watched as Grand Marshall Brigadier-General Walter P. Story, a prominent financier and veteran of World War I, passed by; following him, Colonel Harcourt Harvey of the 160th Infantry led the parade's first division, made up of members of the Coast Artillery out of Fort MacArthur in San Pedro, Hollywood High School, Spanish War veterans, Red Cross nurses, the Filipino Federation of America, and more.

The parade was temporarily disrupted when a fire alarm caused panic near Ninth and Hill streets. The *Evening Express* reported a number of women fainted, and there "was almost a stampede" among the many thousands of spectators as fire engines rushed to fight a non-existent blaze.[6]

The second division, commanded by Colonel W.G. Schreiber, consisted of thirty-eight musical organizations and eight thousand marchers, including the Long Beach Municipal Band, Los Angeles Police Department, Los Angeles Fire Department, Los Angeles Chamber of Commerce, Chinese Chamber of Commerce, and other local groups.

The sight of a giant dragon operated by twenty performers moving to the loud pops of firecrackers proved irresistible to children, who cheered with excitement, as Chinese American women walked alongside in traditional costumes. They were followed by Chinese community leaders "immaculately clad in their morning coats and gleaming silk hats."[7]

"Chinatown has done itself proud," the *Examiner* reported. "More and bigger floats in this division than anywhere else in the parade."[8]

As "great columns of military, fraternal, civic, patriotic, departmental, and industrial organizations"[9] made their way past the old red stone city hall building on Broadway, like seeing an old friend, paraders saluted the aged but gussied up structure draped in bunting for the special occasion.

Spectators cheered and tossed flowers as a gleaming, colossal cake resembling City Hall passed before them. Chef George Wong's oversized dessert with a six-foot-tall tower was the entry of Bing Kong Tong, an influential Chinese community organization. It took 250 pounds of sugar and a thousand eggs to produce the delicacy, and city leaders were so impressed, they asked Wong to postpone its consumption so it could proudly be displayed inside City Hall.[10]

Chef George Wong and Los Angeles City Hall cake that took 375 hours to make.

The third division, with Colonel H.A. Hannigan at the helm, featured the Musicians Mutual Protective Association, organized labor, Municipal Art Commission, and various women's groups, including the Los Angeles League of Women Voters, Daughters of the American Revolution, and Catholic Women's Club. The African American section of the parade was led by a band seventy strong, all dressed in striking white uniforms with purple and gold embellishments.

"Never in Los Angeles's history has there been such a colorful, magnificent municipal celebration for a City Hall," the *Evening Express* marveled hours later. "It seemed as though every man, woman, and child in Los Angeles was taking a part. Either they were marching or in the line of enthusiastic spectators."[11]

The final division, led by film director Cecil B. DeMille, was made up of sixteen floats headed by the Hollywood American Legion, and featured Leo, the MGM lion, along with a host of leading actors and actresses of the day.[12]

Some two hundred mayors joined the parade and were later entertained at an informal lunch at the Biltmore Hotel, along with three hundred other dignitaries invited by the mayor. At 2 p.m., bands began to play at the south entrance to City Hall, and a half-hour later, Mayor Cryer welcomed visiting mayors up to the twenty-seventh floor for an official reception.

Shortly before 3 p.m., a squadron of U.S. Army aircraft from March Field in Riverside circled City Hall and dipped their wings in tribute to Charles Lindbergh and the newly installed aviation beacon named in his honor. As Mayor Cryer led a procession of dignitaries from the south entrance, it signaled to onlookers the beginning of the formal dedication, with a warm-up of lively entertainment, first from the Rangers performance group, "a colorful mob of Westerners" who fired pistol shots in the air before "galloping" down the steps to sing songs to the vast crowd. As commentator Harry

Chef Wong's cake on display inside City Hall.

Mayor Cryer welcomes San Francisco Mayor James Rolph, in white, and three other dignitaries.

Lang observed in the *Examiner*, "From that moment there wasn't a dull moment—not even in the speechmaking, and that's unusual."[13]

Joseph M. Schenck introduced Arthur Eldridge, who told the crowd other projects the Board of Public Works had completed were "dwarf-like" when compared to the towering city hall. "If there were no other material evidence of the phenomenal progress of this community apparent to the casual observer, this monument—the new City Hall—a symbol of the community's faith in the present and the future, this should be sufficient," he remarked. "This sincerely erected structure stands as a beckoning monument to future generations to lay the foundation for civic pride and civic faith. . .."[14]

Eldridge then presented Mayor Cryer with a symbolic golden key to the building, as seven motion picture cameramen "cranked themselves silly." A band played "The Star-Spangled Banner" while a Boy Scout raised the American flag. The crowd then joined performers in singing "America the Beautiful" before the mayor stepped forward to address the multitude of people who had gathered on this important day for the city. With a speech the *Examiner* described as "rich in sincerity, in idealism and in pride," Mayor Cryer spoke to the hushed crowd:

> Let us this day, as we dedicate this building, make the occasion for a rededication of ourselves to better and higher ideals of citizenship.
>
> And best of all my friends, no breath of scandal, no suggestion of graft, has attended any feature of the work. This more remarkable because there are those in this community who do not require a basis in fact upon which to hurl a charge of wrongdoing. . ..It is a privilege to live in this wonderful age of progress and development. It is a double privilege to live in this glorious State of California and in this beautiful progressive city which we love to call home.[15]

A vast network of loudspeakers carried the speeches from the mayor and others to the thousands gathered in the south plaza. The program was also broadcast on radio station KPLA in Los Angeles and KYA in San Francisco.[16] The City Park Department relayed the remarks via its public address system to local parks, including Brookside, Echo, Exposition, Hermosa Beach, Lincoln, Sycamore Grove, and South parks, and the city playgrounds at Venice and Westlake parks.[17]

San Francisco Mayor James Rolph, using what the next day's newspapers called a "booming" voice, spoke of the pride other California cities felt when observing the development of Los Angeles, a city which he predicted would soon become the center of the nation's aviation industry.

Sid Grauman, whose business interests included his namesake Chinese Theatre

COATS
DRESSES
MILLINERY
HOSIERY · SHOES
OUTLET

BALDWIN

Left: Architect John C. Austin and George Eastman, president of the Chamber of Commerce, ready for the dedication festivities.

Below, left: Irving Berlin performs.

Below, right: Mayor Cryer addresses the crowd.

Opposite, top: Members of the Veterans of the Foreign Wars, Ladies Division, march on Broadway near Sixth Street.

Opposite, bottom: The Rangers perform.

A crowd of more than 50,000 gathers at the south end of City Hall.

and Egyptian Theatre, directed the ceremony's entertainment program with performances by celebrated composer Irving Berlin, Chicago Grand Opera Company soprano Elsa Alsen, Utah cowboy-tenor Arnold Blackmer, and a choir of five hundred led by Hugo Kirchhofer.

By 4 p.m., the sound of the military bugle call, "Retreat," could be heard, but the celebration didn't stop, as bands continued to perform until the early evening, when a crowd of more than 50,000 gathered in anticipation of the dedication of the Lindbergh Beacon.

The idea for the beacon had come from George R. Watson, a *Los Angeles Times* staff photographer, who suggested it to the dedication committee as a way of paying tribute to the heroic aviator and highlighting Los Angeles as a center of aviation. Another plus: it could serve as a beacon for planes flying into the city at night.

In September 1927, a crowd of more than 200,000 had welcomed Charles Lindbergh to Southern California when he flew to Vail Field aboard the *Spirit of St. Louis*, the airplane manufactured in Southern California that had famously carried him on his historic journey across the Atlantic. Mayor Cryer had proclaimed September 20 to be Lindbergh Day in Los Angeles, as hundreds of thousands lined the route to the Memorial Coliseum for a hero's welcome and celebration.[18] Lindbergh's much-anticipated visit was organized by the Los Angeles Chamber of Commerce, which supported the idea of the beacon and petitioned the mayor, Board of Public Works, City Council, and Associate Architects to incorporate it into the building's design.

Shortly before Lindbergh arrived, the Board of Public Works informed the Los Angeles City Council it was granting temporary permission for the beacon to be placed atop City Hall. Upon receiving the news, the chamber commissioned the General Electric Company to manufacture the beacon and organized an appeal to raise the $3,000 needed to build it, with an initial $100 contribution coming from Cecil B. DeMille.[19]

The Lindbergh Beacon would be illuminated by a nine-hundred-watt filament lamp positioned in front of a twenty-four-inch mirror, its rays pouring through a twenty-four-inch lens.[20] The power of the mirror was inadvertently demonstrated during the beacon's installation, when sunlight hit the mirror and burned the hair off the arms of workers.[21] The beacon contained two lamps; should one burn out, the other would automatically begin operating.

California U.S. Senator Samuel M. Shortridge and Representatives William E. Evans and Joe Crail requested the president of the United States be the one to inaugurate the beacon, described as "the most powerful light of its kind on the West Coast." President Calvin Coolidge accepted, and promptly at 7 p.m. Pacific Time on April 26, 1928, he pressed a gold telegraph key in the White House, sending the signal cross-country to officially switch on the Lindbergh Beacon, its brilliant beam of light shooting into the night sky. The Western Union Telegraph Company had kept a circuit open for an hour prior to the dedication—free of charge—to enable the commander-in-chief to participate in the ceremony.

According to some estimates, the light was visible for sixty miles. "It seemed as though it were a shaft of pure daylight," the *Express* observed.[22] "That flood of light touched off the tremendous crowd," the *Examiner* reported. "They greeted their new City Hall as they have never greeted anything. Their applause continued for ten deafening minutes before it subsided, and the program could be resumed."[23]

At exactly 7:15 p.m., lights from the entire lighting department of the Metro-Goldwyn-Mayer movie studio, in all representing more than twelve-and-a-half billion beams of candlepower, lit up City Hall for everyone to see. "Here, there, everywhere, from every window flowed radiance," the *Evening Express* rejoiced.[24]

On stage, Judge Leonard Wilson introduced George L. Eastman, president of the Los Angeles Chamber of Commerce, who read a message from President Coolidge proclaiming the beacon would be "a glowing reminder of the fine attributes of him in whose honor it is named."[25]

Responding to the president's message, Eastman told the crowd the building represented the dreams and ideals of the city in "steel, marble, and everlasting beauty."[26] He continued, "May this beacon guide us in the future great development of aviation to which we are all looking forward, and may it be an inspiration to us that real accomplishment carries with it the same calm resolve and willingness to sacrifice that has inspired these early navigators of the air."[27]

As the speeches drew to a close, the Los Angeles Reed and Brass Symphony Orchestra with opera singer Elsa Alsen ended the evening with a rousing rendition of "America the Beautiful" conducted by

Left: Ethlyn Lang and Mildred Montoure from the office of the General Electric Company show how the Lindbergh Beacon is operated.
Right: The Lindbergh Beacon shines atop City Hall.

Glenn M. Tindall, who also served as chairman of the music committee for the event.[28]

As the musical program concluded, fireworks colored the sky, and at 7:30 p.m., the public was finally allowed inside their new City Hall. An estimated 38,000 people explored the building that first night.

The next day, 67,000 more toured the structure and were guided by women from various civic groups who served as hostesses. The *Evening Express* stated the city was still "breathless from the glories of the magnificent parade." It was an event the newspaper predicted would "live forever in the pages of Los Angeles History."[29]

The three-day celebration concluded on Saturday evening, with a parade and pageant titled *The Passing of the Flags* organized by the Native Sons and Native Daughters of the Golden West.

Beginning at 7:30 p.m. at Tenth and Main streets, a parade led by the motor police, police drill team, and firemen's band made its way to City Hall. Behind them were Mayor Cryer and San Francisco Mayor James Rolph, who rode with officers of the Native Sons and Native Daughters of the Golden West, followed by various groups in costumes depicting the romantic history of California.[30]

At 9 p.m., a bugle call signaled the beginning of the pageant, which celebrated the growth of California and included Native American dances, the raising of the Spanish flag by an actor portraying Junipero Serra, Spanish dances by Gabriel Ruiz's dancers, Forty-niners raising the California flag, a performance by singer Edith Barton, and the raising of the Stars and Stripes by a United States Army platoon of the 160th Infantry Regiment.[31]

As Los Angeles embraced its new municipal home, just a few blocks away the old city hall building on Broadway was emptied in anticipation of its demolition. On the morning of January 21, 1929, at around 10 a.m., a chilly wind whipped through the air as a "motley crowd" gathered outside for an auction to sell off the old building's remaining contents.

The sale was organized by the Globe Wrecking Company, which had secured the contract to remove the building with a $5,000 bid to the Board of Public Works. The company planned to gain a profit through the sale of leftover fixtures, stone, and bricks.

The *Los Angeles Times* reported, " . . .curious people picked their way among radiators, globes from light fixtures and bunting, plumbing fixtures, old files, and cubby holes piled about the main lobby with

Auctioneer W.O. Trask takes bids on the contents of City Hall, Broadway.

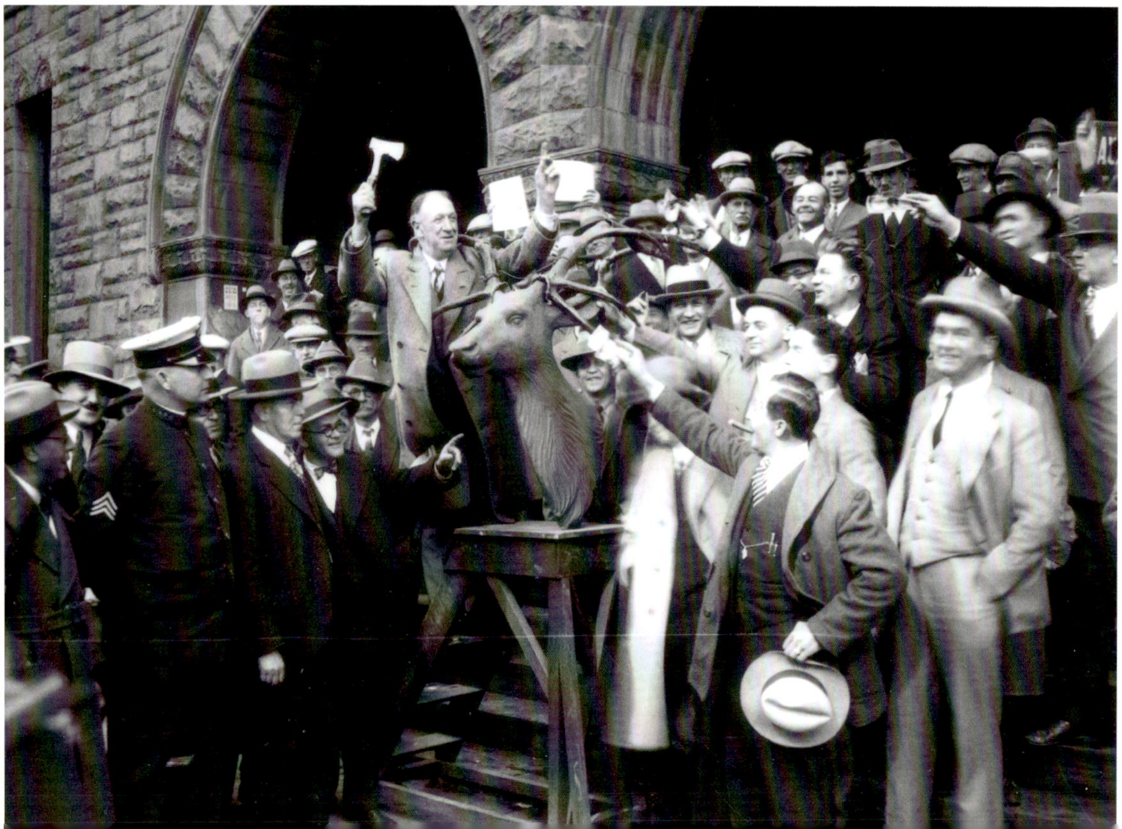

Demolition of City Hall on Broadway.

its solid hardwood grand staircase all ready to be knocked down to the highest bidder."[32]

Among the items up for sale were a moth-eaten elk's head, sets of mailboxes, and an enormous vault that had once held the City's cash and securities. Auctioneer W.O. Trask conducted much of the sale while standing on top of a counter once used by City Clerk Robert Dominguez's office to meet with citizens disputing their property taxes.

The first item on the auction block was a forty-foot steel flagpole that Trask assured would be a "great memento" by which to remember the building and a "great attraction in anybody's front yard." It sold to George R. Kindred of North Hollywood for $155. According to reports, he later changed his mind and attempted to return it.

The Globe Wrecking Company was allowed forty-five days to demolish the building, but finding the task more demanding than they expected, they called in Mission Wrecking to help finish the job. Work continued day and night until March 19, when a steam shovel knocked over the last remaining wall. Soon after, the City Council leased the site as a parking lot to private citizen James Lloyd, who agreed to pay $2,750 for the right to operate a lot.[33]

Following the death of former California U.S. Senator Frank Putnam Flint in February 1929, his friend John Parkinson once again turned his attention to City Hall and the design of a memorial fountain for the former senator and U.S. attorney general that would be ensconced on the south lawn facing

John Parkinson poses with his model for the Frank Putnam Flint Memorial Fountain.

First Street. Flint had played a central role in the development of the Owens River project, Los Angeles Harbor, and the Panama Canal. He was aboard the ocean liner *President Polk* with his wife near the Philippines when he suffered a heart attack.[34]

Parkinson competed with sculptors Howard Swartz and Henry Lion, along with architects Gordon B. Kaufmann and Howard Seidell (on behalf of the Georgia Marble Company), to design the monument. Paying tribute to Flint's contribution to a remarkable effort to build an aqueduct capable of carrying water from the Sierra Nevada mountains to Los Angeles, Parkinson's design revealed a gray granite fountain with panels depicting wisdom, justice, labor, and engineering.[35] It was expected to cost $60,000.

Although Parkinson's concept was favored by the City Park Commission, which was responsible for maintaining the area where it would be located, the Municipal Art Commission felt his "wall-like" design was not "the most appropriate for the location."[36] On hearing the commission's verdict, a member of Parkinson's office asked if the firm could withdraw the plans, restudy the project, and submit an alternative design at a future date.

In November 1931, John and Donald Parkinson appeared before the commission with updated sketches of their original design; however, members debated whether they could legally consider the architects' design, since they had already given preliminary approval to a sketch submitted by Harold Swartz just days earlier. John Parkinson reasoned that since there was no contract in place with Swartz, their design should still be considered.[37]

In a meeting the following week, the Municipal Art Commission read a letter from Deputy City Attorney Loren A. Butts, who made clear the organization had authority to approve one or more designs. Another letter from James R. Martin of the Flint Committee, which was organized to oversee the design, stated the committee had approved the Parkinson design and never offered support to Swartz or any other sculptor.[38]

Since the firm of John and Donald Parkinson had such an "outstanding reputation," Carleton M. Winslow, fellow architect and vice-president of the Municipal Art Commission, suggested the commission should "trust" the Parkinsons' experience. However, Commission President Jules Kauffman was critical of both designs and refused to back down.[39]

In July 1932, Joseph Scott, president of the Flint Committee, appeared before the art commission and withdrew the Parkinson design, presenting instead a plan produced by architect Henry S. MacKay Sr., the father of Henry S. MacKay Jr., Flint's son-in-law.

Sculptor Julia Bracken Wendt and Mayor Frank Shaw in front of the newly dedicated Frank Putnam Flint memorial fountain, 1933

MacKay Sr. told the commission Senator Flint had worked for "unlimited water supply in California" and that he also worked on the Panama Canal project "so that water was considered the most appropriate way to immortalize his name."

He explained he had settled on a design that "would not go out of fashion" and, at seventeen feet high, would be level with the upper terrace of City Hall. Both sides of the fountain would be concave, and the water would be recycled by a series of pumps operated by a timer.[40]

The design included bronze medallions of Flint to be created by renowned sculptor Julia Bracken Wendt, whose early models were in fact criticized by members of the art commission for not adequately capturing "the 'Flint' expression or likeness."[41] In response, Wendt produced a letter from Flint's daughter, Katherine Flint MacKay, saying she, along with her mother and brother, thought the likeness was "splendidly done."[42]

On each end of the fountain was a marble torch in low relief symbolizing leadership. It was constructed of marble from the same Colorado quarry used for the Lincoln Memorial in Washington, D.C., despite warnings from Winslow, who cited potential staining and algae problems.

More than a thousand people attended the dedication ceremony on September 13, 1933. Flint's grandsons, Sandy MacKay and Frank P. Flint II, had the honor of unveiling the fountain.

"Of all this vast western empire which he served so well and faithfully, Los Angeles particularly is indebted to him," Mayor Frank L. Shaw told the crowd. "Our enduring gratitude is for his fine contribution to the success of the Los Angeles Aqueduct, the Los Angeles Harbor, the Panama Canal, and the development and expansion of our international trade, placing Los Angeles in the front rank of the world's ports. These are a few of the achievements for which we honor the memory of this true friend and citizen."[43]

Nearly two decades later, concerns began to grow regarding the pyramidical roof of City Hall. By 1950, the concrete slabs making up the structure's apex were loosening and could potentially be an earthquake hazard, leading the Board of Public Works to advertise for bids to install a new sheet-metal pinnacle to the structure.

The City Council allocated $22,000 for the work, billed as the "highest" repair work ever done in the city.

Frank Putnam Flint Memorial Fountain

TEMPLE

CHAPTER 8

CITY HALL EAST

I will emphasize the contribution of each race and country to the American way of life rather than propagandize tensions which appear to be thoroughly conveyed by press, radio, and television.

—Millard Sheets, Artist, City Hall East Murals[1]

Los Angeles City Hall reigned as the tallest building in the city for thirty-eight years, until the completion of the forty-two-story Union Bank Square in 1966. Voters approved a city charter amendment in 1956 that replaced the existing 150-foot height restriction with a new rule requiring the total floor area of a building to be no more than thirteen times the area of the site.

In the subsequent decade, ninety-eight high-rise structures would go up in the Los Angeles area, but the 516-foot-high Union Bank Square, designed by New York City architects Harrison and Abramowitz and Albert C. Martin and Associates, would be the first to surpass the 452-foot Los Angeles City Hall.[2]

As modern skyscrapers grew taller, Los Angeles City Hall, once a proud symbol of the future, was in serious danger of becoming an outdated relic, unable to keep pace with the demands of an ever-expanding city.

By 1960, history seemed to be on the verge of repeating itself. With a population approaching 2.5 million, the city had once again outgrown its municipal home, resulting in a shortage of space, causing offices and resources to be forced off the premises. When "blunt-talking" Sam Yorty[3] was elected mayor against the odds in 1961, he faced the same problem his predecessor George Cryer had forty years earlier. And like Cryer, Yorty was determined to act.

Rather than demolish the existing structure and start over, the mayor led the effort to construct a new City Hall Annex that would unite various departments "scattered throughout the city in rented quarters."[4]

The responsibility for designing the building was handed to the local firm of Stanton and Stockwell, which would also oversee the mayor's vision to create "the largest civic center mall outside of Washington, D.C." The architects faced a series of challenges, not least of which was the mayor's attempts to add eight floors to the annex after construction had already begun, and the repeated rejection of their plans by the Municipal Art Commission.

The City Hall Annex, later renamed City Hall East, would be linked to City Hall by a pedestrian bridge and decorated on the entry level by two giant tile murals, titled *The Culture Brought to Los Angeles by the Races of the World,* created by celebrated artist Millard Sheets.

The work on the annex and the neighboring mall would take longer than expected and go considerably over budget, causing controversy, but for Mayor Yorty, the project represented a unique opportunity to leave a lasting imprint on the city he would control from 1961 to 1973.

Mayor Sam Yorty
Opposite: Los Angeles City Hall, 1967

Samuel William Yorty won the election for the most powerful office in Los Angeles City Hall in June 1961 by defeating incumbent Norris Poulson, who had the support of downtown businesses and the backing of the *Los Angeles Times.* Commonly known as Sam, he was beloved and reviled in equal measure for his "self-promoting"[5] style and "spontaneous candour."[6]

While in power, he lowered city property taxes and lent his support to a series of ambitious construction projects that included freeways, a new Los Angeles Zoo, and a convention center.

Born in Lincoln, Nebraska, in 1909 to Johanna and Frank Yorty, a one-time farmer and later restaurateur, a young Yorty idolized Woodrow Wilson growing up. After his family moved from the Midwest to Los Angeles, he completed high school, attended Southwestern University, and later graduated from UCLA with a law degree.

An ambitious politician, he won a seat in the California State Assembly in 1936 and then launched an unsuccessful bid for the U.S. Senate four years later. He

temporarily placed his career on hold to join the U.S. Army Air Corps during World War II, where he rose to the rank of captain in the intelligence unit.

After the war, he returned to politics and the California State Assembly before winning a seat in Congress in 1950 as the representative from California's 14th District. He was re-elected in 1952, and two years later, he embarked on yet another failed bid to join the U.S. Senate. He later earned the reputation as a "maverick" after turning his back on fellow Democrat John F. Kennedy to support California candidate Richard Nixon in the 1960 presidential race.

Following his election in 1961 as the thirty-seventh mayor of Los Angeles, Yorty quickly grew frustrated with the way City departments were organized. He made the consolidation of the city and county health departments an early priority, and in 1964, the city's health department was absorbed by the County of Los Angeles. Soon afterward, the City Health Department Administration Building at 200 North Main St., designed by W. Tunstall, senior architect for the Department of Public Works Public Buildings, was converted to, and later renamed, City Hall South.

Examining the needs of the city, Yorty predicted the current Los Angeles City Hall was 100,000 square feet short of what was required.[7] He estimated as much as $300,000 a year could be saved by moving scattered municipal departments into the same new office building. In October 1967, the City Council appropriated $58,300 from the parking meter fund to pay architects Stanton and Stockwell to begin preliminary planning for a new mall and city hall annex.[8]

Jesse Earl Stanton

Born in San Francisco on April 22, 1887, Jesse Earl Stanton was educated at the École des Beaux Arts in Paris. He spent eight months traveling through Europe and Africa before beginning his architectural career with the firm of Daniel H. Burnham and Company and working on Chicago's 1909 city plan. Two years later, he joined the New York City office of architects Whitney Warren and Charles D. Wetmore, known for their work on Grand Central Terminal and numerous extravagant hotels.

Stanton later returned west to work with San Francisco architect Lewis P. Hobart before establishing his own practice in Sacramento. In 1939, he was hired as director of color and lighting at the Golden Gate Exposition, held at San Francisco's Treasure Island. An expert in ceramics, color, and Asian art,[9] he would briefly form a partnership with architect Gordon B. Kaufmann in Los Angeles beginning in 1947. In 1952, he and William Francis Stockwell formed Stanton and Stockwell. Stockwell was born in Genoa, Nebraska, on December 5, 1906. The son of a newspaper editor, he attended the Georgia Institute of Technology, New York University, the Art Students League, and Atelier Airons.[10]

The architects' plans for Los Angeles included a park connecting the City Hall Annex to City Hall South, a sunken Los Angeles Mall, and a bridge extending over Temple Street. It was anticipated the mall would contain "120,000 square feet of beautifully designed shops with public offices, underground parking for approximately two thousand cars, and a magnificently landscaped park"[11] and become "a major factor in attracting people to the downtown area for entertainment, cultural, and recreational purposes."[12] Mayor Yorty would later boast the mall project was "considered as the most imaginative of its kind in the United States by city planners."[13]

He predicted the focal point of the mall would be the *Triforium*, a bold space-age symbol showing Los Angeles's desire to lead the United States into the twenty-first century.

Artist Joseph L. Young created the *Triforium* to be a sixty-ton, three-pronged concrete tower, reflecting man's relationship with the universe. He adorned the six-story public art sculpture with a series of 183 hollow glass tubes ranging from four to eleven feet in length and 1,494 hand-blown Italian glass prisms,

City Hall East, Stanton & Stockwell concept.

illuminated by lasers and operated by a 1975-era computer system that synchronized lights with music.

To make way for the annex and mall construction, the Woolworth variety store on Main Street near Temple Street was closed for demolition, as was a nearby hotel and a branch of the Security First National Bank. As the project advanced, Mayor Yorty asked the City Council to consider a proposal to connect Los Angeles City Hall with the civic center's West Mall by building a pedestrian bridge and plaza area over part of Spring Street. The bridge would connect directly to the structure's Spring Street entrance and would allow the mall to "run unbroken from City Hall to Grand Avenue," where it would "terminate at the west end at the new Water and Power Building and the Music Center complex."[14] The mayor argued the bridge would provide an "even more impressive area" for civic functions staged outside City Hall.[15]

"From the standpoints of utility, safety, aesthetics, this proposal appears to have much merit," Yorty entreated. "I am hopeful that the County of Los Angeles can be persuaded to recognize the mutual benefit which would result."[16] The proposal received unanimous support from the City Planning Commission, although it was never funded.[17]

Yorty's drive to create a new city hall annex was partly fueled by a desire to find a cost-effective new home for the Los Angeles Fire Department, which held ambitions to build its own dedicated structure. When the mayor discovered the department was considering building a new home at Second and Hill streets, he quickly intervened.

"The way they had it planned it was going to be a six-story affair just for the fire people on a site they owned away from the civic center," he recounted in later years. "When I found out about it, I felt the building was too small and that all the factors hadn't been given due weight. Considering the land value it was, uneconomic—an underdevelopment. 'It's got to be bigger,' I told them."

"I insisted on a check with other departments to find out their future needs for additional quarters because of course, for a long time City Hall itself has been inadequate. When the investigation was done we found that it was more economical and efficient to house the fire department in the City Hall Annex back of the City Hall in the Civic Center utilizing other city-owned property."

"I ordered all the department heads to check with the Mayor on things like this so we wouldn't be falling into such mistakes."[18]

On January 8, 1967, the mayor's office issued a press release announcing that Stanton and Stockwell's

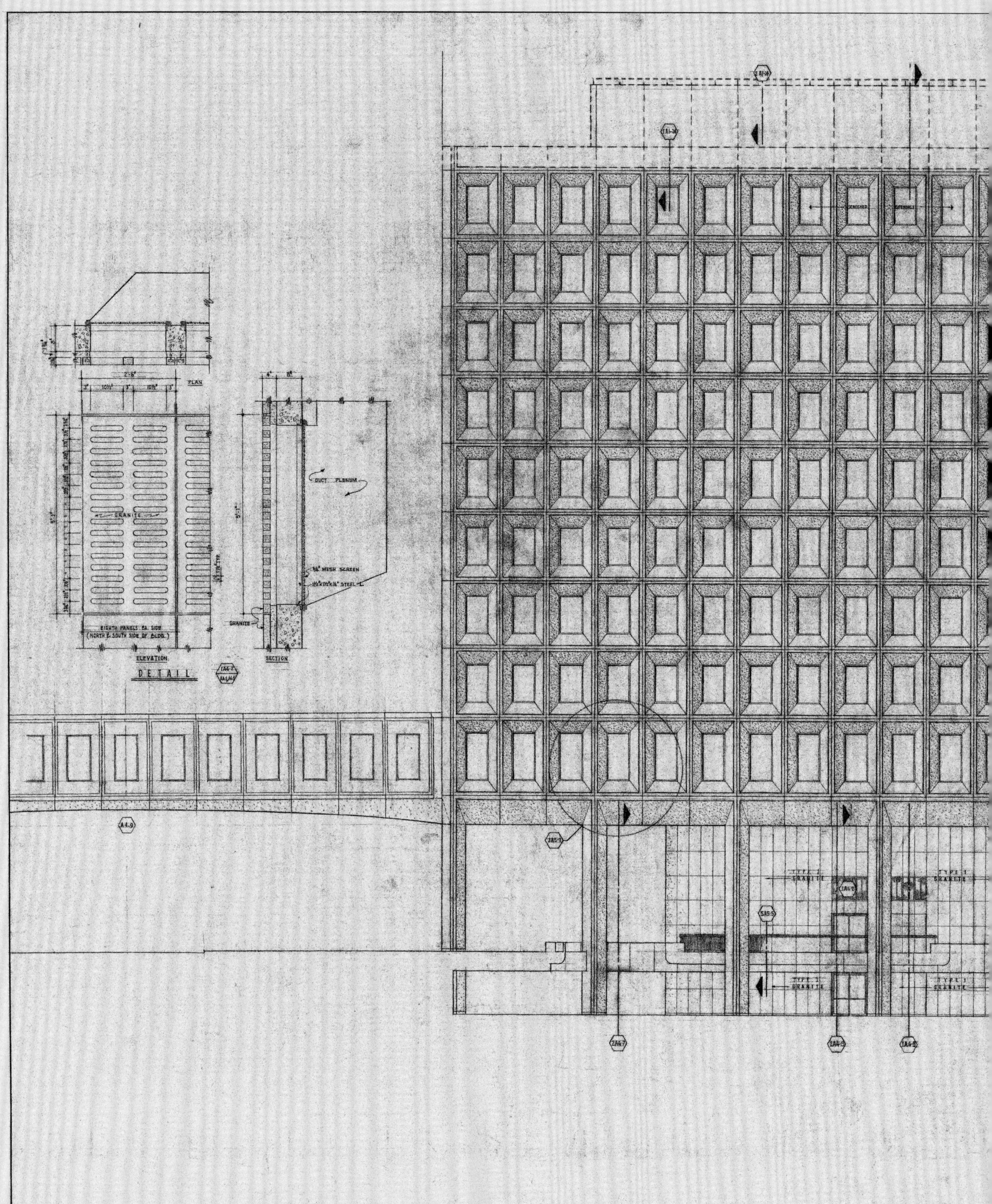
PLAN
2'-6"
3"
10½"
ELEVATION
SECTION
DETAIL
DUCT PLENUM
GRANITE
MESH SCREEN
STEEL L
EIGHTH PANELS EA. SIDE
(NORTH & SOUTH SIDE OF BLDG.)
5'-1"
4"
8"
TYPE 1
GRANITE
JOHN A. MARTIN & ASSOCIATES
STRUCTURAL ENGINEERS
LOS ANGELES, CALIFORNIA
LEVINE & Mc CANN
CONSULTING ENGINEERS
MECHANICAL & ELECTRICAL
LOS ANGELES, CALIFORNIA
CORNELL-BRIDGERS & TROLLER
LANDSCAPE ARCHITECTS
LOS ANGELES, CALIFORNIA
PLAN NORTH
LOS ANGELES STREET
TEMPLE ST.
FIRST STREET
MAIN STREET
CITY HALL
LOCATION PLAN

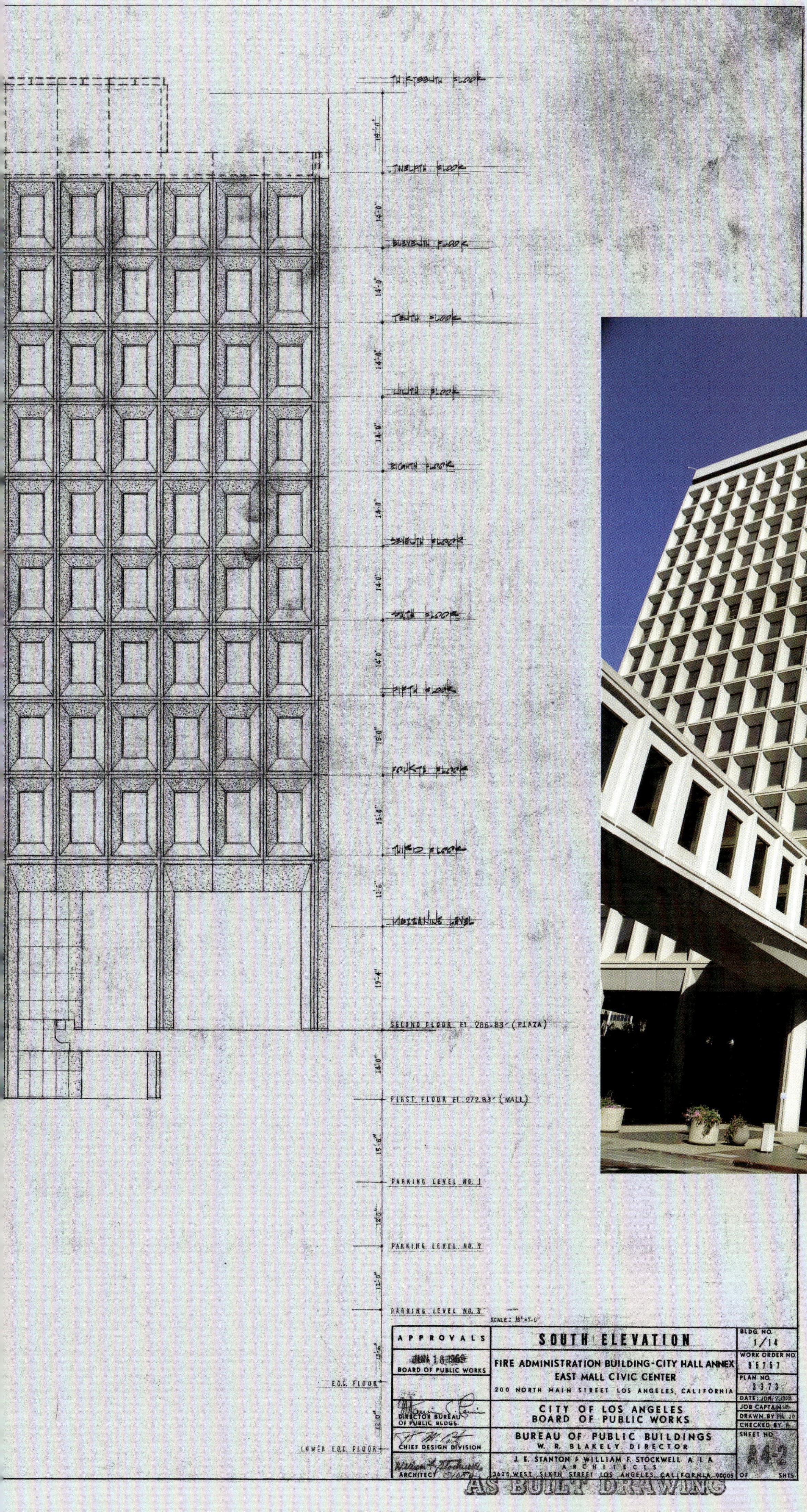
SECOND FLOOR EL. 286.83' (PLAZA)
FIRST FLOOR EL. 272.83' (MALL)
PARKING LEVEL NO. 1
PARKING LEVEL NO. 2
PARKING LEVEL NO. 3
SCALE: 1/8"=1'-0"
APPROVALS
JUN 18 1969
BOARD OF PUBLIC WORKS
DIRECTOR BUREAU OF PUBLIC BLDGS.
CHIEF DESIGN DIVISION
ARCHITECT
SOUTH ELEVATION
FIRE ADMINISTRATION BUILDING-CITY HALL ANNEX
EAST MALL CIVIC CENTER
200 NORTH MAIN STREET LOS ANGELES, CALIFORNIA
CITY OF LOS ANGELES
BOARD OF PUBLIC WORKS
BUREAU OF PUBLIC BUILDINGS
W. R. BLAKELY DIRECTOR
J. E. STANTON & WILLIAM F. STOCKWELL A. I. A.
ARCHITECTS
3625 WEST SIXTH STREET LOS ANGELES, CALIFORNIA 90005
BLDG. NO. 1/14
WORK ORDER NO. 95757
PLAN NO. 3373
DATE
JOB CAPTAIN
DRAWN BY
CHECKED BY
SHEET NO. A4-2
OF SHTS.
AS BUILT DRAWING

Rendering of a proposed pedestrian bridge across Spring Street.

preliminary plans for the city hall annex and fire department administration building had been approved by the Board of Public Works, which authorized the architects to proceed with final plans and specifications.[19]

The architects' preliminary plans revealed a twelve-story modern structure that would offer about 333,000 square feet of floor area above the plaza level. The fire department's administrative offices would be housed on three floors. Below the building, a three-level reinforced-concrete parking structure was planned. A fourth subterranean level was to house the city's Emergency Operating Center (EOC).

The estimated cost of the building was $12 million[20] to be paid for, in part, by a fire bond fund, as well as parking meter funds and revenue bonds. It was anticipated the federal government would contribute matching funds for the EOC.

Stanton and Stockwell submitted their revised plans to the Municipal Art Commission in September, which rejected them and deemed them "not esthetically acceptable." Members of the art commission, who "deplored the monotony of the fenestrated design," had final authority over the arrangement of all City-owned buildings and made it known they wanted a structure that was in "harmony with other civic buildings downtown" and did not "over-power. . .City Hall."[21]

The rejection led to what the mayor described to local newspapers as a "tempest in a teapot." He accused the art commission of "stalling for time to further review the plans" and insisted it was "a fine building." William F. Quinn, vice-president of the commission, confirmed to the *Los Angeles Times* they did indeed require more time to consult with the architects about the "cubical" appearance of the building.

"We want a more horizontal effect or vertical streamlining," Quinn explained, adding the annex was "basically a fine building, especially the first three floors which allow for a lot of open space at ground level for greenery and murals."[22]

The mayor's description of events struck a nerve with Samuel T. Hurst, dean of USC's School of Architecture and Fine Arts. "You are reported as describing the conflict over its design as a 'tempest in a teapot' and stating there is no reason for anyone to take an obstructionist attitude," he wrote to the mayor. "I believe that the architectural professional appropriately feels such a major structure to be of great significance and the question of its appropriate size and location deserving of the most considered discussion."[23]

The mayor promptly responded, "Please be assured that I am most interested and concerned that the civic center for the City of Los Angeles shall be second to none in all aspects, be it function or aesthetics, and at no time do I intend to give it any less attention than a project of such magnitude warrants and deserves."

And he continued, "We agree completely that a structure such as proposed is of outstanding signifi-

Triforium

cance and for that reason we have presented the proposal for the annex in model form to the Civic Center Authority, the Municipal Art Commission, and the executive board of the Southern California Chapter of the American Institute of Architects, and in every case we have considered their professional judgement [*sic*] in the final development of this project."[24]

As the project advanced, the mayor also found himself at odds with the fire department over what to call the new building. In April 1968, he informed the City Council that to avoid confusion, the old City Health Department Administration Building would be renamed City Hall South, and the new city hall annex should be called City Hall East. "I believe names such as these would clarify problems which our citizens have encountered in trying to find various locations by some of the old buildings we have used heretofore," he argued.[25]

However, the Board of Fire Commissioners strongly disagreed with the mayor, arguing the annex should be known instead as the Fire Administration Building as it was partly funded by fire department bonds.

"The name City Hall South could be interpreted by some as South Los Angeles, and City Hall East as East Los Angeles," they argued in a memo to the mayor, adding, "Mayor, we do have a police administration building and I hope the Fire Commission's request will meet with your approval."[26]

Mayor Yorty looked to City Administrative Officer C. Erwin Piper to clarify whether the Fire Commission had just cause for complaint. In November 1969, Piper sent a memo to his boss explaining his understanding of the situation.

"In the event the names of the Civic Center Buildings are to be reconsidered, it does not appear that the Fire Department has sufficient interest, either through financial contribution or through occupancy of the building to justify the designation of the new structure as the Fire Administration Building," he wrote, adding that various City Council committees had also concluded the buildings should continue to be named City Hall, City Hall East, and City Hall South.[27]

In October 1969, the Board of Public Works awarded Montgomery-Ross-Fisher, Inc., the lowest of four bidders, a $17,640,000 contract for the construction of City Hall East, as well as a portion of the adjacent mall and its underground parking. The winning bid was actually considerably higher than what the City Council had anticipated, which delayed the project, as the council would now have to appropriate (and Mayor Yorty approve) additional funds. The firm estimated construction would take eighteen months.[28]

In February 1970, William Stockwell appeared before the Municipal Art Commission to explain the architects' vision for the building and its integration with a number of proposed public art works. Curt Oplinger, the City's art coordinator, agreed with the art commission's general criticism that there was little relationship between the proposed works of art and the structure.

The *Triforium* was described as having "an unhappy marriage of space-age and baroque organ forms," while Stockwell was also forced to defend plans for a proposed "Sun Pool" as merely "an idea and not a final concept."[29] The board voted unanimously to request alternative "concepts of the sun figures and the stainless steel sculpture he submitted."[30]

The following month, with construction well underway, Mayor Yorty began pushing hard for an additional eight floors to be added to the structure. He argued, and the City Council agreed, that the building should be built to its potential to provide much-needed space. The extra floors would add 226,800 square feet of floor space on seven full floors, plus an additional helistop floor of approximately 14,400 square feet atop the building.[31]

"Since architect, Stanton and Stockwell, prepared the plans for the structure currently under construction, I believe that it would be in the best interests of the City to negotiate with the same architect to prepare the documents for the addition and changes to the design," Marvin S. Levin, director of the Bureau of Public Buildings, wrote in a report prepared for the mayor.

Adding floors in the middle of construction would mean having to make modifications to the existing structure and increasing the anticipated cost of the building by an estimated $8,238,840.[32] The mayor brushed off criticism of the escalating expense, arguing it was inevitable that project costs would rise because the economy was in an inflationary period and construction prices had soared.

In October 1970, Stanton and Stockwell's updated plans were rejected by the art commission, which voted 3-0 to ask the architects to go back to the drawing board and prepare "several" new renderings for their review. Commission Vice-President Milton B. Scott told the *Los Angeles Times* all members of the commission who voted agreed the architects should find a way to harmonize their design with the look of City Hall and other nearby government buildings.[33]

Stanton and Stockwell responded with plans for a revised building faced with precast-concrete panels that they maintained linked the building architecturally to City Hall and other municipal structures. The art commission agreed the updated design was an "improvement" that would not add to the cost of construction or reduce the amount of much-needed office space.[34]

Yet more trouble lay ahead.

The project was again thrust into the media spotlight in June 1971, when the *Los Angeles Times* reported Mayor Yorty had requested the removal of three structural columns already in place in the middle of a third-floor corridor. The newspaper estimated the request would add between $200,000 and $500,000 to the cost of the project, now expected to exceed $29 million. It was also reported the action "might weaken the twenty-story building's earthquake stability."[35]

The report led to a flurry of angry correspondence and infuriated the mayor, who was already being heavily criticized for delays in the project. Dorothy W. Burke of San Marino wrote to Mayor Yorty, "So you mean it—or is this pure fiction?. . .Please tell your taxpayers—no money will go for this absurd purpose. . . and you are thinking of running for president?????"[36] While Alden Nash of Hollywood complained, "I'm sure, unsightly as the structure may be, you are still in your right mind (although the *Times* wonders) and realize that the citizens of Los Angeles have more important places to spend half a million than removing some unsightly pillars from a public structure."[37]

Frustrated by the negative coverage, Mayor Yorty fired off an angry letter to the *Times* complaining the journalist had failed to "get his facts straight." He wrote:

> The City Hall East building was designed to have a lobby on the third floor as you enter that building from the bridge going over Main St. It was decided later to remove the lobby as one would not be needed in that building. This resulted in a redesign of the hallway after the structural steel had already been put in place. The result is that three pillars are presently in the middle of the hallway as you enter the third floor corridor of that building.
>
> This matter was called to my attention by the City Administrative Officer. We discussed it at length and decided to request the Bureau of Public Buildings to process a change or-

City Hall East, construction

> der for the purpose of determining whether the structural factors of the building would be affected if those pillars were removed and some other type of support placed in their stead. Secondly, if this could be done on a sound engineering basis, what would be the cost of making the change?
>
> The architect was requested to determine whether the change could be made from an engineering standpoint and then to prepare a design of such change for the Bureau of Public Buildings. Upon receipt of that, the Bureau of Public Buildings will request the contractor constructing City Hall East to give us a cost estimate for the change. Then, and only then, will the determination be made as to whether the change will take place.[38]

The Board of Public Works voted in July 1971 not to spend the estimated $275,000 required to remove the three structural pillars due to the unacceptably high cost, and the mayor agreed. In an effort to diffuse the controversy, Stanton and Stockwell proposed decorating the offending pillars and surrounding spaces with potted flowers and plants.[39]

To embellish the new annex, Stanton and Stockwell turned to celebrated California artist Millard Sheets with a commission for two ceramic-veneer mural panels that would grace the facade of the Main Street and Los Angeles Street entrances.

Sheets, whose work was filled with exotic influences, found success as a muralist, painter, author, teacher, and architectural designer. He created murals and mosaics for numerous buildings, including the Blessed Sacrament Chapel of the National Shrine of the Immaculate Conception in Washington, D.C.; the Mayo Clinic in Minnesota; and the University of Notre Dame near South Bend, Indiana. He also designed the Scottish Rite Masonic Temples in Los Angeles and San Francisco, the Bank and Trust Company building in Beverly Hills, numerous

Millard Sheets

Home Savings and Loan Association buildings, and the downtown Pomona Mall.

Born in Pomona, California, on June 24, 1907, Sheets was raised by his maternal grandparents, Lewis and Emma Owen, after his mother died in childbirth. He received his first art lesson by a neighbor when he was seven, and in 1919 submitted his work for competition at the Los Angeles County Fair fine arts show.[40] A decade later, he traveled to Europe after winning a cash prize in the annual Edgar B. Davis art competition held in San Antonio, Texas. He studied with master printer Dorfinant in Paris before returning to California in 1930, where he soon after married Mary Baskerville. Sheets continued his studies at Scripps College in Claremont, California, and after graduating, he helped establish a new fine arts program at the school. In 1938, he was appointed director of art at Claremont Graduate School.[41] The California native was profoundly influenced by his experience as a wartime artist and journalist for *Life* magazine. From 1943 to 1944, he was stationed on the Burma-India Front, and his postwar work was observed to feature considerably more somber tones.

"I made many, many sketches, though, as well as a real effort to remember each scene that particularly affected me," he later reflected. "Then, once I returned to America, I painted frantically, for months, exorcising demons."[42]

After World War II, Sheets returned to Scripps College before accepting a leadership role with the Los Angeles County Art Institute in 1955. The school was renamed the Otis Art Institute and eventually became part of Parsons School of Design on the West Coast.

In 1953, he founded the Millard Sheets Designs Company. The firm produced murals, mosaics, stained glass, and sculpture for commercial structures and private homes.

In his 1968 proposal, Sheets recommended forming a committee, which would include a philosopher,

Millard Sheets created two tile murals titled *The Culture Brought to Los Angeles by the Races of the World.*

anthropologist, and sociologist, to assist in developing his ideas. "The basic concept is to depict the contribution of the ethnic groups to American culture and economy," he proposed. "The committee would ensure the breadth and depth of the ideas involved and give stature to the program with their personal reputations."[43]

As Sheets later remembered, the project was an opportunity to showcase a new design process he had been perfecting for some time. "We had worked long and hard at developing this technique where we could fire all the colors at one time," he explained. "This was so new, nothing had been done like this before, where you could fire brilliant reds, brilliant yellows, greens, blue, greys, or blacks and earth colors all at the same time. So I was excited about using the tile for this mural.

"I worked up two sketches, more or less depicting the idea of the melting pot, the different cultures that make up our culture. I think there are parts of that are particularly beautiful, and I think the overall effect is interesting."[44]

Sheets's concept for the designs evolved to represent what he described as the "contribution of all races to man's culture and knowledge."

"California is rich in contributions from all corners of the world as well as the separate racial groups," he wrote during the early stages of the design. "I will emphasize the contribution of each race and country to the American way of life rather than propagandize tensions which appear to be thoroughly conveyed by press, radio, and television.

"We need now and always to understand the great cultures of other people. Most of our prejudices and bigotry result from abysmal ignorance of other people. By depicting the dignity of all races and his constructive contributions to life, we create respect for man's infinite variety and purpose to live. . ..This is

Millard Sheets, City Hall East mural.

not merely another interesting assignment—I deeply hope that this commission will be my best work."[45]

Sheets predicted it would take twelve to fifteen months to complete the project. The murals were executed by Interspace Corporation with the aid of his assistant, Mildred Downey.[46]

"I think I must have had eight artists working for me," he recalled. "I had one man that did nothing but wash bottles out of which we squeezed the glaze. It's all hand-squeezed from a bottle with a little nozzle at the end of it.

"We had a variety of nozzles from almost wire-thin tubes that would let the tiniest stream through to some that would come out pretty fast for the big areas. With the techniques that we developed for bringing colors together, but putting on the outlines with one color and then filling between them with another color and so forth, we produced some perfectly beautiful qualities. The color itself is very rich in these glazes that we developed."[47]

His early artistic influences were prominently infused in Sheets's work. He included references to German gothic sculpture, as well as the La Pietà de Villeneuve-lès-Avignon, one of the most celebrated paintings of the fifteenth century, "to suggest the French culture."

He explained, "Sometimes I used people; sometimes I used art—anything that I felt would best symbolize the special cultures."[48]

Construction of the building weathered so many delays that Sheets finished his work before it could even be installed by the contractor, and the murals had to be temporarily moved into storage for several months. "Due to the long delay in the completion of the new City Hall East, I would like to ask your assis-

tance in securing the balance of the money due in our contract in order that I may pay Interspace for the work that they have completed to our satisfaction," Sheets wrote to Stockwell in September 1971.[49]

City Hall East was finally completed in 1972. A year later, Mayor Sam Yorty was defeated in his bid for another mayoral term after a bitterly contested battle with Tom Bradley.

Like many aspects of the mall project, construction of the *Triforium* was subject to constant delays. By the time it was officially dedicated in 1976, the project's escalating costs and electrical problems had made it a political lightning rod.

Angry voters argued the $930,000 price tag would have been better spent financing improvements in rapid transit or cleaning up the postal service.[50] "The *Triforium* is the biggest joke I've ever seen," Councilmember Zev Yaroslavsky told the *Los Angeles Times*. "It's a bigger joke than the Council in my district. It's a wonderful facility, but the one-million-dollar cost is too much."[51]

In the late 1990s,City Hall East would serve temporarily as the primary location for city government while the main structure was emptied during an unprecedented seismic retrofit and restoration.

In 2014, the building was renamed in honor of Los Angeles's fortieth mayor, James K. Hahn, who served as the city's chief executive between 2001 and 2005.

U.S. Representative Janice Hahn, representing California's 44th District, sponsored the motion to rename the building in honor of her brother. "My brother spent twenty years in City Hall East as city attorney before he was elected mayor," she declared. "He did incredible work in that building for our city."[52]

CHAPTER 9

RETURN TO GLORY

City Hall is a symbol that is recognized around the world. It is a symbol to man's noblest achievement in government. This is a temple to democracy.

—Mayor James K. Hahn, April 26, 2002[1]

In a city renowned for reinventing itself, even the most beloved architectural icons are not immune from the forces of time and progress. As Los Angeles moved into the later decades of the twentieth century, it was clear that age and daily use had left "predictable scars" on its City Hall, threatening its "historic integrity."[2]

The building had survived numerous earthquakes over the years, and while its foundation, granite base, and structural steel maintained their integrity, the unreinforced masonry walls were in need of expensive overhaul. Throughout the structure, there was evidence of neglect: cracks in the marble surfaces, chips on the columns in the rotunda and Session Room of the Board of Public Works, damaged floors, deteriorating paintwork, and interior spaces that were "cluttered and over-utilized,"[3] as well as inadequate lighting and outdated plumbing and air conditioning.

As city leaders debated the cost of restoring City Hall and how much of the building required repair, critics questioned whether the time had come, once again, for Los Angeles to create a new municipal home and renew its faith in the future—elsewhere. Still, those who understood the history so steeped in its worn walls and faded floors believed it was worth fighting for.

"This building, which is emblematic of the growth and pride of our people, requires resources far greater than the available public dollars to restore it to its original beauty,"[4] Mayor Tom Bradley wrote in September 1986 to the California Department of Parks and Recreation in seeking funds for the restoration of the Council Chamber and Spring Street forecourt.

It was an effort to revive the Board of Public Works Session Room that gradually led to the formation of Project Restore, a privately funded, nonprofit, public-benefit corporation dedicated to the preservation and restoration of City buildings.

Edward J. Avila, then board commissioner and later president of Project Restore, described the Session Room as in "terrible shape" with "big ugly red curtains" and black cork padding on top of the original white pumice tiles, added years earlier to address acoustical problems. "We took the curtains down, and this incredibly beautiful light started shining in,"[5] he marveled.

Project Restore initially sought to raise $80,000 to reproduce the room's original wooden pews, which had been removed and replaced by theater-style seating. Yet the more the group studied ways to potentially restore the space, the more they started seeing other things that could be improved.

Among those committed to Project Restore's mission was Albert C. Martin Jr., the son of one of City Hall's original trio of architects. Himself an architect, Martin would serve as the organization's founding chairman. "The building belongs to the citizens of Los Angeles," he wrote to Mayor Bradley, "and we hope that restoring it will be a partnership between the private and public sectors."[6]

Following the 1971 Sylmar earthquake, large cracks appeared in the masonry walls at the top of the tower. The building's integrity was again brought into question by the 1987 Whittier Narrows earthquake, which rocked the Los Angeles metropolitan area and left City Hall staffers running for cover as furniture crashed to the ground and cracks opened up in the walls of their offices. Outside, larger cracks could be seen on the building's facade.[7] In 1989, the firm of Hardy, Holzman, Pfeiffer Associates, known for its work on the Los Angeles Central Library, produced a study of the needed restoration work for the building.

Fears over future tremors led voters in 1990 to approve Proposition G, a $376 million bond issue to upgrade municipal buildings in order to meet current earthquake standards. Nearly a third of the funds, or $112 million, would be designated for City Hall to brace the structure's tower, strengthen unreinforced walls, and repair exterior tiling.

In 1991, architect Edward H. Fickett was recruited to provide restoration and design services for the twenty-fourth through twenty-seventh floors and to prepare a "preliminary proposal for structural strengthening of the overall building."[8] Fickett, whose many works include the Los Angeles Police Academy and the former Tower Records store on Sunset Boulevard, later submitted a proposal for a second

A family project. Albert C. Martin Jr. (*front, left*), J. Edward Martin (*front, right*), David Martin (*rear, left*), and Christopher Martin.

phase of seismic rehabilitation, but he was told the City intended to award the service contract to the firm of A.C. Martin and Associates.[9]

In March 1993, A.C. Martin and Associates was recruited along with its consultants to begin a comprehensive seismic, life safety, and accessibility upgrade of City Hall. In August, the firm of Lehrer McGovern and Bovis was engaged for project management services, and along with A.C. Martin and Associates and the City of Los Angeles, began planning the project with nine key objectives:

- To reinforce the building structure to withstand projected seismic forces without collapse and minimize loss of life and injury
- To preserve/repair the building "skin" so that it will withstand projected seismic forces and minimize loss of life and injury
- To design the project to be in compliance with life/safety requirements
- To make the facility accessible to and usable by the physically disabled
- To provide for maximum energy efficiency in the impacted areas
- To preserve and enhance the culturally and historically significant aspects of the original structure
- To promote efficient space utilization
- To provide a safe, secure, and comfortable environment befitting a historical public complex
- To design the project to be within the program budget construction cost limitations.[10]

For Christopher Martin, then managing partner at A.C. Martin and Associates, the project was one of the most significant of his career and a matter of personal pride. His father, structural engineer J. Edward Martin, a retired partner in the firm and another son of Albert C. Martin Sr.,

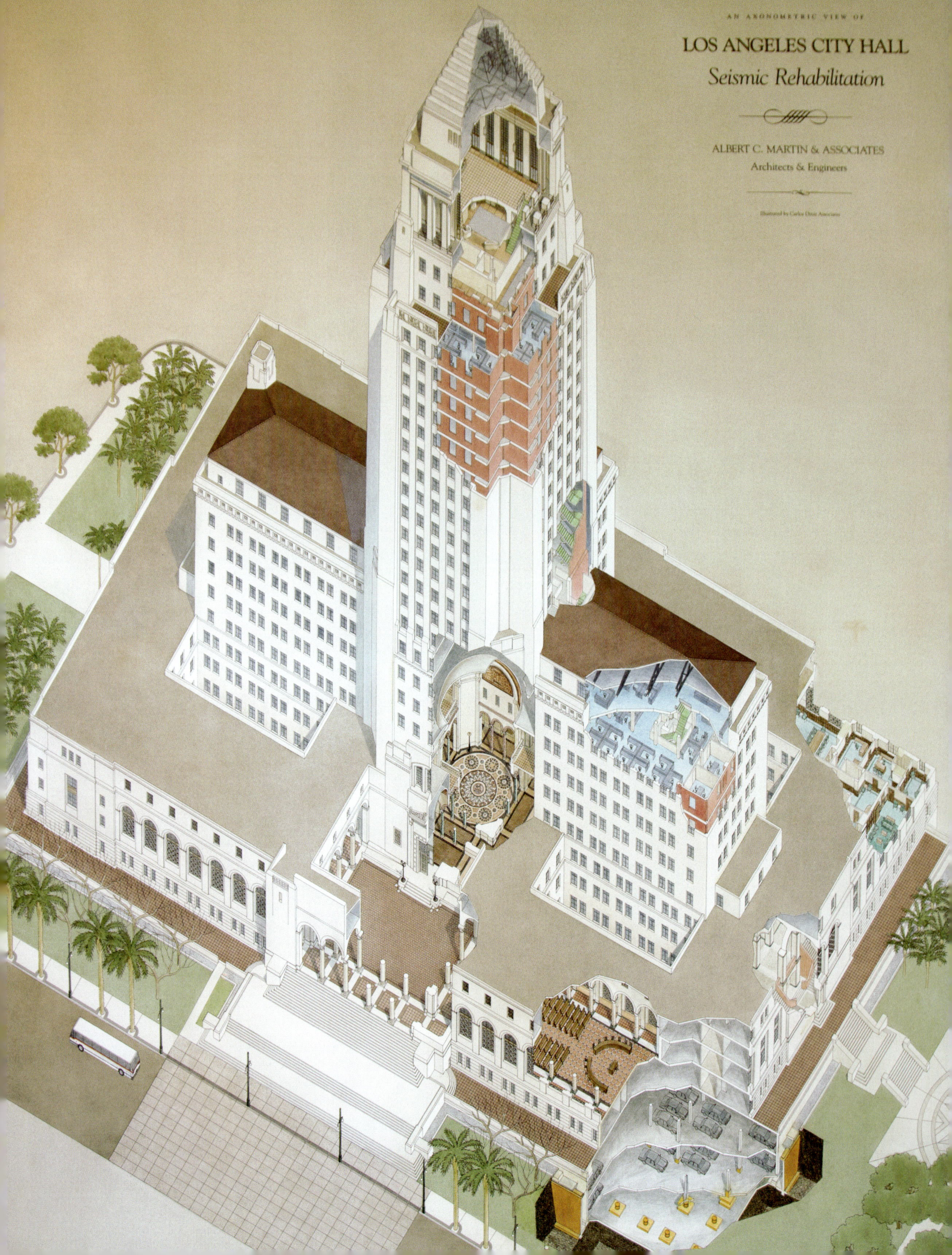
AN AXONOMETRIC VIEW OF
LOS ANGELES CITY HALL
Seismic Rehabilitation
ALBERT C. MARTIN & ASSOCIATES
Architects & Engineers

had observed the original excavation of the building in his youth. Now, these many years later, he could return to witness a new generation of the family business work to secure the building's future.

"It's, first of all, very personal, and it's very comfortable because you're doing something on the basis of what is the right thing to do and it gives you courage," Christopher Martin reflected. "When somebody says, 'Don't do this,' you say, 'No, it's really the right thing to do.'"[11]

Martin began working at the family firm as a junior draftsman in 1967 before graduating from the University of Southern California and joining the firm full time in 1973. He smiled as he recalled how so many city leaders were invested and had scrutinized his work on their beloved building. "I thought I had one client, I thought it was the City of Los Angeles," he said. "I think I had seventeen or eighteen clients. Every City Council member viewed this as their building. The (City) controller viewed this as his building, the city attorney viewed it as his building, the mayor viewed it as his building."

"I grilled Chris Martin pretty carefully on how they expected to stay within the budget," recalled former council member Zev Yaroslavsky, then head of the Council Finance Committee. "Typically, it had been my experience when you try and renovate a building that was built in the 1920s, the costs go up for a variety of reasons... I was skeptical about whether this could be done for the price they had given us."[12]

Shortly after the design of the project began, the building was shaken by the Northridge earthquake on January 17, 1994. "Within hours we were in the building examining it, and we had a terrible problem at the very top," Martin recollected. "A lot of terra cotta had come off, and there was significant damage. We did an emergency cable bracing to keep the top straight. It had almost deformed, or there was enough motion to deform it."

"We had the water drained out of the tank above the observation deck to get that dead load off, because it was acting like an inverted pendulum and was pulling the building over... we were very close to exceeding the elastic limit of the steel." An enormous debris net was placed around the top of the tower as emergency repair work got underway.

Martin's team included the firm's Principal and Director of Engineering Nabih Youssef (who simultaneously headed Nabih Youssef Associates) and Senior Structural Engineer Onik Tahtakran. Working together with City Engineer Robert S. Horii, they confronted another challenge: the walls around the stairwells were made of unreinforced masonry that had partially collapsed.

"While the stairwell was still usable after we cleaned it up, we knew another big jolt, and [the walls of the stairwell] would all fall in, and we wouldn't be able to exit the building well," Martin explained.

It became clear the building would eventually have to be emptied in order for a seismic upgrade and restoration to be possible. While the mayor and City Council moved across the street into City Hall East, many City employees took up offices in nearby locations. By August 1995, all tenants above the fourth floor had moved out to alternative work spaces.

"The original plan, as Christopher Martin's team designed it, was to try and do the restoration with people in the building," the City's project manager, Stan Morimoto, recalled. "The project then evolved into one where we could not keep the building occupied and do the work that was required; therefore, the council had to approve a second budget."[13]

As the estimated cost of the project ballooned to $273 million, the City Council debated whether the expense could be justified. "I thought it was a waste of money," Richard Riordan, who became the city's thirty-ninth mayor in July 1993, remembered.

> They could have bought a building on Grand Avenue where they could have put ten times more employees, compared to spending $300 million on the retrofit. It was a time of deflation in L.A., and you could have bought a building for almost nothing.... You could have kept the City Hall in place, but not spend all the money on it.... I had to accept where we were going. Certainly when you look at City Hall today, it is not a very efficient building.[14]

Opposite: Seismic rehabilitation plan.

The granite steps leading to City Hall were removed for cleaning and more than 20,000 cubic yards of dirt was cleared from beneath the building.

Ronald F. Deaton was the City Council's chief legislative analyst and one of the most powerful people in the city. As he recalled, the mayor's attitude toward the building evolved over time. "As a businessman, he looked at whether to keep City Hall or build a new city hall," Deaton recollected. "To him and his associates, the money and efficiency model said tear City Hall down and build a new building. So it became a fight between those of us who wanted to preserve the culture of City Hall versus those who wanted a new building."

"When it became apparent that the people wanted their city hall to be refurbished and rebuilt to modern earthquake standards, at that point Richard Riordan became aware of the value of maintaining the culture and supported keeping the current city hall."[15] Deaton would play a crucial role behind the scenes to make the project happen. To examine ways to reduce the cost, Riordan and City Controller Rick Tuttle assembled a blue-ribbon panel, and its recommendation was to scale back the work.

"I was told it would be technically possible [for people] to stay in the building and accomplish the seismic retrofit," Tuttle remembered. "There would be some inconvenience, but the job could be done much less expensively than was otherwise being proposed, and so that is what I was for. As I recall, the blue-ribbon committee substantially agreed with my observation."[16]

"There are those who say we ought to tear this building down and build another," Council President John Ferraro conveyed at the time. "Can you imagine the reaction of preservationists if we tried to do that? It would be tied up in the court for years, while nothing was done."[17]

Installation of a seismic base isolator.

Restoration artist Joseph Nicoletti working on the Main Street lobby ceiling.

In October 1996, the City Council voted 11 to 2 in favor of an expanded seismic retrofit and rehabilitation plan. "We've gone for the Cadillac retrofit when we could have done it with a Chevy," complained Councilman Rudy Svorinich Jr., who, along with Joel Wachs, voted against the project.[18] To help fund the work, the City turned to the federal government, namely FEMA, the Federal Emergency Management Agency, for a $126 million grant.

"Los Angeles City Hall is not simply the offices of the mayor and the City Council," President Bill Clinton declared in a FEMA statement, "but a nostalgic icon of the city, rich in history and a symbol of one of America's most important cities. I'm pleased that the federal government can help in the effort to restore this beautiful building."[19]

To secure the building, Nabih Youssef and his colleagues examined various seismic rehabilitation schemes, including "a reinforced-concrete shear wall system; a megabrace with shear walls; and a base-isolation system with shear walls and supplemental dampers."[20]

After an extensive analysis of the alternatives, along with visits to earthquake-affected areas in Japan and New Zealand, extensive testing, and an open debate with leading seismic experts, the base-isolation system with shear walls and supplemental dampers was selected, as it provided the most "flexibility for controlling the building's reaction in different types of earthquakes and protecting the historic resources on the lower floors."[21] It was also considered to be the most cost-effective solution.

To execute the plan, more than 20,000 cubic yards of dirt would have to be cleared from underneath the building to allow workers, with the help of hydraulic jacks, to insert 526 seismic base isolators made of vulcanized rubber and steel into more than four hundred support columns and also beneath walls. Isolators would soften the energy absorbed by the building during an earthquake, allowing for horizontal rather than vertical movement. Additionally, fifty-two viscous dampers acting like giant shock absorbers were added to limit "the maximum displacement at the plane of isolation" and dissipate seismic energy.[22] An additional twelve viscous dampers were installed in the tower to reduce the "whiplash" impact of an earthquake at the top of the structure.

The base-isolation plan would essentially seismically isolate the structure, decoupling it from the ground motion and "greatly reducing the level of seismic force transferred to the upper structure."[23] In the event of an earthquake, "the building, because of its mass, will stand still, and the earth underneath it will move back and forth," Christopher Martin explained.

Upon completion, Los Angeles City Hall would become the tallest building ever to be base isolated.

"Conventionally it would have been a concrete shear-wall system," Nabih Youssef, who championed the base-isolation technology, observed. "The challenge with that is you don't have enough places to put these walls because the more you put walls, the more you stiffen the building—which means it sucks more energy from the earthquake. The more you attract force, the more you crack the masonry."[24]

In addition to the base isolators and reinforced-concrete shear walls, a four-foot-wide and fifteen- to twenty-five-foot-deep underground moat was constructed around the building. Hidden from view by metal grates and planters, it was designed to reduce contact with actively shaking ground during an earthquake. A new steel-truss diaphragm was also added to the roof of the structure's flanking wings to help transfer energy away from the tower.

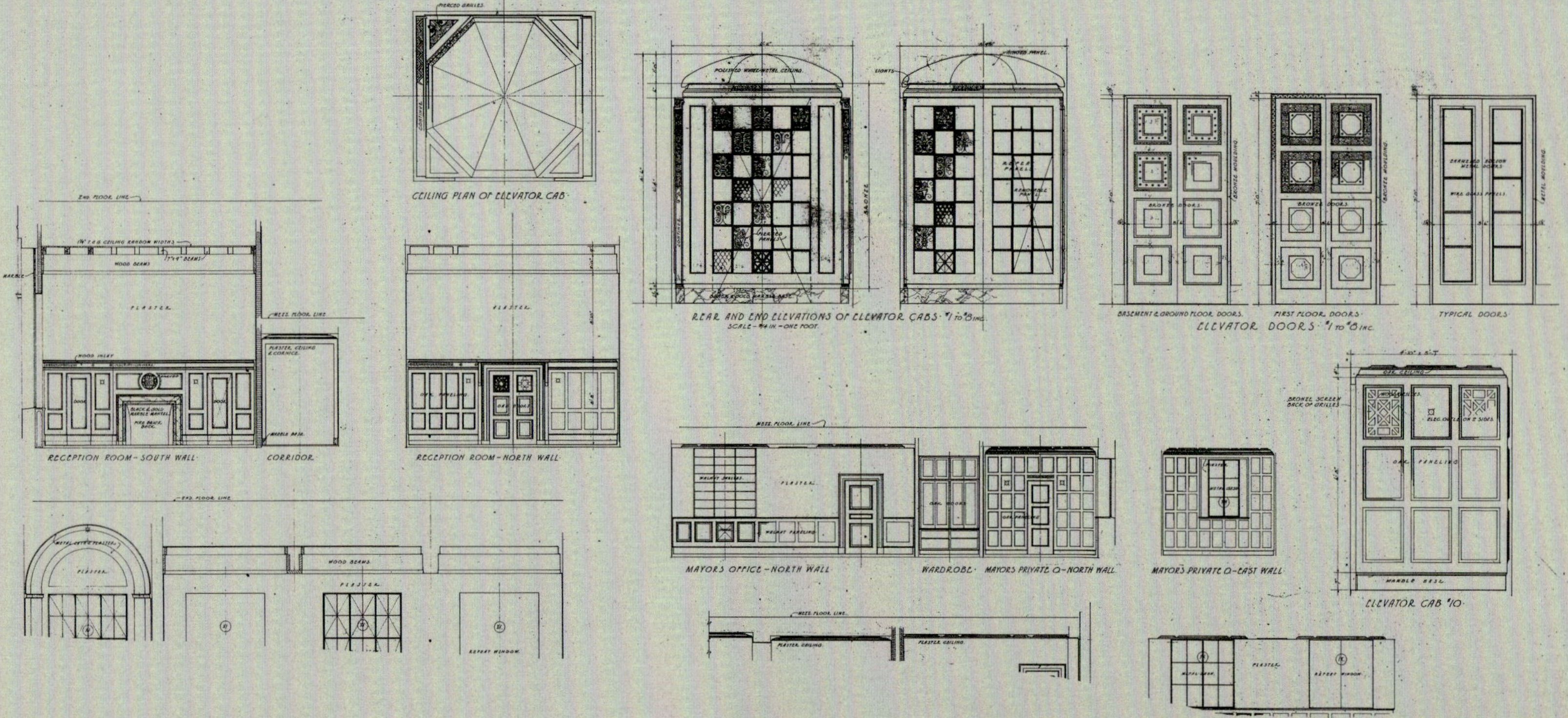

Above and Right: A reproduced elevator cab. The original cabs were removed during a 1960s modernization.

Top: The original elevator cab plans.

Opposite: The restored Council Chamber.

In February 1998, the City hired Clark Construction, a respected building and civic construction firm based in Bethesda, Maryland. Among its many critical tasks was the addition of "30,000 cubic yards of concrete, 3,000 tons of structural steel, 5,000 tons of reinforcing steel, and an additional 68,467 million pounds of deadweight to the structure."[25]

By the end of March 1998, all tenants on the first four floors had been relocated, freeing up space for heavy construction work to begin. At the height of the activity, more than 350 workers labored on site working two shifts, six days a week. Whether it was welding, removing the Spring Street granite steps for cleaning, washing the exterior, or spending hours on top of scaffolding doing intricate paintwork, there was rarely a moment when the building wasn't a hive of activity.

"This building had everything," City Construction Manager James Treadaway reminisced. "It was historic, it had gravitas, it was a technical challenge, it had logistical challenges, and there was politics. It had every degree of complexity."[26]

Brenda Levin of Levin and Associates worked alongside A.C. Martin and Associates as the historic preservation architect for the project.

"Our role really had to do with all the historic materials, interior and exterior; the rotunda, corridors on the second and third floor, Council Chamber, Public Works Chamber, all of the decorative murals, and then the exterior terra cotta and granite," Levin detailed. "What we learned about the terra cotta is that there was substantial cracking and displacement, particularly [in] the area where the observation deck is. That material couldn't be repaired, so it had to be replaced. So much of our energy and effort went into—how do we replace it, and who does the work?"[27]

Although Gladding, McBean and Company had supplied the original tiles decades earlier and even retained the original mold, the task of replicating the tile was awarded to New York-based Boston Valley Terra Cotta. Gladding, McBean did, however, supply replacement tiles for the roof.

As part of a painstaking restoration effort, more than one hundred historic light fixtures were removed, catalogued, cleaned, and rewired to meet contemporary codes. More than 270 new bronzed-and-etched-glass fixtures were produced to replace modern plastic-lensed lighting previously added to corridors and elevator lobbies. While discreet uplighting was added to illuminate the historic ceilings, ten newly created eight-foot-tall torchieres were added in the observation room, and on the twenty-sixth floor.

In the rotunda, the elaborate twelve-foot-tall chandelier that had originally hung from the ceiling, but had long since been removed, was discovered in a disassembled state among different boxes in a City storage facility. The elaborate fixture was professionally cleaned, updated, and returned to its rightful place in City Hall.

"It took about a year, but [the chandelier] was finally located in a warehouse, so we were able to restore it, relamp it, and connect a structural connection to the dome," Levin explained.

The rotunda was filled with scaffolding as workers set about dusting and then cleaning the faience tiles with a mild detergent. Numerous other tasks kept the immense restoration project continuing around the clock, such as the renovation and repainting of 1,600 steel-casement windows, the restoration of the cast-iron grilles in the Board of Public Works Session Room and Council Chamber, and the upgrading of hundreds of doors to meet modern safety codes.

In the Council Chamber, the member desks that previously had faced the council president were reconfigured to face the public. The firm of Kaplan Chen Kaplan designed the new furniture, which additionally included new desks for the city clerk and council president. "The goal was to match the spirit and designs of the old desks," David Kaplan explained.[28] To accomplish this, Kaplan and his team used then-new computer-aided design programs to control computerized wood-carving machines to make modern furniture embellished with period-style carvings and vintage details.

The same firm introduced TV monitor stands and a modern speaker's podium designed to blend in with the historical space, in addition to developing specifications and reviewing the preservation work throughout the building.

The staircase ascending from the 26th floor was added.

Like a lost treasure, an original elevator cab found by Project Restore in a salvage yard proved an exciting find and was eventually used as the model for newly produced cabs. "Project Restore went looking, contacted the owner, and they still had one cab left," Kevin Jew, the organization's chief operating officer, remembered. "They had already recycled, melted, or sold the other parts of the other seven cabs."[29]

When an appeal went out to City employees for any information on missing historical material, a former staff member came forward to say he had been allowed to take home one of the central light fixtures from a cab that was headed to salvage and had installed it as a porch light. Like the old elevator cab, it was used as a valuable model to recreate fixtures for the new cabs.

All decorative ceilings were cleaned and old varnishes removed. The T.D. Patrinos Painting and Contracting Company of Bethel Park, Pennsylvania, worked to bring much of the building's paintwork back to life by matching the rich, authentic colors, which were lighter and more vibrant. "Sometimes we had to go through four and five coats to get back to the original paint," Ray Kraves, the firm's project manager, explained.[30]

Chameleon Paintworks was initially hired to work on the Main Street lobby before moving on to the Board of Public Works Session Room and various other areas. "It was magical," company owner Joseph Nicoletti remembered of his time working on the building. "I am so proud to have worked there and have people look up at what we did."[31] Nicoletti and his crew often worked at night when the building was empty to carefully fulfill the fine-tuned, painstaking task of restoring artwork that had faded, cracked, chipped, or been damaged by smoke and other city grime.

To allow more people to enjoy the majestic views from the twenty-seventh floor and its outdoor observation deck, a grand staircase ascending from the twenty-sixth floor was added.

The twenty-sixth floor, previously used as storage space, was reinvented as a gallery for restored portraits of former mayors. The twenty-seventh floor that had been so rarely used (and previously reached via a cramped elevator) was revitalized and renamed in honor of former Mayor Tom Bradley.

"The architecture is so sublime in that building," Steven Fader, who worked as the project architect for Levin and Associates, reminisced. "There was just so much detail to it, and the colors were so rich, and everything was so much more vibrant after we had finished. . ..To some degree you look at it, and you don't know anything was done, but we spent eight years doing it."[32]

Years earlier, local TV host Huell Howser, producer of KCET's *Videolog*, learned about the story of the Lindbergh Beacon from Project Restore's then-President Georgia Rosenberry. He developed an episode exploring the history of the beacon that first aired on November 11, 1990. After the show aired, the beacon was found stashed away in a City-owned warehouse on Central Avenue, and then was cleaned and taken to Los Angeles International Airport in 1992 to be displayed inside Tom Bradley International Terminal. "It was almost a miracle that this beacon was restored instead of being taken off to scrap," Bradley said in an interview.[33]

The beacon had actually faced criticism from aviation experts almost immediately after it was switched on in 1928, and ironically, it had even confused its namesake Colonel Charles A. Lindbergh. After an all-day flight from Wichita, Kansas, to Los Angeles with Major Thomas G. Lamphier, a co-director of the Transcontinental Air Transport Company, Lindbergh complained they had mistaken the revolving beacon with landing beacons at a nearby airport.[34]

In 1931, federal aviation law required the beacon's clear lens to be replaced by a red alternative, much to the annoyance of Mayor John Clinton Porter and others in his administration. Later requests to upgrade the beacon were rejected, and it was believed to have been removed from the structure in the 1940s following the outbreak of World War II, amid fears it could guide enemy bombers.

Christopher Martin and Edward J. Avila persuaded British Petroleum to fund a $250,000 effort to return the beacon to the top of City Hall. Phoebus Manufacturing of San Francisco restored the iconic fixture, adding numerous upgrades, such as a metal mirror to replace the original glass one and a 2.5kW HMI metal halide short-arc discharge lamp. On September 7, 2001, the historic beacon was eventually returned to its rightful home on top of City Hall via helicopter.

In March 2000, Carrara Marble Company of America began renovation work on the building's exterior, and in September, the last base isolator was installed. "I think really the comforting part—because change is always difficult—is that we're keeping our landmark building," City Council President Ruth Galanter told the *Los Angeles Daily News* in May 2001, as the project neared completion. "We're acknowledging that this new millennium, new council and new mayor are actually part of a long history of city government and that our responsibilities are part of a continuum that goes way back."[35] The first employees soon began moving back into the building, and in June, a ceremony was held to rededicate the Council Chamber in honor of late Council President John Ferraro, the city's longest-serving councilmember and a champion of the renovation effort.

An elaborate formal rededication of the building scheduled for September 23, 2001, was postponed after the terrorist attacks on the East Coast on September 11. Subsequently, a much smaller event was held the following April on the seventy-fourth anniversary of the original dedication in 1928.

The building was once again decorated with red, white, and blue bunting. More than a thousand people gathered. In a demonstration of unity, both the USC and UCLA marching bands made an appearance, and members of the Gabrieleno-Tongva tribes blessed the building. Actor Kent McCord, who appeared in Jack Webb's *Dragnet*, read the 1928 dedication.[36]

It was noted that when the building had originally been dedicated, all fifteen members of the City Council and five members of the Board of Public Works were white males. Seventy-four years later, the council was dominated by minority and women members. Valerie Lynn Shaw, an African American woman, was the chair of the Board of Public Works, leading a five-member commission including three other women and one man.

In December 2001, Mayor Hahn had joined City Council members and representatives of the Los Angeles Department of Water and Power to rededicate the newly restored Flint Fountain, revitalized through the efforts of Project Restore.

Indeed, generations to come will look back to the generations before them, to those who put forth tremendous effort, understanding the history of their city and what the building would mean to all the generations, that City Hall still stands today as the bustling municipal home of Los Angeles.

The building remains a potent symbol of ambition in a dynamic city always ready to exceed expectations. Much has changed since it opened in 1928, and although it may no longer be the city's tallest building, Los Angeles City Hall remains a true American icon and a cherished symbol of civic pride.

Opposite: The UCLA Bruin Marching Band performs at the rededication of Los Angeles City Hall.

Angeles

ACKNOWLEDGMENTS

This book was made possible through the efforts of many people. I am grateful to Mayor Eric Garcetti for his wonderful foreword and his support of this project. I would like to thank Paddy Calistro and Scott McAuley at Angel City Press who graciously published it, the talented Amy Inouye who designed it, and Jim Schneeweis for promoting it. I am grateful to Sandra Stojanovic who worked tirelessly to take the excellent contemporary photographs and I would like to say a personal thank you to Jo for her selfless, inspired efforts editing the text. I'm also grateful for the editorial support provided by Cindy Olnick. I would like to thank Edward J. Avila, Kevin Jew, Nancy Lopez, and Audrey de Leon at Project Restore for all their support, and also Jane Chung in Mayor Garcetti's office. I appreciate the many people interviewed for this book including David Bell, Ronald F. Deaton, Steven Fader, David Kaplan, Austin Keithley, Brenda Levin, Christopher Martin, Stan Morimoto, Joseph Nicoletti, Richard Riordan, Jane Spaulding, James Treadaway, Rick Tuttle, Zev Yaroslavsky, and Nabih Youssef. I am grateful to Dawn Heinsbergen for access to the Heinsbergen family archive and Pamela Parkinson Kellogg for access to the Parkinson family archive. I appreciate all the kind support I received from the Parkinson family. I am grateful to Christopher Martin for access to the A.C. Martin archive, and also his colleagues Izabela Dimitrova and Donna Clandening. Paul Young in the Architectural Division of the Bureau of Engineering helped enormously. I would like to thank Michael Holland and Todd Gaydowski at the Los Angeles City Archives; the staff of the Los Angeles Public Library including City Librarian John Szabo, Glen Creason, Christina Rice, and Terri Garst; the staff of the Huntington Library and Botanical Gardens; Rochele Gomez at the Department of Cultural Affairs; Erica Varela at the *Los Angeles Times*; Simon Elliot and Octavio Olvera at the UCLA Special Collections; Susan K. Hikida in Special Collections at the University of Southern California; John Cahoon at the Seaver Center for Western History Research; Kathleen Correia at the California State Library and Scott Field owner of the Parkinson Archive. I would also like to express my gratitude to Christina Chan, Sally Bettinson, Susan Kwan, Ron Johnson, John Grunewald, Ruth and Bill Mellor, Angela Chan, Frank Simons, Patricia Casado, Shirley Wilson, Shelia Tepper, Sasa Brajovic, Tom LaBonge, Charlotte He, Diane Harstedt, Antoinette Byron, Linda G. Arntzenius, Sheila and Gordon Richards, David Trilling, Avak Keotahian, Chuck Fry, Ellery Deaton, and Liz Stanton. Lastly, this book is dedicated to my beloved parents Dorothy and Harry Gee whose frequent visits to Los Angeles and joyful exploration of the city often reminded me of how fortunate I am to live in such a remarkable place.

BIBLIOGRAPHY

The bibliography on the following page includes books and oral histories I consulted in my research for *Los Angeles City Hall: An American Icon.*

In addition, I found a wealth of information revealing the rich history of City Hall—including scrapbooks, correspondence, designs, and other irreplaceable historical documents—preserved at the following institutions. The **Archives of American Art** at the Smithsonian Institution houses the Millard Sheets Papers and the Henry Lion Papers. The **Huntington Library, Art Collections, and Botanical Gardens Photo Archives** houses the Historical Society of Southern California Collection—Charles Puck Collection of Negatives and Photographs, which also includes important printed material. The **Los Angeles City Archives** houses the Board of Public Works Minutes, the Los Angeles City Council Minutes, and the Sam Yorty Records. The **City of Los Angeles Department of Cultural Affairs** houses the Los Angeles Municipal Art Commission Minutes. The **UCLA Special Collections, Charles E. Young Research Library** houses the Bradley Administrative Papers: Project Restore; the John C. Austin papers ca. 1890–1963, and the Joseph Mesmer papers. The **Regional History Collection, Special Collections, USC Libraries** at USC houses the Los Angeles Union Station Collection. And, of course, the **Los Angeles Central Library**, on its shelves and in its vast Special Collections, preserves an enormous amount of information, not just about City Hall, but the people and the place it serves.

I conducted interviews with these subjects on the dates noted: **Edward J. Avila**, May 9, 2017; **David Bell**, July 20, 2017; **Ronald F. Deaton**, December 9, 2017; **Steven Fader**, November 3, 2017; **Kevin Jew**, May 9, 2017; **David Kaplan**, October 23, 2017; **Austin Keithley**, May 1, 2017; **Brenda Levin**, September 11, 2017; **Christopher Martin**, June 7, 2017; **Stan Morimoto**, November 6, 2017; **Joseph Nicoletti**, July 14, 2017; **Richard Riordan**, January 3, 2018; **Jane Spaulding**, October 5, 2017; **James Treadaway**, November 7, 2017; **Rick Tuttle**, December 13, 2017; **Zev Yaroslavsky**, December 16, 2017; **Nabih Youssef**, October 17, 2017.

—SG

Ainsworth, Ed. *Maverick Mayor, A Biography of Sam Yorty of Los Angeles*. Garden City, New York: Doubleday, 1966.

Deverell, William F., and Tom Sitton, eds. *Metropolis in the Making: Los Angeles in the 1920s*. Berkeley: University of California Press, 2001.

Gee, Stephen. *Iconic Vision: John Parkinson, Architect of Los Angeles*. Santa Monica, California: Angel City Press, 2013.

Gleye, Paul, Julius Shulman, and Bruce Boehner. *The Architecture of Los Angeles*. Los Angeles: Rosebud Books, 1981.

Goodwin, George M. "Los Angeles Art Community: Group Portrait, Millard Sheets." Oral history transcript of Interview of Millard Sheets by George M. Goodwin [1976–1977]. Los Angeles: UCLA Library, Center for Oral History Research, 1977.

Hales, George P. *Los Angeles City Hall*. Times Mirror Printing and Binding House, Los Angeles, 1928.

Hughes, Edan M. *Artists in California, 1786-1940*. Sacramento, California: Crocker Art Museum, 2014.

Kurutz, Gary F. *Architectural Terra Cotta of Gladding, McBean*. Sausalito, California: Windgate Press, 1989.

Laskey, Marlene L. "Evolution of a Metropolitan Skyline." Oral history transcript of Interview of Albert Carey Martin Jr. by Marlene L. Laskey [1980–1981]. Los Angeles: UCLA Library, Center for Oral History Research, 1985.

Lovoos, Janice, Millard Sheets, and Edmund F. Penney. *Millard Sheets: One-Man Renaissance*. Flagstaff, Arizona: Northland Press, 1984.

McGroarty, John S. *Los Angeles from the Mountains to the Sea: With Selected Biography of Actors and Witnesses of the Period of Growth and Achievement*. Chicago: American Historical Society, 1921.

Notables of the Southwest: Being the Portraits and Biographies of Progressive Men of the Southwest. Los Angeles: Los Angeles *Examiner*, 1912.

Notables of the West: Being the Portraits and Biographies of Progressive Men of the West Who Have Helped in the Development and History Making of This Wonderful Country. New York, Chicago, San Francisco, Los Angeles, Boston, Atlanta: International News Service, 1913, 1915.

Oliver, Richard. *Bertram Grosvenor Goodhue*. New York: Architectural History Foundation, 1983.

Parkinson, John. *Incidents by the Way: The Boy! What has the Future in Store for Him? What Will Be His Experience?* Los Angeles: Press of G. Rice & Sons, 1935.

Rindge, Ronald L., Thomas W. Doyle, and Marcia Page. *Ceramic Art of the Malibu Potteries, 1926–1932*. Malibu, California: Malibu Lagoon Museum, 1988.

Rudd, Hynda, ed. *The Development of Los Angeles City Government: An Institutional History, 1850–2000*. Los Angeles: City of Los Angeles Historical Society, 2007.

Schwartzman, Arnold, and Stephen Gee. *Los Angeles Central Library, A History of Its Art and Architecture*. Santa Monica, California: Angel City Press, 2016.

Wingert, Paul S. *The Sculpture of William Zorach*. New York: Pitman Publishing Corporation, 1938.

Wolfe, Wellington C. *Men of California: Western Personalities and Their Affiliations, with Club Memberships and Civic Associations, Illustrated Record of Men, with Biographs of Their Activities*. San Francisco: Western Press Reporter, 1926.

Woodbridge, Sally B. *John Galen Howard and the University of California*. Berkeley: University of California Press, 2002.

Workman, Boyle, and Caroline Walker. *The City That Grew*. Los Angeles: Southland Publishing Co., 1936.

Yorty, Sam. *The Yorty Years, the Story of Sam Yorty's Leadership as Mayor of Los Angeles Since 1961: An 8-Year Report of Dynamic Progress in Los Angeles, Setting the Urban Pattern for the Future*. Los Angeles, 1969.

——. *Los Angeles Progresses into the Seventies: A Continuation of the Yorty Years*. Los Angeles, 1971.

ENDNOTES

Abbreviations used for common sources:

ACM	*American City Magazine*
AIA	American Institute of Architects
A&E	*Architect and Engineer*
AF	*Architectural Forum*
BPW	Board of Public Works
BAP	Bradley Administrative Papers
CSM	*Club and Sports Magazine*
DN	*Daily News* (San Fernando Valley)
EE	*Evening Express*
HLP	Henry Lion papers, 1931–1963
HSSC	Historical Society of Southern California
HDC	*Hollywood Daily Citizen*
HUNT	Huntington Library, Art Collections, and Botanical Gardens Photo Archives
IDN	*Illustrated Daily News*
JCAP	John C. Austin Papers
LAA	*L.A. Architect*
LABJ	*Los Angeles Business Journal*
LACA	Los Angeles City Archives
LACC	Los Angeles City Council
LADN	*Los Angeles Daily News*
LADCA	Los Angeles Department of Cultural Affairs
LAEE	*Los Angeles Evening Express*
LAEH	*Los Angeles Evening Herald*
LAEH&E	*Los Angeles Evening Herald and Express*
LAEHE	*Los Angeles Evening Herald Express*
EXAM	*Los Angeles Examiner*
LAExp	*Los Angeles Express*
LAH	*Los Angeles Herald*
LAH&E	*Los Angeles Herald and Express*
LAMAC	Los Angeles Municipal Art Commission
LAPL	Los Angeles Public Library
LAR	*Los Angeles Record*
LAT	*Los Angeles Times*
MSP	Millard Sheets papers, 1907–1990
NYT	*New York Times*
PCA	*Pacific Coast Architect*
PFA	Parkinson Family Archive
SYR	Sam Yorty Records
SFC	*San Francisco Chronicle*
SN	*Spartan News*
UCLA	University of California, Los Angeles
USC	University of Southern California

Introduction

1. "Cryer Turns 1st Shovel on New City Hall," *EXAM*, Mar 5, 1926.

Chapter 1

1. Boyle Workman. *The City That Grew*: 376.
2. "Our City Halls: A Pictorial History of the City Halls of Los Angeles Showing the Onward Steps of the Administration Buildings of a Great City from 1847 to 1928." HSSC Collection—Charles Puck Collection of Negatives and Photographs; Box 34, Album 6; HUNT. (Herein, "Our City Halls: A Pictorial History . . ." HUNT.)
3. Ira Berthelot Wood. "Beginnings of Los Angeles: Early Events In History of Metropolis Recounted." *LAT*, Mar 27, 1927: B5.
4. Workman: 106.
5. Paul Gleye. *The Architecture of Los Angeles*: 44.
6. H.D. Barrows. "Recollections of the Old Court House and Its Builder." *Annual Publication of the Historical Society of Southern California*, Los Angeles, 1894: 4.
7. *Ibid.*: 40.
8. Ira Berthelot Wood. "Bullard Block Once Towered above City." *LAT*, Jan 10, 1926: C22.
9. Barrows: 42.
10. "Our City Halls: A Pictorial History . . ." HUNT.
11. *Notables of the Southwest*: 459.
12. "The New City Hall," *LAH*, Jul 29, 1884: 5.
13. *Ibid.*
14. Workman: 106.
15. "The City Hall: Full Description of the Projected One." *LAT*, Jul 13, 1887: 1.
16. "The City Hall: Lot Location to be Chosen Tomorrow Evening." *LAT*, Sep 28, 1886: 4.
17. "Early Days in Los Angeles." *LAEHE*, Feb 22, 1954: 16.
18. J.A. Graves. "Letters to the *Times*: The Old City Hall." *LAT*, Jan 25, 1929: A4.
19. *Notables of the West*: 220.
20. "Our City Halls: A Pictorial History . . ." HUNT.
21. "For a City Hall: The Council Building Committee Issues a Circular." *LAT*, May 7, 1887: 2.
22. "Random Jottings about the City Architects." *LAT*, Dec 29, 1886: 6.
23. Sally B. Woodbridge. *John Galen Howard and the University of California*: 6.
24. "Architect of Eighties Astounded: Designer of City Hall on Visit after Thirty-Three Years Amazed at Change." *LAT*, Jan 27, 1926: A1.
25. "The City Hall: Full Description of the Projected One." *LAT*, Jul 13, 1887: 1.
26. "Buildings: How Los Angeles Has Grown and Is Growing." *LAT*, Sep 17, 1888: 4.
27. "Our City Halls: A Pictorial History . . ." HUNT.
28. "Buildings: How Los Angeles Has Grown and Is Growing." *LAT*, Sep 17, 1888: 4.
29. "The City Hall: Full Description of the Projected One." *LAT*, Jul 13, 1887: 1.
30. "Buildings: How Los Angeles Has Grown and Is Growing." *LAT*, Sep 17, 1888: 4.
31. "Our City Halls: A Pictorial History . . ." HUNT.
32. "City Hall Repairs." *LAT*, Mar 30, 1898: 12.
33. "Afternoon Session: City Hall Tower." *LAT*, Jan 15, 1889: 2.
34. "Our City Halls: A Pictorial History . . ." HUNT.
35. *Ibid.*
36. "In Other Times." *LAT*, Dec 1, 1957: B4.
37. "Our City Halls: A Pictorial History . . ." HUNT.
38. "New City Hall—The People Want It." *LAT*, Mar 6, 1912: 114.
39. "Earlier Days in Los Angeles." *LAEHE*, Dec 7, 1959.
40. "People Would Sell the Old City Hall." *LAT*, Jul 1, 1910: 111.
41. "New City Hall—The People Want It." *LAT*, Mar 6, 1912: 114.
42. "Law Permits an Easy Way." *LAT*, Feb 14, 1914: 113.

Chapter 2

1. "For City Hall in North End: Mayor Cryer Calls It the Proper Location." *LAT*, May 31, 1923: 111.
2. "If I Were Broke What?" *EXAM*, Apr 16, 1928: 7.
3. "George Cryer." Local History Collection, Biography. LAPL.
4. "Civic Center Approval to be Asked on Ballot." *LAT*, Mar 16, 1923: 111.
5. "Ask 'Examiner' To Play Fair." *LAT*, Jun 3, 1921: II12.
6. Alma Whitaker. "The Woman Behind Cryer." *LAT*, Jun 26, 1921: 113.
7. "Ex-Mayor Cryer's Wife Passes." *LAT*, Sep 13, 1945: 5.
8. "First After-Election Interview Outlines Policy of New Mayor." *EXAM*, Jun 8, 1921: 2.
9. "New Mayor of L.A. Rides in on Reform Wave." *SFC*, Jun 9, 1921: 2.
10. *Ibid.*
11. John S. McGroarty. *Los Angeles from the Mountains to the Sea*: 395.
12. Meredith P. Snyder. "Message of the Mayor." Jul 7, 1919: 4.
13. "When Bosses Fall Out." *LAT*, Jan 29, 1929: A4.
14. "Last Round in Mayoralty Debate." *LAR*, Jun 6, 1921: 1.
15. "Kent Parrot Accused by Richards as 'Sinister.'" *LAT*, Aug 1, 1923: 111.
16. "Kent Parrot, Political Power Here in 20s, Dies." *LAT*, Mar 24, 1956: 3.
17. "Last Round in Mayoralty Debate." *LAR*, Jun 6, 1921: 1.
18. "Cryer Elected by 5100." *EXAM*, Jun 8, 1921: 1.
19. "Cryer Wins by Majority of 6159 Votes." *EXAM*, Jun 9, 1921: 1.
20. "Snyder Wishes Cryer Success." *LAEE*, Jun 8, 1921: 6.
21. "First After-Election Interview Outlines Policy of New Mayor." *EXAM*, Jun 8, 1921: 2.
22. George E. Cryer, Mayor. "Message of the Mayor." Jan 3, 1922: 5.
23. George E. Cryer, Mayor. "Message of the Mayor." Jan 22, 1923: 9.
24. "New Municipal Building Urged." *LAT*, Nov 15, 1922: 111.
25. "Re-elected Mayor Cryer!" *LAT*, Apr 26, 1923: 114.
26. "City Hall Issue to the Voters." *LAT*, Mar 8, 1923: 119.
27. "Civic Center Approval to be Asked on Ballot." *LAT*, Mar 16, 1923: 111.
28. *Ibid.*
29. "Re-elected Mayor Cryer!" *LAT*, Apr 26, 1923: 114.
30. "For City Hall In North End: Mayor Cryer Calls It the Proper Location." *LAT*, May 31, 1923: 111.
31. "Vote Asked on City Hall Site." *LAT*, May 20, 1923: 111.
32. "New Home for City Hall: Experts Unanimously Indorse [*sic*] Civic Center." *LAT*, Jun 4, 1923: 112.
33. "City's Growth Forces Issues." *LAR*, Jun 4, 1923: 8.

Chapter 3

1. George Cryer, Mayor. "Annual Message." Jan 2, 1925: 8.
2. "New City Hall Plans Nearing." *LAT*, Nov 15, 1923: II1.
3. Edwin Bergstrom. "The Organization and Procedure of Allied Architects, The Allied Architects Association of Los Angeles." *AF*, Feb 1928: 289.
4. "New City Hall Plans Nearing." *LAT*, Nov 15, 1923: II1.
5. *Ibid.*
6. "Bigger Federal Building Likely: Need of New Post Office Here Recognized." *LAT*, Nov 27, 1923: 111.
7. Arnold Schwartzman and Stephen Gee. *Los Angeles Central Library: A History of its Art and Architecture*: 25.
8. George Cryer, Mayor. "Annual Message." Jan 2, 1924: 9.
9. "Will Rush New City Hall." *LAT*, Feb 20, 1925: A1.
10. Wellington C. Wolfe. *Men of California*: 227.
11. "Will Rush New City Hall." *LAT*, Feb 20, 1925: A1.
12. *Ibid.*
13. "Council Acts on City: Instructs Attorney to Draft Contract with Architects; Mayor and Board are Ignored." *LAT*, Mar 7, 1925: A1.
14. *Ibid.*
15. "Architect Row Goes to Court." *LAT*, Mar 10, 1925: A2.
16. BPW. Minutes, Apr 9, 1925, Vol. 139: 194, LACA.
17. LACC. Minutes, Mar 2, 1925.
18. "Deadlock on Architects." *LAT*, Mar 3, 1925: A1.
19. "Keep Cryer." *LAT*, Apr 13, 1925: A1.
20. "City Hall Architects Want Cash." *LAT*, May 13, 1925: A5.
21. *Ibid.*
22. "City Hall Enjoiner Issued." *LAT*, May 17, 1925: 15.
23. "Architects May File Appeal on City Hall Ruling." *LAT*, Aug 3, 1925: A16.
24. BPW. Minutes, Aug 6, 1925, Vol. 144: 238, LACA.
25. BPW. Minutes, Aug 18, 1925, Vol. 145: 50, LACA.
26. "End Hall Row, City's Plea: Parley Brings Decision to Ask Architects to Drop Litigation over Contract Held Invalid." *LAT*, Aug 7, 1925: A1.
27. "Architects to Seek Damages." *LAT*, Aug 8, 1925: A1.
28. BPW. Minutes, Sep 25, 1925, Vol. 146: 274, LACA.
29. *Ibid.*
30. Special Meeting of LAMAC. Minutes, Sep 30, 1925.
31. *Ibid.*
32. *Ibid.*
33. "Obstacle for New City Hall." *LAT*, Oct 7, 1925: 6.
34. *Ibid.*
35. County Adopts Plan for $50,000,000 Civic Center." *LAT*, Nov 3, 1925: A1.

Chapter 4

1. Albert C. Martin. "Evolution of a Metropolitan Skyline: Oral History Transcript." Interviewed by Marlene L. Laskey, 1980–1981. UCLA Center for Oral History Research. (Herein, A.C. Martin, interviewed by Laskey.)
2. *Ibid.*
3. *Notables of the Southwest*: 71.
4. "John Parkinson: John C. Austin." *AF*, Jan 1928, Volume 48: 145.
5. John Parkinson. *Incidents by the Way*: 194.
6. Biography of John C. Austin for AIA. JCAP.
7. *Notables of the Southwest*: 71.
8. Biography of John C. Austin for AIA. JCAP.
9. Parkinson. *Incidents by the Way*: 193.
10. Jane Spaulding. Interview by author Oct 5, 2017.
11. "Austin Chosen Chamber Head." *LAT*, Jan 9, 1930: A1.
12. "Uncle Sam To Be Urged." *LAT*, Jan 8, 1931: A18.
13. Biography of John C. Austin for AIA. JCAP.
14. "John C. Austin, Dean of Architects, Dies." *LAT*, Sep 5, 1963: A3.
15. Marco R. Newmark. "Historical Profiles — IV: John C. Austin." *The Historical Society of Southern California Quarterly*, 36.4 (1954): 342.
16. John C. Austin. Biography, Bibliographic Division Los Angeles Historical Society, LAPL.
17. "John Parkinson: John C. Austin." *AF*, Jan 1928, Volume 48: 145.
18. A.C. Martin, interviewed by Laskey.
19. *Notables of the Southwest*: 231.

20. Frederick Hamilton. "Recent Work of Albert C. Martin, Architect." *A&E*, Jun 1926, Vol. LXXXV, No. 3: 43.
21. *Notables of the Southwest*: 231.
22. A.C. Martin, interviewed by Laskey.
23. *Ibid.*
24. *Ibid.*
25. *Notables of the Southwest*: 417.
26. A.C. Martin, interviewed by Laskey.
27. *Ibid.*
28. *Ibid.*
29. *Ibid.*
30. "A.C. Martin & Associates Fetes Anniversary." *LAT*, Aug 31, 1986: H1.
31. Linda G. Arntzenius. "Architects of Early Twentieth Century Los Angeles and Their Legacy:" 66. (Submitted in fulfillment of final project requirements for the Master of Professional Writing, USC.)
32. Myron Hunt. Letter to John Parkinson. Nov 5, 1935. PFA.
33. "Career Ended, Parkinson Rites Said." *LAT*, Dec 11, 1935: A1.
34. "Parkinson, Famed Architect, Dies." *LAEH&E*, Dec 10, 1935: 1.
35. "John Parkinson: John C. Austin." *AF*, Jan 1928, Volume 48: 145.
36. Parkinson. *Incidents by the Way*: 194.
37. Stephen Gee. *Iconic Vision: John Parkinson, Architect of Los Angeles*: 109.
38. John Parkinson. Letter to Donald B. Parkinson. Dec 1926. PFA.
39. John Donovan. Letter to John Parkinson. Oct 9, 1935. PFA.

Chapter 5

1. "Stories Sure, Some Day," *IDN*, Apr 13, 1926: 28.
2. "Old Landmarks Crumble to Make Way for Era of Beautification." *LAT*, Jan 3, 1926: C23.
3. *Ibid.*
4. Joseph Mesmer Papers.
5. "Our City Halls: A Pictorial History . . ." HUNT.
6. BPW. Minutes, Feb 1, 1926: 297, Vol.151. LACA.
7. "City Hall Work Rushed." *LAT*, Oct 24, 1926: E7.
8. "Hall Contract Blow to Unions: Open-Shop Steel Company Winner of Award." *LAT*, Jan 25, 1926: A2.
9. "Cryer Turns 1st Shovel on New City Hall." *EXAM*, Mar 5, 1926: 9.
10. *Ibid.*
11. "Ground Broken for New City Hall." *LAT*, Mar 5, 1926: A1.
12. *Ibid.*
13. *Ibid.*
14. John C. Austin. "New Ordinance is for Benefit of Whole City." Untitled, JCAP.
15. Ray Herbert. "L.A.'s Low Skyline was a Matter of Aesthetics, Not Fear of Earthquakes." *LAT*, Jul 8, 1985: OC_A4.
16. "Voters to Pass on 28 Stories for City Hall." *IDN*, Apr 4, 1926.
17. *Ibid.*
18. "Politics: The Watchman." *LAT*, Apr 4, 1926: B5.
19. "Mayor Urges Aid for New City Hall." *IDN*, Apr 9, 1926.
20. "High City Hall Idea Explained." *LAExp*, Apr 19, 1926.
21. "Says Mammoth Tower Won't Dim Buildings." *LAR*, Apr 14, 1926.
22. "Voters to Pass on 28 Stories for City Hall," *IDN*, Apr 4, 1926.
23. "City Hall Architect Explains Reason for 28-Story Building." *LAExp*, Apr 10, 1926.
24. "Height-Limit Reason Given." *LAT*, Apr 25, 1926: E4.
25. "Mayor Cryer Recommends Twenty-Eight Story New City Hall." *SN*, Apr 22, 1926.
26. "Logical Reasons For High City Hall." *IDN*, Apr 22, 1926.
27. "City Claims Right to Fix Limit Height." *LAR*, Apr 19, 1926.
28. Rube Borough. "Hot Balloting Is Predicted." *LAR*, Apr 29, 1926.
29. "Polls Open At Six O'Clock for City Election." *IDN*, Apr 30, 1926.
30. "Pouring the Foundation for the New Los Angeles City Hall." *ACM*, Nov 1926: 666.
31. "C.J. Kubach, General Contractor." *Southwest Contractor and Manufacturer*, Oct 5, 1912, Volume IX, Number 22: 10.
32. "Great Structures Commemorate Him: Builder of City Hall Succumbs." *LAT*, Nov 30, 1929: A1.
33. "Hall Contract Blow to Unions: Open-Shop Steel Company Winner of Award." *LAT*, Jan 25, 1926: A2.
34. "High Court to Rule on Hall." *LAT*, Aug 1, 1926: 3.
35. "Court Upholds High City Hall." *LAT*, Aug 10, 1926: A1.
36. BPW. Minutes, Mar 26, 1926: 389, Vol.153, LACA.
37. BPW. Minutes, Aug 27, 1926: 361, Vol.160, LACA.
38. *Ibid.*
39. A.C. Martin, interviewed by Laskey.
40. BPW. Minutes, Nov 22, 1926: 302, Vol.164, LACA.
41. "New City Hall Ceremony Set." *LAT*, Feb 7, 1927: A1.
42. "New City Hall Work Speeded." *LAT*, Mar 14, 1927: A1.
43. "New City Hall Progress Rapid." *LAT*, May 18, 1927: A5.
44. "Impressive Ceremonies Mark Laying of Structure's Cornerstone." *LAT*, Jun 23, 1927: A1.
45. "Los Angeles City Hall Cornerstone Ceremony Program."
46. "New City Hall Rises Rapidly." *LAT*, Jul 10, 1927: E8.
47. "New City Hall about Finished." *LAT*, Nov 6, 1927: E8.
48. Los Angeles City Hall, BPW Information Card.

Chapter 6

1. "Los Angeles City Hall." *AF*, Jan 1928: 25.
2. George P. Hales. "*Los Angeles City Hall*." *PCA*, Volume XXXIII, May 1928, No. 5: 14.
3. Los Angeles City Hall, BPW Information Card.
4. John C. Austin. "Los Angeles City Hall." *AF*, Jan 1928: 25.
5. Albert C. Martin. "New Hall Will Symbolize City: Architects Plan Building to Reflect Greatness." *LAT*, Apr 11, 1926: B3.
6. *Ibid.*
7. "Distinction for San Francisco Bay." *A&E*, Jul 1922, Vol. LXX, No. 1: 110.
8. J. Donald Prouty, quoted in Ronald L. Rindge, *et al. Ceramic Art of the Malibu Potteries, 1926–1932*: 87.
9. Hales. *Los Angeles City Hall*: 63.
10. *Ibid.*: 59.
11. Albert C. Martin. "New Hall Will Symbolize City: Architects Plan Building to Reflect Greatness." *LAT*, Apr 11, 1926: B3.

12. Edward Alden Jewell. "William Zorach: Sculpture for Architecture." *NYT*, Feb 1, 1931: 119.
13. "This Work May Be Carved on Public Building: Art Model For City Hall." *LAT*, Nov 13, 1941: A1.
14. Special Meeting of LAMAC. Minutes, Nov 26, 1926. LADCA.
15. BPW. Minutes, Nov 29, 1926: 25, Vol. 165, LACA.
16. BPW. Minutes, Feb 17, 1926: 221, Vol. 164, LACA.
17. Special Meeting of LAMAC. Minutes, Mar 8, 1927. LADCA.
18. Edan M. Hughes. *Artists in California*: 225.
19. "Sculptor Completing Municipal Edifice Labors." *LAT*, Feb 22, 1927: A1.
20. BPW. Minutes, Oct 29, 1926: 332, Vol. 163, LACA.
21. LAMAC. Minutes, Nov 26, 1926. LADCA.
22. LAMAC. Minutes, Dec 21, 1926. LADCA.
23. *Ibid.*
24. LAMAC. Minutes, Sep 7, 1927. LADCA.
25. "Henry Lion." Exhibition program, Los Angeles Museum Park, Dec 1937. HLP.
26. *The Western Woman*, Los Angeles, California: 38, HLP.
27. "Henry Lion." Exhibition program, Los Angeles Museum Park, Dec 1937. HLP.
28. LAMAC. Minutes, Feb 7, 1928. LADCA.
29. "Noted Architect Taken by Death." *LAT*, Sep 19, 1927: A9.
30. "Date Dispute Decision Due." *LAT*, Feb 14, 1928: 16.
31. LAMAC. Minutes, Feb 14, 1928. LADCA.
32. "Panel Models for Historical Door in New City Hall are Complete." *LAT*, Jan 17, 1928: A12.
33. John C. Austin. "Los Angeles City Hall." *AF*, Jan 1928: 26.
34. "The Los Angeles City Hall." *Through The Ages*, Vol. 6, No. 10, Feb 1929: 6.
35. George P. Hales. "Los Angeles City Hall." *PCA*, Vol. XXXIII, May 1928, No. 5: 14.
36. Hales. *Los Angeles City Hall*: 26.
37. J. Donald Prouty, quoted in Rindge *et al.*: 86.
38. John C. Austin. "Los Angeles City Hall." *AF*, Jan 1928: 26.
39. "The Los Angeles City Hall." *Through The Ages*, Vol. 6, No. 10, Feb 1929: 7.
40. Los Angeles City Hall, BPW Flyer.
41. *Our City Halls: A Pictorial History . . ."* HUNT.
42. "The Los Angeles City Hall." *Through The Ages*, Vol. 6, No. 10, Feb 1929: 6.
43. "Los Angeles City Hall." *Shapes of Clay*, Jun 1928, Vol. IV, Number 3.
44. *Ibid.*
45. Jeff Glass. "Artist Was Famous for Deliberate Excess." *LAT*, Jun 22, 1981: B14.
46. *Ibid.*
47. Kay Wood. "Meet 'Tony' Heinsbergen." *CSM*, Apr 1955: 4, Heinsbergen Family Archive.
48. *Ibid.*
49. Herman Sachs. Letter to H.L. Gilman, Jun 16, 1937. Los Angeles Union Station Collection, USC Libraries.
50. Edan M. Hughes. *Artists in California*: 487.
51. Donald B. Parkinson. Letter to M.C. Blanchard, Jul 21, 1937. Los Angeles Union Station Collection, USC Libraries.
52. "The Los Angeles City Hall." *Through The Ages*, Vol. 6, No. 10, Feb 1929: 8.
53. Hales. *Los Angeles City Hall*: 38.
54. "The Los Angeles City Hall." *Through The Ages*, Vol. 6, No. 10, Feb 1929: 8.
55. Hales. *Los Angeles City Hall*: 44.
56. Albert C. Martin. "New Hall Will Symbolize City: Architects Plan Building to Reflect Greatness." *LAT*, Apr 11, 1926: B3.
57. Hales. *Los Angeles City Hall*: 50.
58. John C. Austin. "Los Angeles City Hall." *AF*, Jan 1928: 27.
59. Albert C. Martin. "New Hall Will Symbolize City: Architects Plan Building to Reflect Greatness." *LAT*, Apr 11, 1926: B3.
60. John C. Austin. "Los Angeles City Hall." *AF*, Jan 1928: 28.
61. Hales. *Los Angeles City Hall*: 57.

Chapter 7

1. "Native Sons Will Present Colorful Pageant Ending Fete on Saturday Night." *EE*, Apr 27, 1928: 1.
2. "New Landmark for Sky Pilots." *LAT*, Apr 11, 1928: A22.
3. "Cryer Proclamation Urges Holiday Here." *EXAM*, Apr 25, 1928: 5.
4. "Dedication of New City Home is Begun." *LAEH*, Apr 26, 1928: 1.
5. *Ibid.*
6. "Dedication of City Hall Gala Affair." *EE*, Apr 26, 1928: 1.
7. *Ibid.*
8. Marjorie Driscoll. "Huge Parade Sets Mark For All Big Cities." *EXAM*, Apr 27, 1928: 5.
9. "Dedication of City Hall Gala Affair." *EE*, Apr 26, 1928: 1.
10. "Our City Halls: A Pictorial History . . ." HUNT.
11. "Dedication of City Hall Gala Affair." *EE*, Apr 26, 1928: 1.
12. "Thousands View Parade, Attend at Ceremonies." *HDC*, Apr 26, 1928: 2.
13. Harry Lang. "Dedication Ceremony City's Most Impressive." *EXAM*, Apr 27, 1928: 5.
14. *Ibid.*
15. "Mayor Cryer Voices City's High Ideals." *EXAM*, Apr 27, 1928: 5.
16. "Cryer Proclamation Urges Holiday Here." *EXAM*, Apr 25, 1928: 5.
17. "Broadcast Planned In All City Parks." *EXAM*, Apr 26, 1928: 2.
18. "Los Angeles Thunders Greeting To Lindbergh." *LAT*, Sep 21, 1927: A1.
19. "Lindbergh Light Fund Requested." *LAT*, Sep 25, 1927: B1.
20. "City Hall Fete to Depict Cal. History." *LAEH*, Apr 18, 1928: 1.
21. "Beacon to Shine Thursday." *LAT*, Apr 21, 1928: A1.
22. "Native Sons Will Present Colorful Pageant Ending Fete on Saturday Night." *EE*, Apr 27, 1928: 1.
23. "Key Touched and Air Guide Flashes Here." *EXAM*, Apr 27, 1928: 1.
24. "Native Sons Will Present Colorful Pageant Ending Fete on Saturday Night." *EE*, Apr 27, 1928: 1.
25. Harry Lang. "Dedication Ceremony City's Most Impressive." *EXAM*, Apr 27, 1928: 5.
26. *Ibid.*
27. "Lindbergh Light Also Dedicated." *LAT*, Apr 27, 1928: A1.
28. *Ibid.*
29. "Native Sons Will Present Colorful Pageant Ending Fete on Saturday Night." *EE*, Apr 27, 1928: 1.
30. *Ibid.*
31. "Mayor Cryer Voices City's High Ideals." *EXAM*, Apr 27, 1928: 5.
32. "Ghosts of Past Stalk At Sale." *LAT*, Jan 22, 1929: 14.
33. "Our City Halls: A Pictorial History . . ." HUNT.
34. "Governor To Honor Flint." *LAT*, Mar 13, 1929: A12.

35. "Flint Memorial Site Favored." *LAT*, Mar 24, 1930: A17.
36. LAMAC. Minutes, Jul 9, 1930. LADCA.
37. LAMAC. Minutes, Nov 25, 1931. LADCA.
38. LAMAC. Minutes, Dec 2, 1931. LADCA.
39. *Ibid.*
40. LAMAC. Minutes, Jul 20, 1932. LADCA.
41. LAMAC. Minutes, Jul 5, 1933. LADCA.
42. LAMAC. Minutes, Aug 14, 1933. LADCA.
43. "Fountain Unveiling Today." *LAT*, Sep 13, 1933: A2.

Chapter 8

1. Millard Sheets. Handwritten note. MSP.
2. Henry Sutherland. "L.A.'s Going Up—Question Is 'How High?'" *LAT*, Jan 8, 1967: I1.
3. Don Terry. "Sam Yorty, Maverick Mayor of Los Angeles, Dies at 88." *NYT*, Jun 6, 1998.
4. "Yorty Urges 20 Stories for City Hall East." *LAT*, Mar 4, 1970: B2.
5. Terry. "Sam Yorty. . ." *NYT*, Jun 6, 1998.
6. Ed Ainsworth. *Maverick Mayor: A Biography of Sam Yorty of Los Angeles*: 2.
7. Sam Yorty. *Los Angeles Progresses into the Seventies: A Continuation of the Yorty Years*: 11.
8. Council File No. 129,840. Civic Center Development. SYR.
9. "J.E. Stanton Named PBA Architect." *National Architect*, Vol. 2, No. 2, Feb 1946: 1.
10. "Obituary: William F. Stockwell." *LAA*, Sep 1981: 2.
11. Yorty. *Los Angeles Progresses. . .*: 11.
12. *Ibid.*
13. Yorty. *Los Angeles Progresses. . .* : 1.
14. Office of Mayor Sam Yorty, Press Release, Apr 22, 1966. SYR.
15. Sam Yorty. *The Yorty Years: The Story of Sam Yorty's Leadership as Mayor of Los Angeles since 1961*: 20.
16. Office of Mayor Sam Yorty, Press Release, Apr 22, 1966. SYR.
17. City Planning Department, Staff Report to the Director of Planning, Jan 27, 1966. SYR.
18. Ainsworth: 147.
19. Office of Mayor Sam Yorty, News Release, Jan 8, 1967. SYR.
20. Millard Sheets. Proposal, Los Angeles City Hall Annex. Nov 5, 1968. MSP.
21. "Arts Commission Turns Down City Hall Annex Plan." *LAT*, Sep 26, 1967: A1.
22. John Dreyfuss. "Annex Rejection Called Just Stalling for Time." *LAT*, Sep 28, 1967: A8.
23. Samuel T. Hurst. USC, Letter to Mayor Sam Yorty, Oct 3, 1967. SYR.
24. Sam Yorty, Letter to Samuel T. Hurst, Nov 8, 1967. SYR.
25. Office of Mayor Sam Yorty, News Release, Apr 30, 1968. SYR.
26. Memorandum, From: Ethel C. Bryant to Mayor Sam Yorty, Oct 7, 1969. SYR.
27. Memorandum, From: C. Erwin Piper to Mayor Sam Yorty, Nov 7, 1969. SYR.
28. LAMAC. Minutes, Feb 18, 1970. LADCA.
29. *Ibid.*
30. Report of the Director of the Bureau of Public Buildings, Fire Administration Building—City Hall Annex, May 15, 1970. SYR.
31. Report of the Director of the Bureau of Public Buildings of the advised logistics to add eight (8) floors to the City Hall East, May 27, 1970. SYR.
32. Erwin Baker. "Dispute Over Esthetics Halts City Hall Work." *LAT*, Oct 16, 1970: D23.
33. Erwin Baker. "Compromise 'Star-Step' Profile: City Hall East Esthetic Snag Appears Over." *LAT*, Oct 29, 1970: A1.
34. LAMAC. Minutes, Feb 18, 1970. LADCA.
35. "Yorty Requests Removal of 3 Columns in City Hall East." *LAT*, Jun 18, 1971: 3.
36. Dorothy W. Burke. Letter to Mayor Yorty, Jun 23, 1971. SYR.
37. Alden Nash. Letter to Mayor Yorty, Jun 18, 1971. SYR.
38. "Yorty Objects to *Times* Story on Pillars in City Hall East." *LAT*, Jun 26, 1971: A4.
39. "Removal of 3 City Hall East Pillars Too Costly, Board Says." *LAT*, Jul 22, 1971: A1.
40. Millard Sheets. Letter to Stanton and Stockwell, Nov 5, 1968. MSP.
41. Biographical Note, MSP.
42. *Ibid.*
43. *Ibid.*
44. Millard Sheets, Interviewed by George M. Goodwin, "Los Angeles Art Community: Group Portrait, Millard Sheets:" 438.
45. Millard Sheets, Interviewed by Goodwin: 482.
46. Millard Sheets. Handwritten note. MSP.
47. Millard Sheets, Interviewed by Goodwin: 484.
48. *Ibid.*
49. *Ibid.*
50. Dave Smith. "Sound and the Fury: The Triforium on the Mall." *LAT*, Jan 13, 1976: E1.
51. *Ibid.*
52. Rick Orlov. "Los Angeles' City Hall East Named After Former Mayor James K. Hahn." *LADN*, Sep 4, 2014.

Chapter 9

1. Rick Orlov. "Spotlight on City Hall; Redone 1928 Structure Dedicated After Face Lift." *DN*, Apr 27, 2002: N4.
2. Georgia Rosenberry, President, Project Restore. Letter to Mayor Tom Bradley, Jun 7, 1991. BAP.
3. David C. Martin, Onik Tahtakran, A.C. Martin Partners. *The Structural Design of Tall and Special Buildings, Special Issue: Great Structural Engineering Firms*, Sep 2003, Vol. 12, Issue 3.
4. Tom Bradley, Mayor. Letter to Kathryn Gualtieri, State historic preservation officer, Sep 14, 1986. BAP.
5. Edward J. Avila. Interview by author, May 9, 2017.
6. Albert C. Martin Jr. Letter to Mayor Tom Bradley, Jan 21, 1988. BAP.
7. Eric Malnic. "The Los Angeles Earthquake: 6.1 Quake Jolts L.A., Three Dead." *LAT*, Oct 2, 1987: 6.
8. Edward H. Fickett. "Qualifications For Design Services," Dec 14, 1992. Edward H. Fickett, FAIA, records, Special Collections, USC Libraries.
9. William A. Holland. Letter to Edward H. Fickett, Jan 19, 1993. Edward H. Fickett, FAIA, records, University Archives, Special Collections, USC Libraries.
10. *The Restoration Alliance* (Newsletter for the Los Angeles City Hall Restoration Project), Issue 1, Volume 1, Dec 1993: 2, Nabih Youssef and Associates Archive.
11. Christopher Martin. Interview by author, Jun 7, 2017.
12. Zev Yaroslavsky. Interview by author, Dec 16, 2017.
13. Stan Morimoto. Interview by author, Nov 6, 2017.
14. Richard Riordan. Interview by author, Jan 3, 2018.
15. Ronald F. Deaton. Interview by author, Dec 9, 2017.
16. Rick Tuttle. Interview by author, Dec 13, 2017.

17. Kenneth Reich. "Council OKs Seismic Retrofitting of City Hall." *LAT*, Oct 31, 1996.
18. *Ibid.*
19. Kenneth Reich. "$264 Million OK'd for Quake Repair." *LAT*, Jul 18, 1996.
20. Nabih Youssef, Brent Nuttall, Owen Hata, Onik Tahtakran, and Gary C. Hart. *The Structural Design of Tall Buildings, Los Angeles City Hall*, Vol. 9, No. 1, Mar 1, 2000: 3–24.
21. David C. Martin and Onik Tahtakran, A.C. Martin Partners. *The Structural Design of Tall and Special Buildings, Special Issue.*
22. Nabih Youssef. "Tall Order." *Civil Engineering*, Oct 1999: 59.
23. Nabih Youssef, *et al. The Structural Design of Tall Buildings, Los Angeles City Hall*: 3–24.
24. Nabih Youssef. Interview by author, Oct 17, 2017.
25. Clark Construction Website: www.clarkconstruction.com.
26. Treadaway, James. Interview by author, Nov 7, 2017.
27. Brenda Levin. Interview by author, Sep 11, 2017.
28. David Kaplan. Interview by author, Oct 23, 2017.
29. Kevin Jew. Interview by author, May 9, 2017.
30. Howard Fine. "Return to Glory." *LABJ*, May 28, 2001: 56.
31. Joseph Nicoletti. Interview by author, Jul 14, 2017.
32. Steven Fader. Interview by author, Nov 3, 2017.
33. Tom Bradley, Mayor. Interviewed by Huell Howser. KCET *Videolog*, Nov 11, 1990.
34. "Revolving Lights Are Misleading." *LAT*, Oct 26, 1928: A10.
35. "Face Lift Nearly Done; City Hall Redo Restores Sparkle to Jewel of City." *LADN*, May 29, 2001: N1.
36. Rick Orlov. "Spotlight on City Hall. . ." *LADN*, Apr 27, 2002: N4.

IMAGE CREDITS

Contemporary architectural images of Los Angeles City Hall were photographed for this book by Sandra Stojanović. Except as noted below, all other images in *Los Angeles City Hall* are from the author's collection. Please contact the publisher with any comments or questions.

AC Martin Partners, Inc.: 134, 192
The American Architect, 1927: 42, 54 (top), 54 (bottom), 55, 82
Architectural Forum, January 1928: 112
Board of Public Works, City of Los Angeles: 52, 74, 76, 84, 88 (bottom), 89 (bottom), 92, 98, 99, 100, 106, 108, 117, 130 (left), 138 (inset), 140, 142, 147, 149 (bottom), 150 (top), 154 (inset), 178, 196 (top), 178
Robert J. Burdette. From *Greater Los Angeles & Southern California Portraits & Personal Memoranda* (The Lewis Publishing Company, 1910): 20 (inset)
California State Library: 2, 28, 58, 80, 81, 90, 141, 144, 152, 167 (right), 175
Stephen Gee photographs: 85, 88 (top), 89 (top), 91, 95, 118, 119, 120, 121, 148, 149 (top), 171 (bottom), 179 (inset), 204, 216
George P. Hales. From *Los Angeles City Hall*, 1928: 122
Heinsbergen Family Archive: 130 (right), 131, 137 (top), 153, 157, 162 (bottom)
Huntington Library, San Marino, California: Ralph Arnold Papers, George E. Cryer, Republican Mayor, Los Angeles (1921–1929): 26; Historical Society of Southern California Collection: Charles Puck Collection of Negatives and Photographs: 12, 14, 16, 17, 20, 23, 29, 59, 60, 65, 69, 70, 71 (top), 77, 162 (top), 164 (top), 166, 169
Amy Inouye: 201
Levin and Associates: 194
Library of Congress: 38
Los Angeles City Archives: 18; Mayor Sam Yorty Collection: 172, 177, 180
Los Angeles County Museum of Natural History, Seaver Center for Western History Research: 56, 63
Los Angeles Modern Auctions: 156
Los Angeles Public Library Photograph Collection: 30, 66, 67, 68, 96, 104, 167 (left), 168, 183 (top)
Los Angeles Times: 191, copyright © 1998, used with permission. Photograph by Con Keyes.
Joseph Nicoletti: 195
From *Notables of the Southwest*, 1912: 27
Office of Los Angeles Mayor Eric Garcetti: 8
The Parkinson Archives: courtesy of William Scott Field, owner: 41, 61 (left), 78; courtesy Linda G. Arntzenius: 61 (right)
Parkinson Family Archives: 37, 44, 50, 51, 132 (top), 170
John Parkinson. From *Incidents by the Way*, 1935: 39
Project Restore: 196 (bottom left)
Smithsonian Institution, Archives of American Art, Millard Sheets papers (1907–1990): 183 (bottom)
Stanton Family Archive: 176
University of California Los Angeles, Charles E. Young Research Library, Department of Special Collections: John C. Austin Papers (Collection 904): 32, 46, 105, 160, 165 (top left), 165 (top right); *Los Angeles Times* Photographic Archives: 71 (bottom), 86, 102, 158, 161, 163 (right), 164 (bottom), 165 (bottom left and right), 171 (top)
University of Southern California, Doheny Memorial Library, Special Collections, California Historical Society Collection (1860–1960): 64
Wellington Wolfe. From *Men of California*, 1926: 35 (left), 35 (right), 48

INDEX

Los Angeles City Hall: An American Icon

By Stephen Gee

Design by Amy Inouye, Future Studio, Los Angeles

10 9 8 7 6 5 4 3 2 1

ISBN-13 978-1-62640-051-1 (print edition)
ISBN-13 978-1-62640-052-8 (e-pub edition)

Library of Congress Cataloging-in-Publication Data is available

Printed in Canada

ACP ANGEL CITY PRESS

Published by Angel City Press
2118 Wilshire Blvd. #880
Santa Monica, California 90403
+1.310.395.9982